MANAGING INVESTMENT PORTFOLIOS WORKBOOK

A DYNAMIC PROCESS

The **CFA Institute** is the premier association for investment professionals around the world, with over 85,000 members in 129 countries. Since 1963 the organization has developed and administered the renowned Chartered Financial Analyst® Program. With a rich history of leading the investment profession, CFA Institute has set the highest standards in ethics, education, and professional excellence within the global investment community, and is the foremost authority on investment profession conduct and practice.

Each book in the CFA Institute Investment Series is geared toward industry practitioners along with graduate-level finance students and covers the most important topics in the industry. The authors of these cutting-edge books are themselves industry professionals and academics and bring their wealth of knowledge and expertise to this series.

MANAGING INVESTMENT PORTFOLIOS WORKBOOK

A DYNAMIC PROCESS

Third Edition

John L. Maginn, CFA

Donald L. Tuttle, CFA

Dennis W. McLeavey, CFA

Jerald E. Pinto, CFA

John Wiley & Sons, Inc.

Published by John Wiley & Sons, Inc., Hoboken, New Jersey.
Published simultaneously in Canada.

ISBN 978-0-470-10493-4

Printed in the United States of America.

10 9 8 7 6 5 4 3

CONTENTS

PART I

LEARNING OUTCOMES, SUMMARY OVERVIEW, AND PROBLEMS

CHAPTER 1

THE PORTFOLIO MANAGEMENT PROCESS AND THE INVESTMENT POLICY STATEMENT

John L. Maginn, CFA

Maginn Associates, Inc.
Omaha, Nebraska

Donald L. Tuttle, CFA

CFA Institute
Charlottesville, Virginia

Dennis W. McLeavey, CFA

CFA Institute
Charlottesville, Virginia

Jerald E. Pinto, CFA

CFA Institute
Charlottesville, Virginia

LEARNING OUTCOMES

After completing this chapter, you will be able to do the following:

- Justify the importance of the portfolio perspective.
- Formulate the steps of the portfolio management process and the components of those steps.
- Compare and contrast the types of investment objectives.
- Contrast the types of investment constraints.
- Justify the central role of the investment policy statement in the portfolio management process.
- Review the elements of an investment policy statement and distinguish among the components within (1) the risk objective, (2) the return objective, and (3) the time horizon constraint.
- Compare and contrast passive, active, and semiactive approaches to investing.
- Discuss the role of capital market expectations in the portfolio management process.
- Discuss the role of strategic asset allocation in the portfolio management process.
- Discuss the roles of portfolio selection/composition and portfolio implementation in the portfolio management process.
- Contrast the elements of performance evaluation.
- Explain the purpose of monitoring and rebalancing.
- Formulate the elements of portfolio management as an ongoing process.
- Formulate and justify a risk objective for an investor.
- Formulate and justify a return objective for an investor.
- Determine the liquidity requirement of an investor and evaluate the effects of a liquidity requirement on portfolio choice.
- Contrast the types of time horizons, determine the time horizon for an investor, and evaluate the effects of the investor's time horizon on portfolio choice.
- Determine the tax concerns, legal and regulatory factors, and unique circumstances for an investor and evaluate their effects on portfolio choice.
- Justify ethical conduct as a requirement for managing investment portfolios.

SUMMARY OVERVIEW

In Chapter 1, we have presented the portfolio management process and the elements of the investment policy statement.

- According to the portfolio perspective, individual investments should be judged in the context of how much risk they add to a portfolio rather than on how risky they are on a stand-alone basis.
- The three steps in the portfolio management process are the planning step (objectives and constraint determination, investment policy statement creation, capital market expectation formation, and strategic asset allocation creation); the execution step (portfolio selection/composition and portfolio implementation); and the feedback step (performance evaluation and portfolio monitoring and rebalancing).

- Investment objectives are specific and measurable desired performance outcomes, and constraints are limitations on the ability to make use of particular investments. The two types of objectives are risk and return. The two types of constraints are internal (posed by the characteristics of the investor) and external (imposed by outside agencies).
- An investment policy statement (IPS) is a written planning document that governs all investment decisions for the client. This document integrates a client's needs, preferences, and circumstances into a statement of that client's objectives and constraints.
- A policy or strategic asset allocation establishes exposures to IPS-permissible asset classes in a manner designed to satisfy the client's long-run objectives and constraints. The plan reflects the interaction of objectives and constraints with long-run capital market expectations.
- In a passive investment strategy approach, portfolio composition does not react to changes in expectations; an example is indexing, which involves a fixed portfolio designed to replicate the returns on an index. An active approach involves holding a portfolio different from a benchmark or comparison portfolio for the purpose of producing positive excess risk-adjusted returns. A semiactive approach refers to an indexing approach with controlled use of weights different from the benchmark.
- The portfolio selection/composition decision concerns portfolio construction and often uses portfolio optimization to combine assets efficiently to achieve return and risk objectives. The portfolio implementation decision concerns the trading desk function of implementing portfolio decisions and involves explicit and implicit transaction costs.
- The elements of performance evaluation are performance measurement, attribution, and appraisal. Performance measurement is the calculation of portfolio rates of return. Performance attribution is the analysis of those rates of return to determine the factors that explain how the return was achieved. Performance appraisal assesses how well the portfolio manager performed on a risk-adjusted basis, whether absolute or relative to a benchmark.
- Portfolio monitoring and rebalancing use feedback to manage ongoing exposures to available investment opportunities in order to continually satisfy the client's current objectives and constraints.
- Portfolio management is an ongoing process in which the investment objectives and constraints are identified and specified, investment policies and strategies are developed, the portfolio composition is decided in detail, portfolio decisions are initiated by portfolio managers and implemented by traders, portfolio performance is evaluated, investor and market conditions are monitored, and any necessary rebalancing is implemented.
- The steps to determine a risk objective include: (1) specify a risk measure (or measures) such as standard deviation, (2) determine the investor's willingness to take risk, (3) determine the investor's ability to take risk, (4) synthesize the investor's willingness and ability into the investor's risk tolerance, and (5) specify an objective using the measure(s) in the first step above.
- The steps to determine a return objective include: (1) specify a return measure such as total nominal return, (2) determine the investor's stated return desire, (3) determine the investor's required rate of return, and (4) specify an objective in terms of the return measure in the first step above.
- A liquidity requirement is a need for cash in excess of the contribution rate or the savings rate at a specified point in time. This need may be either anticipated or unanticipated.
- A time horizon is the time period associated with an investment objective. Investment objectives and associated time horizons may be short term, long term, or a combination

of these two. A multistage horizon is a combination of shorter-term and longer-term horizons. A time horizon can be considered a constraint because shorter time horizons generally indicate lower risk tolerance and hence constrain portfolio choice, making it more conservative.

- A tax concern is any issue arising from a tax structure that reduces the amount of the total return that can be used for current needs or reinvested for future growth. Tax concerns constrain portfolio choice. If differences exist between the tax rates applying to investment income and capital gains, tax considerations will influence the choice of investment.
- Legal and regulatory factors are external considerations that may constrain investment decision making. For example, a government agency may limit the use of certain asset classes in retirement portfolios.

Unique circumstances are internal factors (other than a liquidity requirement, time horizon, or tax concerns) that may constrain portfolio choices. For example, an investor seeking to avoid investments in tobacco companies will place an internal constraint on portfolio choice.

PROBLEMS

1. A. An individual expects to save €50,000 during the coming year from income from non-portfolio sources, such as salary. She will need €95,000 within the year to make a down payment for a house purchase. What is her liquidity requirement for the coming year?

   B. Endowments are funds that are typically owned by nonprofit institutions involved in educational, medical, cultural, and other charitable activities. Classified as institutional investors, endowments are almost always established with the intent of lasting into perpetuity.

   The Wilson-Fowler Endowment was established in the United States to provide financial support to Wilson-Fowler College. An endowment's spending rate defines the fraction of endowment assets distributed to the supported institution. The Wilson-Fowler Endowment has established a spending rate of 4 percent a year; the endowment follows the simple rule of spending, in a given year, an amount equal to 4% × (Market value of the endowment at the end of the prior year). This amount is committed to the budgetary support of the college for the coming year. At the end of the prior year, the market value of the Wilson-Fowler Endowment's assets stood at $75 million. In addition, the Wilson-Fowler Endowment has committed to contribute $1 million in the coming year to the construction of a new student dormitory. Planners at the endowment expect the endowment to receive contributions or gifts (from alumni and other sources) of $400,000 over the coming year. What is the anticipated liquidity requirement of the Wilson-Fowler Endowment for the coming year?

2. The Executive Director of the Judd University Endowment estimates that the capital markets will provide a 9 percent expected return for an endowment portfolio taking above-average risk, and a 7 percent expected return for an endowment portfolio taking average risk. The Judd Endowment provides tuition scholarships for Judd University students. The spending rate has been 4 percent, and the expected tuition inflation rate is 3 percent. Recently, university officials have pressured the endowment to increase the spending rate to 6 percent. The endowment has an average to below-average ability to accept risk and only an average willingness to take risk, but a university official claims

that the risk tolerance should be raised because higher returns are needed. Discuss an appropriate return objective and risk tolerance for the Judd Endowment.

3. Stux (1994) describes a country allocation strategy across five major equity markets: the United States, the United Kingdom, Germany, France, and Japan. In this strategy, a measure of relative attractiveness among the five equity markets is used as a factor in determining the weights of the five equity markets in the overall portfolio. The investment in each country, however, whatever the country's weight, is an indexed investment in the equity market of that country. The weights of the five equity markets in the overall portfolio generally are expected to differ from benchmark weights (the weights of the countries in an appropriate benchmark for the international equity market), within limits.

   A. Characterize the two components (portfolio weights and within-country investments) of the country allocation strategy using the text's framework for classifying investment strategies.
   B. Characterize the country allocation strategy overall.

4. Characterize each of the investment objectives given below as one of the following: an absolute risk objective, a relative risk objective, an absolute return objective, or a relative return objective.

   A. Achieve a rate of return of 8 percent a year.
   B. Limit the standard deviation of portfolio returns to 20 percent a year or less.
   C. Achieve returns in the top quartile of the portfolio's peer universe (the set of portfolios with similar investment objectives and characteristics).
   D. Maintain a 10 percent or smaller probability that the portfolio's return falls below the threshold level of 5 percent per annum over a one-year time horizon.
   E. Achieve a tracking risk of no more than 4 percent per annum with respect to the portfolio's benchmark.

Questions 5 through 10 relate to James Stephenson. Select and justify the best answer.

James Stephenson, age 55 and single, is a surgeon who has accumulated a substantial investment portfolio without a clear long-term strategy in mind. Two of his patients who work in financial markets comment as follows:

- James Hrdina: "My investment firm, based on its experience with investors, has standard investment policy statements in five categories. You would be better served to adopt one of these standard policy statements instead of spending time developing a policy based on your individual circumstances."
- Charles Gionta: "Developing a long-term policy can be unwise given the fluctuations of the market. You want your investment adviser to react continuously to changing conditions and not be limited by a set policy."

Stephenson hires a financial adviser, Caroline Coppa. At their initial meeting, Coppa compiles the following notes:

Stephenson currently has a $2.0 million portfolio that has a large concentration in small-capitalization U.S. equities. Over the past five years, the portfolio has averaged 20 percent annual total return on investment. Stephenson hopes that, over the long term, his portfolio will continue to earn 20 percent annually. When asked about his risk tolerance, he described it as "average." He was surprised when informed that U.S. small-cap portfolios have experienced extremely high volatility.

He does not expect to retire before age 70. His current income is more than sufficient to meet his expenses. Upon retirement, he plans to sell his surgical practice and use the proceeds to purchase an annuity to cover his postretirement cash flow needs.

Both his income and realized capital gains are taxed at a 30 percent rate. No pertinent legal or regulatory issues apply. He has no pension or retirement plan but does have sufficient health insurance for postretirement needs.

5. The comments about investment policy statements made by Stephenson's patients are *best* characterized as

	Hrdina	Gionta
A.	Correct	Correct
B.	Correct	Incorrect
C.	Incorrect	Correct
D.	Incorrect	Incorrect

6. In formulating the return objective for Stephenson's investment policy statement, the *most* appropriate determining factor for Coppa to focus on is

   A. Return desires
   B. Ability to take risk
   C. Return requirement
   D. Stephenson's returns over past five years

7. Stephenson's willingness and ability to accept risk can be *best* characterized as

	Willingness to Accept Risk	Ability to Accept Risk
A.	Below average	Below average
B.	Below average	Above average
C.	Above average	Below average
D.	Above average	Above average

8. Stephenson's tax and liquidity constraints can be *best* characterized as

	Tax Constraint	Liquidity Constraint
A.	Significant	Significant
B.	Significant	Insignificant
C.	Insignificant	Significant
D.	Insignificant	Insignificant

9. Stephenson's time horizon is best characterized as

   A. Short-term and single-stage
   B. Short-term and multistage

C. Long-term and single-stage
D. Long-term and multistage

10. Stephenson's return objective and risk tolerance are most appropriately described as

	Return Objective	Risk Tolerance
A.	Below average	Below average
B.	Below average	Above average
C.	Above average	Below average
D.	Above average	Above average

11. James Stephenson Investment Profile

Case Facts	
Type of investor	Individual; surgeon, 55 years of age, in good health
Asset base	$2 million
Stated return desire *or* investment goal	10 percentage points above the average annual return on U.S. small-capitalization stocks
Annual spending needs	$150,000
Annual income from nonportfolio sources (before tax)	$350,000 from surgical practice
Other return factors	Inflation is 3%
Risk considerations	Owns large concentration in U.S. small-capitalization stocks
Specific liquidity requirements	$70,000 charitable donation in 10 months
Time specifications	Retirement at age 70
Tax concerns	Income and capital gains taxed at 30 percent

Questions

1. Underline the word at right that best describes the client's:

A. *Willingness to accept risk*	Below average	Above average
B. *Ability to accept risk*	Below average	Above average
C. *Risk tolerance*	Below average	Above average
D. *Liquidity requirement*	Significant	Not significant
E. *Time horizon*	Single stage	Multistage
F. *Overall time horizon*	Short to intermediate term	Long term
G. *Tax concerns*	Significant	Not significant

2. Discuss appropriate client objectives:
   A. *Risk*
   B. *Return*

12. Foothill College Endowment Fund

Case Facts

Type of investor	Institutional; endowment
Purpose	Provide annual scholarships currently totaling $39.5 million
Asset base	$1 billion
Stated return desire	6 percent, calculated as spending rate of 4 percent plus previously expected college tuition inflation of 2 percent
Other return factors	Revised expectation of college tuition inflation is 3 percent
Tax concerns	Tax exempt

Questions

1. Underline the word at right that best describes the client's:

A. *Risk tolerance*	Below average	Above average
B. *Liquidity requirement*	Significant	Not significant
C. *Time horizon*	Single stage	Multistage
D. *Overall time horizon*	Short to intermediate term	Long term
E. *Tax concerns*	Significant	Not significant

2. Discuss appropriate client objectives:
   A. *Risk*
   B. *Return*

13. Vincenzo Donadoni Investment Profile (adapted from 1998 CFA Level III exam)

Case Facts

Type of investor	Individual; 56 year old male in good health
Asset base	13.0 million Swiss francs (CHF)
Stated return desire *or* investment goal	Leave a trust fund of CHF 15.0 million for three children
Annual spending needs	CHF 250,000 rising with inflation
Annual income from other sources (after tax)	CHF 125,000 consulting income for next two years only
Ability to generate additional income	No
Willingness to accept risk	Impulsive, opinionated, successful with large bets as a businessman, believes success depends on taking initiative
Specific liquidity requirements	CHF 1.5 million immediately to renovate house CHF 2.0 million in taxes due in nine months
Time specifications	Long term except for liquidity concerns
Legal and regulatory factors	None
Unique circumstances	None

Questions

1. Underline the word at right that best describes the client's:

A. *Willingness to accept risk*	Below average	Above average
B. *Ability to accept risk*	Below average	Above average
C. *Risk tolerance*	Below average	Above average
D. *Liquidity requirement*	Significant	Not significant
E. *Time horizon*	Single stage	Multistage
F. *Overall time horizon*	Short to intermediate term	Long term

2. Discuss appropriate client objectives:
   - A. *Risk*
   - B. *Return*

CHAPTER 2

MANAGING INDIVIDUAL INVESTOR PORTFOLIOS

James W. Bronson, CFA

Northern Trust Bank
Newport Beach, California

Matthew H. Scanlan, CFA

Barclays Global Investors
San Francisco, California

Jan R. Squires, CFA

CFA Institute
Hong Kong

LEARNING OUTCOMES

After completing this chapter, you will be able to do the following:

- Review situational profiling for individual investors and discuss source of wealth, measure of wealth, and stage of life as approaches to situational profiling.
- Prepare an elementary situational profile for an individual investor.
- Discuss the role of psychological profiling in understanding individual investor behavior.
- Formulate the basic principles of the behavioral finance investment framework.
- Discuss the influence of investor psychology on risk tolerance and investment choices.
- Discuss the use of a personality-typing questionnaire for identifying an investor's personality type.
- Formulate the relationship of risk attitudes and decision-making styles with individual investor personality types.
- Discuss the potential benefits for both clients and investment advisers of having a formal investment policy statement.
- Review the process involved in creating an investment policy statement for a client.

- Discuss each of the major objectives that an individual investor's investment policy statement includes.
- Distinguish between an individual investor's ability to take risk and willingness to take risk.
- Discuss how to set risk and return objectives for individual investor portfolios.
- Discuss each of the major constraints that an individual investor's investment policy statement includes.
- Formulate and justify an investment policy statement for an individual investor.
- Demonstrate the use of a process of elimination to arrive at an appropriate strategic asset allocation for an individual investor.
- Determine the strategic asset allocation that is most appropriate given an individual investor's investment objectives and constraints.
- Compare and contrast traditional deterministic versus Monte Carlo approaches in the context of retirement planning.
- Discuss the advantages of the Monte Carlo approach to retirement planning.

SUMMARY OVERVIEW

Chapter 2 has presented an overview of portfolio management for individual investors, including the information-gathering process, situational and psychological profiling of clients, formulation of an investment policy statement, strategic asset allocation, and the use of Monte Carlo simulation in personal retirement planning.

- Situational profiling seeks to anticipate individual investors' concerns and risk tolerance by specifying the investor's source of wealth, measure or adequacy of wealth in relationship to needs, and stage of life.
- Psychological profiling addresses human behavioral patterns and personality characteristics and their effect on investment choices. It is particularly important in assessing risk tolerance.
- Underlying behavioral patterns often play an important role in setting individual risk tolerance and return objectives.
- Based on their responses to a questionnaire, individual investors may be classified into descriptive personality types, such as *cautious, methodical, spontaneous*, or *individualist.*
- Using the results of situational and psychological profiling, and the financial information gathered in the interviewing process, an adviser can formulate an investment policy statement (IPS).
- A carefully formulated IPS serves as the keystone to the relationship between investor and investment adviser. The process of creating an IPS mirrors the process of portfolio management. The policy statement reconciles investment goals with the realities of risk tolerance and investment constraints, resulting in operational guidelines for portfolio construction and a mutually agreed-upon basis for portfolio monitoring and review. By necessity, the investor and adviser must discuss the construction of an IPS in a linear fashion. In practice, the process is dynamic, similar to solving simultaneously for multiple variables.
- The return objective for an investment portfolio must ultimately be made consistent with the investor's risk tolerance and the portfolio's ability to generate returns. The traditional division of return requirements between "income" and "growth" objectives may seem intuitive, but these terms blur the distinction between return goals and risk tolerance. The "total return" approach seeks to identify a portfolio return that will meet the investor's objectives without exceeding the portfolio's risk tolerance or violating its investment constraints.

- Risk tolerance reflects both an investor's ability and willingness to accept risk. Ability to accept risk is a probabilistic assessment of the investment portfolio's ability to withstand negative investment outcomes and still meet the investor's objectives. Willingness to accept risk is a more subjective assessment of the investor's propensity for risk taking. Because many individuals are unfamiliar with the quantitative terminology of risk tolerance, the investment adviser may use psychological or situational profiling to anticipate client attitudes toward risk.
- Investment constraints include the following:

  1. *Liquidity.* Liquidity needs may be categorized as ongoing expenses, emergency reserves, and negative liquidity events. Liquidity is the ease and price certainty with which assets can be converted into cash. Because assets with stable prices and low transaction costs are generally low-risk investments, an increasing need for liquidity will constrain the investment portfolio's ability to accept risk. Significant illiquid holdings and their associated risks should be documented. For many investors, the home or residence represents a large percentage of total net worth and is relatively illiquid. Although the primary residence may be viewed as offsetting long-term needs for care and housing, it should be discussed as a source of investment risk and as a source of funding for future cash flow needs. The investor and adviser should together thoroughly review the risks associated with any concentration of net worth. Large "positive" liquidity events should also be documented, even though they will not act as a constraint.
  2. *Time horizon.* The investor's time horizon also constrains his ability to accept risk; shorter investment horizons allow less time to make up portfolio losses. The time horizon constraint may be categorized as short term, intermediate term, or long term and as single stage or multistage. With sufficient assets and multigenerational estate planning, even older investors may retain a long-term investment perspective.
  3. *Taxes.* The basic principles of tax deferral, avoidance, and reduction underlie all tax-driven portfolio strategies, but individual solutions are highly country specific and client specific. Taxes relevant to portfolio management generally fall into four major categories: income, gains, wealth transfer, and property.
  4. *Legal and regulatory environment.* The investment portfolio's legal and regulatory environment is ultimately country and client specific. A basic knowledge of English and American trust law is often valuable, however, as the terminology is widely recognized and the framework widely applied.
  5. *Unique circumstances.* The IPS should capture all unique investment considerations affecting the portfolio. Unique circumstances might include guidelines for social investing, trading restrictions, and privacy concerns.

- As a general rule, only certain asset allocations will be consistent with the client's return objectives, risk tolerance, and investment constraints. The adviser can use a process of elimination to arrive at an appropriate long-term strategic allocation.
- For individual investors, investment decisions, including asset allocation, are made on an after-tax basis. This is a key distinction in contrast to tax-exempt institutions.
- Monte Carlo simulation has certain advantages over deterministic approaches: It more accurately portrays risk–return trade-offs, can illustrate the trade-offs between the attainment of short-term and long-term goals, provides more realistic modeling of taxes, and is better suited to assessing multiperiod effects.

PROBLEMS

Problems 1 through 8 relate to the Inger family: father (Peter), mother (Hilda), son (Hans), and daughter (Christa) and her child (Jürgen). Peter is the founder and majority owner of IngerMarine.

Christa estimates that her revised annual living expenses, including a new studio and apartment, will average €132,500 (excluding Jürgen's educational costs). If necessary, she could combine her apartment and studio to reduce spending by €32,500. She does not want her financial security to be dependent on further gifting from her parents and is pleased that, after the sale of IngerMarine, she will be able to meet her new living expenses with proceeds from art sales (€50,000) and the expected total return of the proposed investment portfolio (€82,500). Because of the uncertainty of art sales, Christa plans to establish an emergency reserve equal to one year's living expenses. Her after-tax proceeds from the sale of IngerMarine are expected to be $€1,200,000 \times (1 - 0.15) = €1,020,000$. She also holds €75,000 in balanced mutual funds and €25,000 in a money market fund. Christa intends to reevaluate her policy statement and asset allocation guidelines every three years.

1. Discuss Christa's liquidity requirements.
2. Determine Christa's return requirement and evaluate whether her portfolio can be expected to satisfy that requirement if inflation averages 3 percent annually and she reduces her annual living expenses to €100,000 by combining her apartment and studio.
3. Explain why an analysis of Christa's investment policy statement might become necessary before the next three-year review.

Hans's increasingly irresponsible lifestyle has become a burden to his parents. Hans was recently arrested for reckless driving—he crashed his car into a restaurant, causing considerable damage and injuring a patron. As a result of Hans's behavior, Peter has placed him on probationary leave of absence from IngerMarine but will allow him to retain his annual salary of €100,000. The restaurant patron is suing Hans for €700,000 in damages, and the restaurant owner estimates that it will take €500,000 to repair damages to his building. Hans's insurance will cover costs to a maximum of only €200,000.

4. Assess the impact of these events on Hans's liquidity and his personal financial statement. What course of action should he pursue?
5. Assess Hans's probable future ability to assume risk, based on information about his background and current living situation.

Peter and Hilda are considering an investment of €1,000,000 in one of the following investment funds:

Investment	Projected Income	Projected Price Appreciation	Projected Turnover
High-growth stock fund	2.0%	12%	75%
Equity value fund	2.5%	10%	25%
Municipal bond fund	5.0% (tax free)	2%	15%

6. Evaluate each investment fund based only on its after-tax return. *Note:* Capital gains tax = Price appreciation ×15% × Turnover rate

IngerMarine has experienced a catastrophic event from which it cannot recover. Damage claims resulting from a design flaw are expected to leave IngerMarine bankrupt and its stock worthless. Peter's pension is also lost.

7. Assess the probable impact on Peter's and Hilda's return requirement.
8. Assess the probable impact on Peter's and Hilda's portfolio constraints.
9. Adapted from the 2001 CFA Level III examination:

   James Stephenson, 55 years old and single, is a surgeon. He has accumulated a \$2.0 million investment portfolio with a large concentration in small-capitalization U.S. equities. During the past five years, his portfolio has averaged a 20 percent annual total return on investment. Stephenson's current portfolio of \$2.0 million is invested as shown in Exhibit 2-1.

EXHIBIT 2-1 Summary of Stephenson's Current Portfolio

	Value	Percent of Total	Expected Annual Return	Annual Standard Deviation
Short-term bonds	\$ 200,000	10%	4.6%	1.6%
Domestic large-cap equities	600,000	30	12.4	19.5
Domestic small-cap equities	1,200,000	60	16.0	29.9
Total portfolio	\$2,000,000	100%	13.8%	23.1%

His newly hired financial adviser, Caroline Coppa, has compiled the following notes from her meetings with Stephenson:

> Stephenson hopes that long term, his investment portfolio will continue to earn 20 percent annually. For the remainder of this year, he would like to earn a return greater than the 5 percent yield to maturity currently available from short-term government notes. When asked about his risk tolerance, he described it as "average." He was surprised when informed that U.S. small-cap portfolios have historically experienced extremely high volatility.
>
> Stephenson does not expect to retire before age 70. His current annual income from his surgical practice is \$250,000, which is more than sufficient to meet his current yearly expenses of \$150,000. Upon retirement, he plans to sell his surgical practice and use the proceeds to purchase an annuity to cover his postretirement cash flow needs. He could not state any additional long-term goals or needs.
>
> Stephenson's income and realized capital gains are taxed at a 30 percent rate. No pertinent legal or regulatory issues apply. He has no pension or retirement plan but does have sufficient health insurance for postretirement needs.

Stephenson soon expects to receive an additional \$2.0 million from an inheritance and plans to invest the entire amount in an index fund that best complements the current portfolio. Coppa is evaluating the four index funds shown in Exhibit 2-2 for their ability to produce a portfolio that will meet the following two criteria relative to the current portfolio:

EXHIBIT 2-2 Index Fund Characteristics

Index Fund	Expected Annual Return	Expected Annual Standard Deviation	Correlation of Returns with Current Portfolio
A	15%	25%	+0.80
B	11%	22%	+0.60
C	16%	25%	+0.90
D	14%	22%	+0.65

1. Maintain or enhance expected return.
2. Maintain or reduce volatility.

Each fund is invested in an asset class that is not substantially represented in the current portfolio.

A. Formulate the following elements of Stephenson's investment policy statement and justify your response for each element with two arguments:

   i. Return objective
   ii. Risk tolerance
   iii. Liquidity requirements
   iv. Time horizon

B. State which fund Coppa should recommend to Stephenson. Justify your choice by describing how your chosen fund best meets both of the criteria set forth by Coppa. (No calculations are required.)

10. Adapted from the 2000 CFA Level III examination:

Robert Taylor, 50 years old and a U.S. resident, recently retired and received a $500,000 cash payment from his employer as an early retirement incentive. He also obtained $700,000 by exercising his company stock options. Both amounts are net of tax. Taylor is not entitled to a pension; however, his medical expenses are covered by insurance paid for by his former employer. Taylor is in excellent health and has a normal life expectancy.

Taylor's wife died last year after a long illness, which resulted in devastating medical expenses. All their investments, including a home, were liquidated to fully satisfy these medical expenses.

Taylor has no assets other than the $1.2 million cash referenced above, and he has no debts. He plans to acquire a $300,000 home in three months and insists on paying cash given his recent adverse experience with creditors. When presented with investment options, Taylor consistently selects the most conservative alternative.

After settling into his new home, Taylor's living expenses will be $2,000 per month and will rise with inflation. He does not plan to work again.

Taylor's father and his wife's parents died years ago. His mother, Renee, is 72 years old and in excellent physical health. Her mental health, however, is deteriorating and she has relocated to a long-term-care facility. Renee's expenses total $3,500 per month. Her monthly income is $1,500 from pensions. Her income and expenses will rise with inflation. She has no investments or assets of value. Taylor, who has no siblings, must cover Renee's income shortfall.

EXHIBIT 2-3 Robert Taylor Investment Policy Statement

Return objective	• Income requirement is $2,000 monthly. • Total return requirement is 2.7% annually ($24,000/$900,000).
Risk tolerance	• Substantial asset base and low return requirement provide ample resources to support an aggressive, growth-oriented portfolio.
Time horizon	• Client is 50 years old, recently retired, and in excellent health. • Time horizon exceeds 20 years.
Liquidity needs	• $300,000 is needed in three months for purchase of home. • Modest additional cash is needed for normal relocation costs. $100,000 may be needed for possible investment in son's business. • A normal, ongoing cash reserve level should be established.
Tax concerns	• There is little need to defer income. • Mother's expenses may have an effect.
Legal and regulatory factors	• No special considerations exist.
Unique circumstances	• Client desires to support mother. • Client insists that any investment in son's business be excluded from long-term planning. • Client has strong aversion to debt.

Taylor has one child, Troy. Troy and a friend need funds immediately for a start-up business with first-year costs estimated at $200,000. The partners have no assets and have been unable to obtain outside financing. The friend's family has offered to invest $100,000 in the business in exchange for a minority equity stake if Taylor agrees to invest the same amount.

Taylor would like to assist Troy; however, he is concerned about the partners' ability to succeed, the potential loss of his funds, and whether his assets are sufficient to support his needs and to support Renee. He plans to make a decision on this investment very soon. If he invests $100,000 in Troy's business, he insists that this investment be excluded from any investment strategy developed for his remaining funds.

With the above information, portfolio manager Sarah Wheeler prepared the investment policy statement for Taylor shown in Exhibit 2-3.

A. Evaluate the appropriateness of Taylor's investment policy statement with regard to the following objectives:

   i. Return requirement
   ii. Risk tolerance
   iii. Time horizon
   iv. Liquidity requirements

After revising the investment policy statement and confirming it with Taylor, Wheeler is now developing a long-term strategic asset allocation for Taylor. Wheeler will use the following revised information to recommend one of the allocations in Exhibit 2-4.

- Taylor has decided to invest $100,000 in his son's business but still insists that this investment be disregarded in making his allocation decision.
- Taylor's total cash flow needs have changed to $4,200 a month.
- The available asset base is $800,000.
- Wheeler estimates that the inflation rate will be 1 percent next year.

EXHIBIT 2-4 Potential Long-Term Strategic Asset Allocations

	Allocation			
	A	B	C	D
Asset Class Weighting				
Stocks	20%	40%	60%	80%
Bonds	75%	55%	35%	15%
Cash	5%	5%	5%	5%
Total	100%	100%	100%	100%
Expected Annual				
Return	6.7%	7.5%	8.2%	9.1%
Standard Deviation	9.0%	11.5%	15.3%	19.0%
Potential for Growth				
Asset Growth	Very low	Low	Moderate	High
Income Growth	Very low	Low	Moderate	High
Current Income	High	High	Low	Very low
Stability	Very high	High	Moderate	Low

- Taylor is determined to maintain the real value of his assets because he plans to set up a charitable foundation in the future.
- Taylor insists on taking no more risk than absolutely necessary to achieve his return goals.

B. Select the strategic asset allocation that is most appropriate for Taylor and justify your selection with two supporting reasons related to the revised information shown above.

11. Adapted from the 1999 CFA Level III examination:

Mark and Andrea Mueller, U.S. residents, are reviewing their financial plan. The Muellers, both 53 years old, have one daughter, 18 years old. With their combined after-tax salaries totaling $100,000 a year, they are able to meet their living expenses and save $25,000 after taxes annually. They expect little change in either their incomes or expenses on an inflation-adjusted basis other than the addition of their daughter's college expenses. Their only long-term financial goal is to provide for themselves and for their daughter's education. The Muellers both wish to retire in 10 years.

Their daughter, a talented musician, is now entering an exclusive five-year college program. This program requires a $50,000 contribution, payable now, to the college's endowment fund. Thereafter, her tuition and living expenses, to be paid entirely by the Muellers, are estimated at $40,000 annually.

The Mueller's personal investments total $600,000, and they plan to continue to manage the portfolio themselves. They prefer "conservative growth investments with minimal volatility." One-third of their portfolio is in the stock of Andrea's employer, a publicly traded technology company with a highly uncertain future. The shares have a very low cost basis for tax purposes. The Muellers, currently taxed at 30 percent on income and 20 percent on net realized capital gains, have accumulated losses from past unsuccessful investments that can be used to fully offset $100,000 of future realized gains.

In 10 years, Mark will receive a distribution from a family trust. His portion is now $1.2 million and is expected to grow prior to distribution. Mark receives no income from the trust and has no influence over, or responsibility for, its management. The Muellers know that these funds will change their financial situation materially but have excluded the trust from their current financial planning.

A. Construct the objectives and constraints portion of an investment policy statement for the Muellers, addressing each of the following:

   i. Return objective
   ii. Risk tolerance
   iii. Time horizon
   iv. Liquidity requirements
   v. Tax concerns
   vi. Unique circumstances

Ten years have passed. The Muellers, now both aged 63, will retire this year. The distribution from Mark's family trust will occur within the next two weeks. The Muellers' current circumstances are summarized below:

Personal Circumstances and Assets

- Pension income will total $100,000 a year and will not increase with inflation.
- Annual expenses will total $180,000 initially and will increase with inflation.
- Inflation is expected to be 2 percent annually.
- Their personal investments now total $1 million (excluding trust distribution).
- The Muellers will rely on this $1 million portfolio to support their lifestyle and do not wish to reduce their level of spending.
- The Muellers have health problems and neither is expected to live more than 10 years. All health care expenses will be covered by employer-paid insurance.
- The Muellers' daughter is now financially independent, and the Muellers' sole investment objective is to meet their spending needs.
- The Muellers are not concerned with growing or maintaining principal. The income deficit may be met with both investment income and by invading principal.

Trust Distribution Assets

- The trust distribution totals $2 million and will occur within the next two weeks. No tax liability is created by the distribution.
- The Muellers will maintain separate accounts for their personal assets and the trust distribution.
- They do not plan to withdraw income or principal.
- Tax liabilities produced by these assets will be paid from this portfolio.
- The Muellers plan to donate these assets to an arts society when the surviving spouse dies. They have made a minimum pledge of $2.6 million toward construction of a new building.
- An after-tax annual return of 5.4 percent is required over five years to meet the minimum pledge.
- The Muellers are concerned only that a minimum gift of $2.6 million is available. The Muellers assume that at least one of them will live at least five years and that neither will live more than 10 years.

Alternative portfolios for the Muellers' consideration appear in Exhibit 2-5.

EXHIBIT 2-5

	Portfolio			
Asset Allocation	A	B	C	D
Domestic large-cap stocks	14%	30%	40%	30%
Domestic small-cap stocks	3	5	10	25
Foreign stocks	3	5	10	25
Intermediate-term fixed income	70	60	30	20
Cash equivalents	10	0	10	0
Total	100%	100%	100%	100%
Expected annual return[a]	4.2%	5.8%	7.5%	8.5%
Annual standard deviation	6.0%	8.0%	13.0%	18.0%

[a]Nominal after-tax returns.

B. Select and justify with three reasons the most appropriate of the four portfolios from Exhibit 2-5 as an asset allocation for the Muellers' $1 million in personal assets.

C. Select and justify with three reasons the most appropriate of the four portfolios from Exhibit 2-5 as an asset allocation for the Muellers' $2 million in trust distribution assets.

12. Adapted from the 1997 CFA Level III examination:

John Mesa, CFA, is a portfolio manager in the Trust Department of BigBanc. Mesa has been asked to review the investment portfolios of Robert and Mary Smith, a retired couple and potential clients. Previously, the Smiths had been working with another financial adviser, WealthMax Financial Consultants (WFC). To assist Mesa, the Smiths have provided the following background information:

Family. We live alone. Our only daughter and granddaughter are financially secure and independent.

Health. We are both 65 years of age and in good health. Our medical costs are covered by insurance.

Housing. Our house needs major renovation. The work will be completed within the next six months, at an estimated cost of $200,000.

Expenses. Our annual after-tax living costs are expected to be $150,000 for this year and are rising with inflation, which is expected to continue at 3 percent annually.

Income. In addition to income from the Gift Fund and the Family Portfolio (both described below), we receive a fixed annual pension payment of $65,000 (after taxes), which continues for both of our lifetimes.

Financial Goals. Our primary objective is to maintain our financial security and support our current lifestyle. A secondary objective is to leave $1 million to our grandchild and $1 million to our local college. We recently completed the $1 million gift to the college by creating a "Gift Fund." Preserving the remaining assets for our granddaughter is important to us.

Taxes. Our investment income, including bond interest and stock dividends, is taxed at 30 percent. Our investment returns from price appreciation (capital gains) are taxed at 15 percent, at the time of sale. We have no other tax considerations.

General Comments. We needed someone like WFC to develop a comprehensive plan for us to follow. We can follow such a plan once it is prepared for us. We invest only in companies with which we are familiar. We will not sell a security for less than we paid for it. Given our need for income, we invest only in dividend-paying stocks.

Investments. We benefit from two investment accounts:

- The Gift Fund ($1 million) represents our gift to the college. During our lifetimes, we will receive fixed annual payments of $40,000 (tax free) from the Gift Fund. Except for the annual payments to us, the Gift Fund is managed solely for the benefit of the college—we may not make any other withdrawals of either income or principal. Upon our deaths, all assets remaining in the Gift Fund will be transferred into the college's endowment.
- The Family Portfolio ($1.2 million) represents the remainder of our lifetime savings. The portfolio is invested entirely in very safe securities, consistent with the investment policy statement prepared for us by WFC as shown in Exhibit 2-6:

EXHIBIT 2-6 WFC Investment Policy Statement for Smith Family Portfolio

The Smith Family Portfolio's primary focus is the production of current income, with long-term capital appreciation a secondary consideration. The need for a dependable income stream precludes investment vehicles with even modest likelihood of losses. Liquidity needs reinforce the need to emphasize minimum-risk investments. Extensive use of short-term investment-grade investments is entirely justified by the expectation that a low-inflation environment will exist indefinitely into the future. For these reasons, investments will emphasize U.S. Treasury bills and notes, intermediate-term investment-grade corporate debt, and select "blue chip" stocks with assured dividend distributions and minimal price fluctuations.

To assist in a discussion of investment policy, Mesa presents four model portfolios used by BigBanc; Exhibit 2-7 applies the bank's long-term forecasts for asset class returns to each portfolio.

A. Prepare and justify an alternative investment policy statement for the Smiths' Family Portfolio.
B. Describe how your IPS addresses three specific deficiencies in the WFC investment policy statement.
C. Recommend a portfolio from Exhibit 2-7 for the Family Portfolio. Justify your recommendation with specific reference to:

   i. Three portfolio characteristics in Exhibit 2-7 other than expected return or yield.
   ii. The Smiths' return objectives. Show your calculations.

EXHIBIT 2-7 BigBanc Model Portfolios

Asset Class	Total Return	Yield	Portfolios			
			A	B	C	D
U.S. large-cap stocks	13.0%	3.0%	0%	35%	45%	0%
U.S. small-cap stocks	15.0	1.0	0	5	15	0
Non-U.S. stocks	14.0	1.5	0	10	15	10
U.S. corporate bonds (AA)	6.5	6.5	80	20	0	30
U.S. Treasury notes	6.0	6.0	0	10	5	20
Non-U.S. government bonds	6.5	6.5	0	5	5	0
Municipal bonds (AA)[a]	4.0	4.0	0	10	0	10
Venture capital	20.0	0.0	0	0	10	25
U.S. Treasury bills	4.0	4.0	20	5	5	5
Total			100%	100%	100%	100%
After-tax expected return			4.2%	7.5%	13.0%	6.4%
Sharpe ratio			0.35	0.50	0.45	0.45
After-tax yield			4.2%	2.9%	1.9%	3.3%
Expected inflation: 3.0%						

[a]Tax-exempt.

13. Adapted from the 2004 CFA Level III examination:

Louise and Christopher Maclin live in London, United Kingdom, and currently rent an apartment in the metropolitan area. Christopher Maclin, aged 40, is a supervisor at Barnett Co. and earns an annual salary of £80,000 before taxes. Louise Maclin, aged 38, stays home to care for their newborn twins. She recently inherited £900,000 (after wealth-transfer taxes) in cash from her father's estate. In addition, the Maclins have accumulated the following assets (current market value):

- £5,000 in cash
- £160,000 in stocks and bonds
- £220,000 in Barnett common stock

The value of their holdings in Barnett stock has appreciated substantially as a result of the company's growth in sales and profits during the past 10 years. Christopher Maclin is confident that the company and its stock will continue to perform well.

The Maclins need £30,000 for a down payment on the purchase of a house and plan to make a £20,000 non-tax-deductible donation to a local charity in memory of Louise Maclin's father. The Maclins' annual living expenses are £74,000. After-tax salary increases will offset any future increases in their living expenses.

During discussions with their financial adviser, Grant Webb, the Maclins express concern about achieving their educational goals for their children and their own retirement goals. The Maclins tell Webb:

- They want to have sufficient funds to retire in 18 years when their children begin their four years of university education.
- They have been unhappy with the portfolio volatility they have experienced in recent years. They state that they do not want to experience a loss in portfolio value greater than 12 percent in any one year.

- They do not want to invest in alcohol and tobacco stocks.
- They will not have any additional children.

After their discussions, Webb calculates that in 18 years the Maclins will need £2 million to meet their educational and retirement goals. Webb suggests that their portfolio be structured to limit shortfall risk (defined as expected total return minus two standard deviations) to no lower than a negative 12 percent return in any one year. Maclin's salary and all capital gains and investment income are taxed at 40 percent and no tax-sheltering strategies are available. Webb's next step is to formulate an investment policy statement for the Maclins.

A. i. Formulate the risk objective of an investment policy statement for the Maclins.
   ii. Formulate the return objective of an investment policy statement for the Maclins. Calculate the pre-tax rate of return that is required to achieve this objective. Show your calculations.

B. Formulate the constraints portion of an investment policy statement for the Maclins, addressing *each* of the following:
   i. Time horizon
   ii. Liquidity requirements
   iii. Tax concerns
   iv. Unique circumstances

Note: Your response to Part B should not address legal and regulatory factors.

CHAPTER 3

MANAGING INSTITUTIONAL INVESTOR PORTFOLIOS

R. Charles Tschampion, CFA

CFA Institute
New York, New York

Laurence B. Siegel

The Ford Foundation
New York, New York

Dean J. Takahashi

Yale University
New Haven, Connecticut

John L. Maginn, CFA

Maginn Associates, Inc.
Omaha, Nebraska

LEARNING OUTCOMES

After completing this chapter, you will be able to do the following:

- Contrast a defined-benefit plan to a defined-contribution plan from the perspectives of both the employee and employer.
- Discuss investment objectives and constraints for defined-benefit plans.
- Evaluate pension fund risk tolerance when risk is considered from the perspective of the (1) plan surplus, (2) sponsor financial status and profitability, (3) sponsor and pension fund common risk exposures, (4) plan features, and (5) workforce characteristics.

- Formulate an investment policy statement for a defined-benefit plan.
- Evaluate the risk management considerations in investing pension plan assets.
- Formulate an investment policy statement for a defined-contribution plan.
- Discuss hybrid pension plans (e.g., cash balance plans) and employee stock ownership plans.
- Distinguish among the types of foundations with respect to their description, purpose, source of funds, and annual spending requirements.
- Discuss investment objectives and constraints for foundations, endowments, insurance companies, and banks.
- Formulate an investment policy statement for a foundation, an endowment, an insurance company, and a bank.
- Contrast investment companies, commodity pools, and hedge funds to other types of institutional investors.
- Evaluate the factors that affect the investment policies of pension funds, foundations, endowments, life and non–life insurance companies, and banks.
- Differentiate among the return objectives, risk tolerances, liquidity requirements, time horizons, tax considerations, legal and regulatory environment, and unique circumstances of pension funds, foundations, endowments, insurance companies, and banks.
- Compare and contrast the asset/liability management needs of pension funds, foundations, endowments, insurance companies, and banks.
- Compare and contrast the investment objectives and constraints of institutional investors given relevant data such as descriptions of their financial circumstances and attitudes toward risk.

SUMMARY OVERVIEW

Chapter 3 has described the investment contexts in which institutional investors operate. Our chief focus has been the development of an investment policy statement for defined-benefit pension plans, defined-contribution pension plans, endowments, foundations, life insurance companies, non–life insurance companies, and banks. We have discussed the specific considerations that enter into the development of appropriate return and risk objectives. We then addressed liquidity requirements, time horizon, tax concerns, legal and regulatory factors, and unique circumstances.

- The two major types of pension plan are defined benefit (DB) plans and defined contribution (DC) plans. A defined-benefit plan specifies the plan sponsor's obligations in terms of the benefit to plan participants. In contrast, a defined-contribution plan specifies the sponsor's obligations in terms of contributions to the pension fund rather than benefits to participants.
- DB pension assets fund the payment of pension benefits (liabilities). The investment performance of a DB plan should be judged relative to its adequacy in funding liabilities even if it is also judged on an absolute basis. The funded status of a DB plan is the relationship of the plan assets to the present value of plan liabilities, and is usually measured with respect to the projected benefit obligation (PBO) definition of plan liabilities.
- In setting a risk objective, DB plan sponsors need to consider plan funded status, sponsor financial status and profitability, sponsor and pension fund common risk exposures, plan features (such as provision for lump-sum distributions), and workforce characteristics.

- A DB pension plan's broad return objective is to achieve returns that adequately fund its pension liabilities on an inflation-adjusted basis. An appropriate return requirement for a fully funded plan is the discount rate applied to pension liabilities. The pension fund's stated return desire may be higher and may reflect considerations relating to reducing pension contributions or increasing pension income.
- For DB plans, liquidity requirements relate to the number of retired lives, the size of contributions in relation to disbursements, and plan features. Factors affecting the time horizon length include whether the plan is a going concern, the age of the workforce, and the proportion of retired lives.
- Defined-contribution plans fall into two types: those in which the plan sponsor sets investment policy, and those in which the plan participants individually set policy. The investment process for the sponsor-directed plans is a simpler version of the process for DB plans.
- For participant-directed DC plans, the principal issues are offering participants sufficient investment choices and avoiding inadequate diversification because of holdings of the sponsor company's stock.
- Hybrid pension plans combine features of DB and DC plans. A cash balance plan is a hybrid plan in which the promised benefit is shown as a balance in a participant-individualized statement. Another important type of hybrid plan is the employee stock ownership plan (ESOP), a type of DC plan entirely or primarily invested in the employer's stock.
- Foundations are grant-making institutions. Private foundations are typically subject to a payout requirement that specifies a minimum level of spending. Endowments are generally not subject to a legal spending requirement. Endowments typically provide vital support of ongoing operations and programs of institutions such as universities, hospitals, museums, and religious organizations.
- The return objective for most foundations (and endowments) can be stated as the sum of the annual spending rate, the cost of generating returns (managing assets), and the expected inflation rate. A multiplicative formulation of the components is more precise than an additive one in specifying the return level that should allow the foundation or endowment to preserve the inflation-adjusted value of assets over many periods.
- A foundation's investment policy can often be more risk tolerant than the investment policy of DB plans because foundation assets need not be managed with respect to a stream of legal liabilities, in general. Endowment risk tolerance often depends on the importance of the endowment to the supported institution's operating budget as reflected in the spending rate, and the use of a smoothing rule for spending, which dampens the portfolio's sensitivity to short-run volatility.
- A foundation or endowment's liquidity requirements come from both anticipated and unanticipated cash needs in excess of contributions received. Anticipated needs are captured in the periodic distributions prescribed by a foundation's or endowment's spending rate. Generally, time horizons are long. A variety of legal and regulatory issues can affect a foundation or endowment's investment activities.
- Insurance companies play a role in absorbing personal and business risks. Insurers are broadly divided into life insurers and non–life insurers (casualty insurers); the two groups have distinct investment concerns.
- Historically, return requirements for life insurers have been tied to the interest rates used by actuaries to determine policyholder reserves or accumulation rates for the funds being held by a company for future disbursement. Actual return objectives have been less clearly defined but may relate to an interest rate spread concerning liabilities.

- Insurers have moved toward segmenting their portfolios in relation to associated liabilities and setting return objectives by major line of business. The result is that a single company's investment policy may incorporate multiple return objectives. Furthermore, many companies have established separate investment policies and strategies for each segment of their portfolios.
- Because of public policy concerns related to payment of insurance benefits, insurer portfolios are viewed as quasi–trust funds from a public policy perspective. As a result, conservative fiduciary principles limit the risk tolerance of both life and non–life insurers.
- As one consequence of the need for managing risk with respect to their contractual liabilities, insurers use a variety of asset/liability management techniques.
- Life insurance companies have valuation concerns (related to prescribed valuation reserves), reinvestment risk, credit risk, and cash flow volatility.
- The liquidity concerns associated with disintermediation of cash value policies, asset/liability mismatch, and asset marketability risk have increased insurers' traditionally relatively minimal liquidity requirements.
- Life insurers have been viewed as the classic long-term investor. As a result of portfolio segmentation, life insurers may establish relatively shorter time horizons for some portfolio segments (e.g., group annuities).
- As a regulated industry, life insurers face many regulatory and legal constraints including those relating to eligible investments, the prudent investor rule, and valuation methods.
- In contrast to life insurers, non–life insurers typically have shorter-term liabilities. The underwriting (profitability) cycle may require non–life insurers to liquidate investments to supplement cash flow shortfalls. For both of these reasons, non–life insurers have much shorter investment time horizons than do life insurers.
- Return requirements reflect competitive pricing policy, profitability concerns, and the requirement for a growing surplus to support the writing of new business.
- A bank's portfolio investments are a residual use of funds after loan demand has been met. The portfolio's overall objectives are to manage the interest rate risk of the balance sheet, manage liquidity, produce income, and manage credit risk. The bank's return objective is to earn a positive spread over the cost of funds. Banks typically have below-average risk tolerance, and liquidity is a key concern. Bank investment is subject to a range of legal and regulatory factors.
- Investment companies such as mutual funds as well as commodity pools and hedge funds are institutional investors that function as investment intermediaries. In contrast to other types of institutional investors, one cannot generalize about the investment objectives and constraints of these types of investors.
- Among institutional investors, asset/liability management (ALM) considerations are particularly important for DB pension funds, insurance companies, and banks.

PROBLEMS

1. Worden Technology, Inc.:

   Based in London, Worden Technology, Inc. is an established company with operations in North America, Japan, and several European countries. The firm has £16 billion in total assets and offers its employees a defined-benefit pension plan.

   Worden's pension plan currently has assets of £8.88 billion and liabilities of £9.85 billion. The plan's goals include achieving a minimum expected return of 8.4 percent

EXHIBIT 3-1 Investment Policy Statements

	IPS X	IPS Y
Return requirement	Plan's objective is to outperform the relevant benchmark return by a substantial margin.	Plan's objective is to match relevant benchmark return.
Risk tolerance	Plan has a high risk tolerance because of the long-term nature of the plan and its liabilities.	Plan has a low risk tolerance because of its limited ability to assume substantial risk.
Time horizon	Plan has a very long time horizon because of its infinite life.	Plan has a shorter time horizon than in the past because of plan demographics.
Liquidity requirement[a]	Plan has moderate liquidity needs to fund monthly benefit payments.	Plan has minimal liquidity needs.

[a]Assume Worden will not contribute to its pension plan over the next several years.

with expected standard deviation of return no greater than 16.0 percent. Next month, Worden will reduce the retirement age requirement for full benefits from 60 years to 55 years. The median age of Worden Technology's workforce is 49 years.

Angus Williamson, CFA, manages the pension plan's investment policy and strategic asset allocation decisions. He has heard an ongoing debate within Worden Technology about the pension plan's investment policy statement (IPS). Exhibit 3-1 compares two IPSs under consideration.

Identify which investment policy statement, X or Y, contains the appropriate language for each of the following components of Worden Technology's pension plan:

i. Return requirement
ii. Risk tolerance
iii. Time horizon
iv. Liquidity

Justify your choice in each instance.

2. LightSpeed Connections (adapted from the 2000 CFA Level III Exam):

Hugh Donovan is chief financial officer (CFO) of LightSpeed Connections (LSC), a rapidly growing U.S. technology company with a traditional defined-benefit pension plan. Because of LSC's young workforce, Donovan believes the pension plan has no liquidity needs and can thus invest aggressively to maximize returns. He also believes that U.S. Treasury bills and bonds, yielding 5.4 percent and 6.1 percent, respectively, have no place in a portfolio with such a long time horizon. His strategy, which has produced excellent returns for the past two years, has been to invest the portfolio as follows:

- 50 percent in a concentrated pool (15 to 20 stocks) of initial public offerings in technology and Internet companies, managed internally by Donovan.
- 25 percent in a small-capitalization growth fund.
- 10 percent in a venture capital fund.
- 10 percent in an S&P 500 index fund.
- 5 percent in an international equity fund.

Working with LSC's Investment Committee, the firm's president, Eileen Jeffries has produced a formal investment policy statement, which reads as follows:

"The LSC Pension Plan's return objective should focus on real total returns that will fund its long-term obligations on an inflation-adjusted basis. The "time-to-maturity" of the corporate workforce is a key element for any defined pension plan; given our young workforce, LSC's Plan has a long investment horizon and more time available for wealth compounding to occur. Therefore, the Plan can pursue an aggressive investment strategy and focus on the higher return potential of capital growth. Under present U.S. tax laws, pension portfolio income and capital gains are not taxed. The portfolio should focus primarily on investments in businesses directly related to our main business to leverage our knowledge base."

A. Evaluate Donovan's investment strategy with respect to its effect on each of the following:

   i. LSC's pension plan beneficiaries.
   ii. Managing pension assets in relation to LSC's corporate strength.

B. Evaluate LSC's investment policy statement in the context of the following:

   i. Return requirement
   ii. Risk tolerance
   iii. Time horizon
   iv. Liquidity

3. Gwartney International:

U.S.-based Gwartney International (GI) is a financially healthy, rapidly growing import/export company with a young workforce. Information regarding GI's defined-benefit pension plan (which is subject to the Employee Retirement Income Security Act [ERISA]) appears in Exhibits 3-2 and 3-3.

In accordance with GI policy, the plan discounts its liabilities at the market interest rate for bonds of the same duration. GI's risk objectives include a limitation on volatility of surplus.

EXHIBIT 3-2

Asset Class	Actual and Target Allocation	Prior-Year Total Return
Large-capitalization U.S. equities	35%	10.0%
Small-capitalization U.S. equities	10	12.0
International equities	5	7.0
Total equities	50	
U.S. Treasury bills (1-year duration)	10	4.5
U.S. intermediate-term bonds and mortgage-backed securities (4-year duration)	17	1.0
U.S. long-term bonds (10-year duration)	23	19.0%[a]
Total fixed income	50%	
Total	100%	10.0%

[a] Income element 7.0%; price gain element 12.0%.

EXHIBIT 3-3

Present value of plan liabilities	$298 million
Market value of plan assets	$300 million
Surplus	$2 million
Duration of liabilities	10 years
Actuarial return assumption	7.0%
GI board's long-term total return objective	9.0%

Giselle Engle, the newly appointed CFO, must explain to the board of directors why the surplus declined in a year when the actual investment return was 100 basis points more than the long-term objective stated by the board.

A. Explain how the plan surplus could decline in a given year despite an actual return in excess of the long-term return objective.
B. Explain the importance of an appropriate investment time horizon when setting investment policy for GI's corporate pension plan.
C. Discuss the risk tolerance of GI's corporate pension plan.

4. Food Processors Inc. (adapted from the 1994 CFA Level III exam):

Food Processors Inc. (FPI) is a mature U.S. company with declining earnings and a weak balance sheet. Its defined-benefit pension plan (which is subject to ERISA) has total assets of $750 million. The plan is underfunded by $200 million by U.S. standards—a cause for concern by shareholders, management, and the board of directors.

The average age of plan participants is 45 years. FPI's annual contribution to the plan and the earnings on its assets are sufficient to meet pension payments to present retirees. The pension portfolio's holdings are equally divided between large-capitalization U.S. equities and high-quality, long-maturity U.S. corporate bonds. For the purpose of determining FPI's contribution to the pension plan, the assumed long-term rate of return on plan assets is 9 percent per year; the discount rate applied to determine the present value of plan liabilities, all of which are U.S. based, is 8 percent. As FPI's Treasurer, you are responsible for oversight of the plan's investments and managers and for liaison with the board's Pension Investment Committee.

At the committee's last meeting, its chair observed that both U.S. stocks and U.S. bonds had recorded total returns in excess of 12 percent per year over the past decade. He then made a pointed comment: "Given this experience, we seem to be overly conservative in using only a 9 percent future return assumption. Why don't we raise the rate to 10 percent? This would be consistent with the recent record, would help our earnings, and should make the stockholders feel a lot better."

You have been directed to examine the situation and prepare a recommendation for next week's committee meeting. Your assistant has provided you with the background information shown in Exhibit 3-4.

Assume that consensus forecast total returns for bonds are at least approximately equal to the bonds' yields.

A. Explain what is meant when a pension plan is said to be "underfunded" and use FPI to illustrate.
B. Discuss the risk–return dilemma that FPI faces.
C. Explain a rationale for reducing the discount rate from its current level of 8 percent.

EXHIBIT 3-4 Capital Markets Data

Asset Class	Total Return 1929–1993	Total Return 1984–1993	Annualized Monthly Standard Deviation 1984–1993	Consensus Forecast Total Return 1994–2000
U.S. Treasury bills	3.7%	6.4%	2.2%	3.5%
Intermediate-term Treasury bonds	5.3	11.4	5.6	5.0
Long-term Treasury bonds	5.0	14.4	11.7	6.0
U.S. corporate bonds (AAA rated)	5.6	14.0	8.9	6.5
U.S. common stocks (S&P 500)	9.5	14.9	18.0	8.5
U.S. inflation rate (annual rate)	3.2%	5.5%	N/A	3.3%

D. Explain how the underfunded condition of FPI's plan would be affected if the discount rate were reduced to 7 percent from the current 8 percent.

5. Medical Research Foundation (adapted from the 1993 CFA Level III exam):

The Medical Research Foundation (MRF), based in the United States, was established to provide grants in perpetuity. MRF has just received word that the foundation will receive a $45 million cash gift three months from now. The gift will greatly increase the size of the foundation's endowment from its current $10 million. The foundation's grant-making (spending) policy has been to pay out virtually all of its annual net investment income. Because its investment approach has been conservative, the endowment portfolio now consists almost entirely of fixed-income assets. The finance committee understands that these actions are causing the real value of foundation assets and the real value of future grants to decline because of inflation effects. Until now, the finance committee believed it had no alternative to these actions, given the large immediate cash needs of the research programs being funded and the small size of the foundation's capital base. The foundation's annual grants must at least equal 5 percent of its assets' market value to maintain MRF's U.S. tax-exempt status, a requirement that is expected to continue indefinitely. The foundation anticipates no additional gifts or fundraising activity for the foreseeable future.

Given the change in circumstances that the cash gift will make, the finance committee wishes to develop new grant-making and investment policies. Annual spending must at least meet the 5 percent of market value requirement, but the committee is unsure how much higher spending can or should be. The committee wants to pay out as much as possible because of the critical nature of the research being funded; however, it understands that preserving the real value of the foundation's assets is equally important in order to preserve its future grant-making capabilities. You have been asked to assist the committee in developing appropriate policies.

A. Identify and discuss the three key elements that should determine the foundation's grant-making (spending) policy.
B. Formulate and justify an investment policy statement for the foundation.

6. James Children's Hospital (adapted from the 1998 CFA Level III Exam):

   The James Children's Hospital (JCH), based in Washington, D.C., has an operating budget of $15 million and has been operating at a budget surplus for the last two years. JCH has a $20 million endowment (JCHE) whose sole purpose is to provide capital equipment for the hospital. The endowment's long-term expected total return is 8.6 percent, which includes a 3.3 percent income component. JCHE has no minimum payout requirement and expects no future contributions. Traditionally, the JCHE board of directors has determined the annual payout based on current needs. Payouts have been rising steadily—to $1,375,000 two years ago and to $1,400,000 last year.

   Michelle Parker, CFO of JCHE, has asked the board's guidance in establishing a long-term spending policy for JCHE. She has received $1.6 million in requests to buy equipment and is concerned about the inflation rate for medical equipment prices, which is 4 percent, versus 2.5 percent for the U.S. Consumer Price Index.

   A. Discuss the implications of the current pressure on JCHE to increase spending.
   B. Discuss how JCHE's time horizon affects its risk tolerance.
   C. Determine a long-term spending policy for JCHE, including a spending rate as a percentage of assets, and justify the policy.

7. Donner Life Insurance (adapted from the 2000 CFA Level III Exam):

   Susan Leighton, treasurer for U.S.-based Donner Life Insurance, has just joined the board of a charitable organization that has a large endowment portfolio. She is researching how the investment policy for an endowment differs from that of life insurance companies and has thus far reached the following conclusions:

   1. Both endowments and life insurance companies have aggressive return requirements.
   2. Endowments are less willing to assume risk than life insurance companies because of donor concerns about volatility and loss of principal.
   3. Endowments are less able to assume risk than life insurance companies because of expectations that endowments should provide stable funding for charitable operations.
   4. Endowments have lower liquidity requirements than life insurance companies because endowment spending needs are met through a combination of current income and capital appreciation.
   5. Both endowments and life insurance companies are subject to stringent legal and regulatory oversight.

   Evaluate each of Leighton's statements in terms of accuracy and justify your conclusions.

8. Hannibal Insurance Company (adapted from the 1997 CFA Level III Exam):

   U.S.-based Hannibal Insurance Company sells life insurance, annuities, and guaranteed investment contracts (GICs) and other protection- and savings-based products. The company has traditionally managed its investments as a single portfolio, neither segmenting the assets nor segregating the surplus. The data in Exhibit 3-5 describe the portfolio.

   The company attributes the decline in the duration of its liabilities to increases in interest rates and the passage of time.

   Hannibal's CFO has instructed the portfolio manager as follows: "The rapidly increasing popularity of our two-year fixed-rate GIC product has increased our asset base substantially during the last year. Interest rates have been rising and will probably rise another 100 basis points this year. You should continue to take advantage of this situation by investing in higher-yielding, investment-grade, longer-duration bonds in order to

EXHIBIT 3-5 Hannibal Insurance Portfolio Data

	Four Years Ago	Last Year
Assets (reserves and surplus portfolio)	$450 million	$500 million
Duration of assets	6.0 years	6.0 years
Liabilities	$390 million	$470 million
Estimated duration of liabilities	5.5 years	4.0 years

maximize our spread and maintain a constant duration of the assets. This strategy will ensure the delivery of a competitive return to our customers."

A. Judge the appropriateness of Hannibal's investment strategy as stated by the CFO. Prepare two arguments that support your position.
B. Evaluate two factors that would affect liability duration for a life insurance company other than changes in interest rates and the passage of time. Relate the two factors to the specific situation at Hannibal. Assume stable mortality rates.
C. Determine the suitability of the segmentation approach to portfolio management at Hannibal Insurance Company. Prepare three arguments that support your position.
D. Contrast the return requirement of the surplus portfolio to the return requirement of policyholder reserves, in regard to U.S. life insurance companies in general.

9. Winthrop Bank:

Winthrop Bank is a commercial bank with operations in North America. Evaluate the effect of each of the following scenarios on the bank's investment objectives, constraints, or risk-taking ability.

A. The target average maturity of loans is increased, with overall risk tolerance unchanged.
B. The asset/liability risk management committee (ALCO) decides to increase Winthrop Bank's credit standards for loans although Winthrop Bank's overall risk tolerance is unchanged.
C. Winthrop decides to sell its mortgage loans as soon as they are booked.
D. More opportunities exist for expanding net interest margins with low risk in Winthrop's loan portfolio than in its securities portfolio.

CHAPTER 4

CAPITAL MARKET EXPECTATIONS

John P. Calverley

American Express Bank
London, England

Alan M. Meder, CFA

Duff & Phelps Investment Management Co.
Chicago, Illinois

Brian D. Singer, CFA

UBS Global Asset Management
London, England

Renato Staub

UBS Global Asset Management
Chicago, Illinois

LEARNING OUTCOMES

After completing this chapter, you will be able to do the following:

- Discuss the role of capital market expectations in the portfolio management process.
- Review a framework for setting capital market expectations.
- Identify and discuss the following as they affect the setting of capital market expectations: the limitations of economic data, data measurement errors and biases, the limitations of historical estimates, *ex post* risk as a biased measure of *ex ante* risk, biases in analysts'

methods, the failure to account for conditioning information, the misinterpretation of correlations, psychological traps, and model uncertainty.
- Review and demonstrate formal tools for setting capital market expectations, including statistical tools (sample estimators, shrinkage estimators, time-series estimators, multifactor models), discounted cash flow models, the risk premium approach, and financial equilibrium models.
- Explain the use of survey and panel methods and judgment in setting capital market expectations.
- Distinguish between the inventory cycle and the business cycle.
- Identify and interpret business cycle phases and their relationship to short- and long-term capital market returns.
- Review the relationship of inflation to the business cycle and characterize the relationship between inflation/deflation and cash, bonds, equity, and real estate.
- Discuss the effects on the business cycle of the following factors: consumer spending, business investment and spending on inventories, and monetary and fiscal policy.
- Demonstrate the use of the Taylor rule to predict central bank behavior.
- Review the shape of the yield curve as an economic predictor and the relationship between the yield curve and fiscal and monetary policy.
- Distinguish between business cycles and economic growth trends and demonstrate the application of business cycle and economic growth trend analysis to the formulation of capital market expectations.
- Identify and interpret the components of economic growth trends and explain how governmental policies and exogenous shocks can affect economic growth trends.
- Identify and interpret macroeconomic and interest and exchange rate linkages between economies.
- Review the differences between emerging market and developed economies and explain the country risk analysis techniques used to evaluate emerging markets.
- Compare and contrast the major approaches to economic forecasting.
- Demonstrate the use of economic information in forecasting returns for cash and equivalents, nominal default-free bonds, defaultable debt, emerging market debt, inflation-indexed bonds, common shares (developed and emerging market), real estate, and currencies.
- Evaluate how economic and competitive factors affect investment markets, sectors, and specific securities.
- Identify and interpret the major approaches to forecasting exchange rates.
- Recommend and justify changes in the component weights of a global investment portfolio based on trends and expected changes in macroeconomic factors.

SUMMARY OVERVIEW

In Chapter 4, we have discussed how investment professionals address the setting of capital market expectations.

- Capital market expectations are essential inputs to deciding on a strategic asset allocation. The process of capital market expectations setting involves the following steps:

  1. Specify the final set of expectations that are needed, including the time horizon to which they apply.

2. Research the historical record.
3. Specify the method(s) and/or model(s) that will be used and the information needs for developing expectations.
4. Determine the best sources for information needs.
5. Interpret the current investment environment using the selected data and methods, applying experience and judgment.
6. Formulate the set of expectations that are needed, documenting conclusions.
7. Monitor actual outcomes and compare to expectations, providing feedback to improve the expectations-setting process.

- Among the challenges in setting capital market expectations are *the limitations of economic data* (including lack of timeliness as well as changing definitions and calculations); *data measurement errors and biases* (including transcription errors, survivorship bias, and appraisal [smoothed] data); *the limitations of historical estimates* (including nonstationarity); *ex post risk as a biased risk measure* (historical prices may reflect expectations of a low-probability catastrophe that did not occur); *biases in analysts' methods* (including data-mining bias and time-period bias); *the failure to account for conditioning information; the misinterpretation of correlations*; and *psychological traps* (including the anchoring trap, the status quo trap, the confirming evidence trap, the overconfidence trap, the prudence trap, and the recallability trap); and *model uncertainty*.
- The tools for formulating capital market expectations include formal tools, survey and panel methods, and judgment. Formal tools include statistical tools, discounted cash flow models, the risk premium approach, and financial market equilibrium models. Analyst judgment includes economic and psychological insight.
- Economic output has cyclical and growth trend components. The cyclical components include the inventory cycle (measured in terms of fluctuation of inventory) and the business cycle (representing fluctuations in gross domestic product [GDP] in relation to long-term trend growth). A typical business cycle has five phases: initial recovery, early upswing, late upswing, slowdown, and recession. Each of the two cyclical components has implications for variables such as interest rates and corporate profits, which are important for capital market expectations. The economic trend growth component (the long-term growth path of GDP) is important particularly for setting long-term expectations.
- Consumer spending is typically the most important factor affecting GDP (it often accounts for 60 to 70 percent of GDP). Retail sales and consumer consumption are closely watched for indications of consumer spending.
- Business investment has a smaller weight in GDP than consumer spending but is more volatile. Data on business investment and spending on inventories reveal recent real business activity.
- Fiscal policy and monetary policy are means by which governments attempt to influence the business cycle.
- Monetary policy makers often target inflation rates and use the central bank's influence over interest rates to achieve policy goals. The Taylor rule gives the optimal short-term interest rate as the neutral rate plus an amount that is positively related to the excess of the GDP and inflation growth rates above their respective trend and target values.
- If monetary and fiscal policies are both tight, the yield curve is typically inverted. When monetary policy is tight but fiscal policy is loose, the yield curve tends to be flat. An inverted yield curve has often preceded a recession.
- In managing cash and equivalents, central bank actions are closely watched.

- For investors buying and selling nominal default-free bonds for the short term, developments in the business cycle and changes in short-term interest rates must be closely watched. News of stronger economic growth usually makes bond yields rise. For long-term investors, inflation expectations are of great importance. For holders of corporate bonds and other defaultable debt, the spread over Treasuries in relation to the business cycle is an important factor.
- Investing in emerging-market debt involves special considerations, such as country risk analysis. Emerging-market governments borrow in a foreign currency and so cannot simply inflate their way out of a problem in servicing the debt; this limitation increases the risk of default.
- Inflation-indexed bonds are not exposed to the risk of unexpected inflation. Generally, yields on such instruments rise with real economic growth and the level of short-term interest rates.
- Investors in common shares should analyze economic factors, first, in the way that they affect company earnings and, second, in the way that they affect interest rates, bond yields, and liquidity. The trend growth in the aggregate economy largely determines the trend growth in aggregate corporate earnings.
- During the economic cycle, the price-to-earnings (P/E) ratio tends to be high and rising when earnings are expected to rise but low and falling if the outlook for earnings worsens. P/E ratios are usually lower for an economy stuck on a slower growth path. High inflation often tends to depress P/E ratios.
- Among the systematic factors affecting real estate returns are growth in consumption, real interest rates, the term structure of interest rates, and unexpected inflation.
- Among the factors affecting exchange rate movements are purchasing power parity, relative economic strength, capital flows, and savings–investment imbalances.

PROBLEMS

1. An analyst is assembling data for use in her firm's expectations-setting process. Several historical measures have been collected and used to set expectations on inflation and consumer consumption trends. Previously, only the most recent 25 years of historical data concerning these measures had been collected and analyzed. Now, an executive has suggested extending the starting point of the data 25 years further back to make the overall analysis more robust. Discuss why the inclusion of the additional data may present problems for the expectations-setting process despite the request's objective of making the analysis more robust.
2. Seth Bildownes is an analyst who has prepared forecasts regarding the current capital market environment. He recently gave his presentation to the managing directors of his firm. Excerpts of his presentation follow:

   "Noting that year-end holiday sales have been weak over the past several years, I believe that current expectations should be likewise muted. In fact, just last week, I had an occasion to visit Harrods and noticed that the number of shoppers seemed quite low. The last time I saw a retail establishment with so little pedestrian traffic at the beginning of December was in 1990, and that coincided with one of the worst holiday sales periods in the past 50 years. Thus, there will be no overall year-over-year retail sales growth this holiday season."

A. Identify any psychological traps that may be interfering with the creation of Bildownes's forecasts.
B. Recommend a way to mitigate the bias caused by any trap identified in Part A.

3. An investor is considering adding three new securities to his internationally focused fixed-income portfolio. The securities under consideration are as follows:

- 1-year U.S. Treasury note (noncallable)
- 10-year BBB/Baa rated corporate bond (callable)
- 10-year mortgage-backed security (MBS) (callable; government-backed collateral)

The investor will invest equally in all three securities being analyzed or will invest in none of them at this time. He will make the added investment provided that the expected spread/premium of the equally weighted investment is at least 0.5 percent (50 bps) over the similar-term Treasury bond. The investor has gathered the following information:

Real risk-free interest rate	1.2%
Current inflation rate	2.2%
Spread of 10-year over 1-year Treasury note	1.0%
Long-term inflation expectation	2.6%
10-yr MBS prepayment risk spread (over 10-year Treasuries)*	95 bps
10-yr call risk spread	80 bps
10-yr BBB credit risk spread (over 10-year Treasuries)	90 bps

*This spread implicitly includes a maturity premium in relation to the 1-year T-note as well as compensation for prepayment risk.

Using only the information given, address the following problems using the risk premium approach:

A. Calculate the expected return that an equal-weighted investment in the three securities could provide.
B. Calculate the expected total risk premium of the three securities, and determine the investor's probable course of action.

4. An Australian investor currently holds an A$240 million equity portfolio. He is considering rebalancing the portfolio based on an assessment of the risk and return prospects facing the Australian economy. Information pertaining to the Australian investment markets and the economy has been collected in the following table:

10-Year Historical	Current	Capital Market Expectations
10-yr avg govt bond yield: 6.6%	10-yr govt bond yield: 5.6%	
Avg annual equity return: 7.3%	Year-over-year equity return: 2.6%	
Avg annual inflation rate: 2.6%	Year-over-year inflation rate: 3.3%	Expected annual inflation: 3.5%

(continued)

10-Year Historical	Current	Capital Market Expectations
Equity market P/E (beginning of period): 15.0X	Current equity market P/E: 14.5X	Expected equity market P/E: 14.0X
Avg annual income return: 2.0%		Expected annual income return: 1.5%
Avg annual real earnings growth: 6.0%		Expected annual real earnings growth: 5.0%

Using the information in the table, address the following problems:

A. Calculate the historical Australian equity risk premium using the bond-yield-plus-risk-premium method.
B. Calculate the expected annual equity return using the Grinold–Kroner model (assume no change in the number of shares outstanding).
C. Using your answer to Part B, calculate the expected annual equity risk premium.

5. An analyst is reviewing various asset alternatives and is presented with the following information directly pertaining to the broad equity market in Switzerland and various industries within the Swiss market that are of particular investment interest.

Expected risk premium for overall global investable market (GIM) portfolio	3.5%
Expected standard deviation for the GIM portfolio	8.5%
Expected standard deviation for Swiss health care industry equity investments	12.0%
Expected standard deviation for Swiss watch industry equity investments	6.0%
Expected standard deviation for Swiss consumer products industry equity investments	7.5%

- Assume that the Swiss market is perfectly integrated with world markets.
- The Swiss health care industry has a correlation of 0.7 with the GIM portfolio.
- The Swiss watch industry has a correlation of 0.8 with the GIM portfolio.
- The Swiss consumer products industry has a correlation of 0.8 with the GIM portfolio.

A. Basing your answers only on the data presented in the table above and using the international capital asset pricing model—in particular, the Singer–Terhaar approach—estimate the expected risk premium for the following:

   i. Swiss health care industry
   ii. Swiss watch industry
   iii. Swiss consumer products industry

B. Judge which industry is most attractive from a valuation perspective.

6. Consider the information given in the following table:

Eurodollar Short Rates (as of start of month)

Month	1-Month Rates	6-Month Rates	Spread: 6-Month vs 1-Month
Jan 2000	5.71%	6.14%	43 bps
Feb 2000	5.80	6.26	46
Mar 2000	5.97	6.35	38
Apr 2000	6.07	6.48	41
May 2000	6.47	6.93	46
Jun 2000	6.58	6.90	32
Jul 2000	6.54	6.84	30
Aug 2000	6.53	6.75	22
Sep 2000	6.54	6.68	14
Oct 2000	6.53	6.64	11
Nov 2000	6.54	6.61	07
Dec 2000	6.58	6.28	−30
Jan 2001	5.48	5.16	−32
Feb 2001	5.13	4.82	−31
Mar 2001	4.98	4.58	−40

A. Determine the implicit economic forecast in the interest rate data given.
B. For a one-year holding period extending from March 1, 2000, to March 1, 2001, determine the relative merits of buying a six-month security now and then another one in six months, or purchasing a one-month Eurodollar security and then rolling that security over each month at the then-prevailing yield.

7. A. How might an analyst use the data reflected below to confirm her suspicion that Brazil is currently experiencing an output gap?
   B. Given your response in Part A, would you expect inflation over the next year to accelerate or decline?

Variable	3/31/2002	3/31/2003	3/31/2004
GDP (index)	129.0	128.5	128.0
Unemployment rate	10.5%	11.0%	11.5%
Capacity utilization rate	80.5%	80.0%	80.0%
Inflation rate	9.0%	8.5%	7.0%

8. Based on the trends that may be calculated from the following economic measures, determine which of the countries below would be expected to achieve higher economic growth rates over the next year if current trends are sustained? Justify your response.

Economic Measures	Croatia (millions of kuna) Qtr 1	Croatia (millions of kuna) Qtr 2	Czech Republic (millions of koruna) Qtr 1	Czech Republic (millions of koruna) Qtr 2
Consumer spending	28	30	350	386
Business capital investment	12	13	205	250
Government investment/ fiscal spending	10	11	110	140
Other miscellaneous GDP factors	−1	−2	−58	−111
Total GDP	49	52	607	665

9. A. Based on targets for inflation and overall economic growth rate and on actual observations of inflation and economic growth rates, apply the Taylor rule to estimate what short-term interest rate level should be an appropriate target for monetary authorities.
   B. Explain why the monetary action suggested by the Taylor rule output may not actually be taken by central bank authorities.

Economic Measures:	GDP Trend/ Inflation Target	Forecast
Year-over-year increase in GDP	3.2%	2.6%
Inflation rate	2.0%	4.0%
Short-term interest rate (neutral value)	4.0%	

10. Pharmavest is an investment advisory firm that focuses solely on companies within the health care (HC) sector. The firm conducts research and manages several commingled health sector funds. Pharmavest is conducting an analysis of health sector companies that have business exposures to the economies of Europe and the United States. The tables below show current and historical economic data and Pharmavest's forecasts of the most likely economic outcomes for the next year in Europe and the United States. In the tables, "Y/Y" is short for "year-over-year."

Europe

	3-Year Trend	1-Year Trend	Current Measure	1-Year Forecast
Broad economic output measure	Stable	Improving	1.3% Y/Y GDP growth in HC	3.0% Y/Y GDP growth in HC
Economic impact of consumers	Stable	Improving	8.9% consumer spending HC % of GDP	10.0% consumer spending HC % of GDP

	3-Year Trend	1-Year Trend	Current Measure	1-Year Forecast
Economic impact of businesses	Weakening	Improving	4.0% HC business profits 3.6% HC sales	5.5% HC business profits 8.0% HC sales
Economic impact of central bank	Improving/ stimulative	Stable	2.7% avg short interest rates 2.6% inflation	2.8% avg short interest rates 2.7% inflation
Economic impact of government	Stimulative	Stimulative but stable	5.0% government spending % of GDP (fiscal stimulus)	5.0% government spending % of GDP (fiscal stimulus)
Other unique economic factors, population growth, demographics	Stable	Stable	49 average age of aggregate population	49 average age of aggregate population

United States

	3-Year Trend	1-Year Trend	Current Measure	1-Year Forecast
Broad economic output measure	Stable	Improving	3.8% Y/Y GDP growth in HC	2.8% Y/Y growth in HC
Economic impact of consumers	Stable	Improving	9.6% consumer spending HC % of GDP	9.5% consumer spending HC % of GDP
Economic impact of businesses	Stable	Improving	5.2% HC business profits 9.0% HC sales	5.0% HC business profits 9.0% HC sales
Economic impact of central bank	Stimulative	Stable	1.0% avg short interest rates 2.2% inflation	2.2% avg short interest rates 2.5% Inflation
Economic impact of government	Stimulative	Increasingly stimulative	6.0% government spending % of GDP (fiscal stimulus)	6.5% government spending % of GDP (fiscal stimulus)
Other unique economic factors, population growth, demographics	Stable	Stable	44 average age of aggregate population	44 average age of aggregate population

Using the economic categories shown in the table, compare and contrast European and U.S. economic trends and forecasts. Indicate and justify which economic region is expected to provide a relative advantage for the health care sector (Europe or the United States).

11. Plim Ltd. Is a manufacturing company in Finland that is a defined-benefit pension plan sponsor. Plim intends to increase its overall plan diversification by making an investment in Brazil. The table below provides Brazilian data for indices representing various economic variables.

Economic Index Data for Brazil

Variable	Year-end 2001	Year-end 2002	Year-end 2003	Year-end 2004	20-Yr L/T Average Annual % Increase
GDP	118.3	121.3	124.3	127.4	4.2%
Consumer spending	1,569.2	1,596.2	1,584.3	1,647.7	2.5
Business spending	650.1	632.0	707.8	726.9	2.6
Inflation	2,749.8	2,901.1	3,133.1	3,446.4	14.3
Government spending (% of GDP)	16.2	16.5	16.0	15.8	3.6

Based only on the data presented, from the perspective of year-end 2004, indicate whether the 1-year trend for each of the economic variables is stronger than, weaker than, or the same as its 3-year and 20-year data trend growth rates.

12. A. List five general elements of a pro-growth government structural policy.
    B. For each of the variables given below, describe the change or changes in the variable that would be pro-growth and determine the element of a pro-growth government structural policy that would best describe the change or changes:
       i. Tax receipts as a percent of GDP.
       ii. Government tariff receipts.
       iii. Number of publicly funded schools.
       iv. Number of state-owned businesses.
       v. Long-term average budget deficit as a percent of GDP.
13. Identify four differences between developed economies and emerging market economies.
14. In late 2004, K.C. Sung is planning an asset allocation strategy but would first like to assess Australia's current economic environment, then make a forecast for the economic conditions expected over the succeeding six- to nine-month period. Sung has learned that the leading indicator measures that he has compiled are indicative of current economic activity. However, Sung has seen over time that these specific measures impact many parts of the economy and thus are also predictive of potential longer-term (six- to nine-month) economic impacts as the initial economic activities create jobs and other beneficial output throughout the Australian economy.

Leading Indicators: Component Contributions and Total Index	June 2004	July 2004	August 2004 (most current period)
Consumer orders growth	−0.01	0.02	0.07
Business capital goods orders growth	0.04	0.05	0.04
Central bank money supply growth	0.12	0.15	0.16
Total index value	111	115	116

Using the leading indicator approach to forecasting, draw a conclusion for the Australian economy for the next six to nine months using only the above table.

15. Other than changes in the rate of inflation, specify two factors that impact the yields available on inflation-indexed bonds.
16. J. Wolf is an individual investor who intends to make an additional investment in various South Korean–based assets based on the outcome of your capital market expectations-setting framework analysis. Your analysis should use the data provided in the table below. However, each measure should be analyzed independently of the other measures. While examining the forward-looking one-year forecast relative to the data provided for the recent trends, indicate whether the equity market impact and the corporate fixed-income market impact would be positive or negative. Justify your answer considering the likely risk premium impact that would result if the one-year forecast actually occurred.

Index Data (South Korea)	Current Index Measure	Index 1-Year Forecast	South Korean Equity Market Impact	Corporate Fixed-Income Market Impact
GDP	159	173		
Consumer spending	432	430		
Business profits	115	100		
Central bank money supply	396	455		
Government spending relative to tax receipts	1,385	1,600		

17. Discuss four approaches to forecasting exchange rates.
18. Looking independently at each of the economic observations below, indicate the country where an analyst would expect to see a strengthening currency for each observation.

Observation	Canada	United Kingdom
Expected inflation over next year	2.0%	3.0%
Real (inflation-adjusted) government 10-year bond rate	4.8%	5.1%
Short-term (1-month) government rate	1.9%	5.0%

(continued)

Observation	Canada	United Kingdom
Expected (forward-looking) GDP growth over next year	2.0%	3.3%
New national laws have been passed that enable foreign direct investment in real estate/financial companies	Yes	No
Government surplus (deficit)	3.0%	−1.0%
Current account surplus (deficit)	8.0%	−1.0%

19. Fap is a small country whose currency is the fip. Ten years ago, the exchange rate with the Swiss franc (CHF) was 3 fips per 1 CHF, the inflation indices were equal to 100 in both Switzerland and Fap, and the exchange rate reflected purchasing power parity (PPP). Now, the exchange rate is 2 fips per 1 CHF. The Swiss inflation index level is at 150, and the Fap inflation index is at 140.

    A. What should the current exchange rate be if PPP prevails?
    B. Are fips over- or undervalued, according to PPP, relative to CHF?

CHAPTER 5

ASSET ALLOCATION

William F. Sharpe
Stanford University and Financial Engines, Inc.
Palo Alto, California

Peng Chen, CFA
Ibbotson Associates
Chicago, Illinois

Jerald E. Pinto, CFA
CFA Institute
Charlottesville, Virginia

Dennis W. McLeavey, CFA
CFA Institute
Charlottesville, Virginia

LEARNING OUTCOMES

After completing this chapter, you will be able to do the following:

- Summarize the function of strategic asset allocation in portfolio management.
- Discuss the role of strategic asset allocation in relation to exposures to systematic risk.
- Compare and contrast strategic and tactical asset allocation.
- Appraise the importance of asset allocation for portfolio performance.
- Contrast asset-only and asset/liability management (ALM) approaches to asset allocation.
- Explain an advantage and a disadvantage of implementing a dynamic versus a static approach to strategic asset allocation.
- Discuss and interpret the specification of return and risk objectives in relation to strategic asset allocation.

- Evaluate whether an asset class or set of asset classes has been appropriately specified.
- Select and justify an appropriate set of asset classes for an investor.
- Evaluate the theoretical and practical effects of including an additional asset class such as inflation-protected securities, international developed markets or emerging market securities, or alternative assets in an asset allocation.
- Formulate the major steps in asset allocation.
- Compare and contrast the following approaches to asset allocation: mean–variance, resampled efficient frontier, Black–Litterman, Monte Carlo simulation, ALM, and experience based.
- Discuss the structure of the minimum-variance frontier with a constraint against short sales.
- Determine and justify a strategic asset allocation, given an investment policy statement and capital market expectations.
- Summarize the characteristic issues relating to asset allocation for individual investors and for institutional investors (i.e., defined-benefit plans, foundations, endowments, insurance companies, banks) and critique a proposed asset allocation in light of those issues.
- Critique and revise a strategic asset allocation, given an investment policy statement and capital market expectations.
- Determine and justify tactical asset allocation (TAA) adjustments to asset-class weights, given a description of a TAA strategy and expectational data.

SUMMARY OVERVIEW

Portfolio management involves steps of planning, execution, and feedback. In the planning step, strategic asset allocation plays a pivotal, top-level role in converting the investor's objectives, constraints, and long-term capital market expectations into an appropriate portfolio. Tactical asset allocation is a major discipline for attempting to capitalize on perceived disequilibria among asset-class relative values. In this chapter we have presented and illustrated the fundamentals of both disciplines.

- Strategic asset allocation is the allocation of funds among different asset classes so as to satisfy an investor's long-term objectives and constraints.
- The strategic asset allocation specifies the investor's desired exposures to systematic risk.
- Tactical asset allocation involves making short-term adjustments to asset-class weights based on short-term predictions of relative performance among asset classes.
- Asset allocation appears to explain a large fraction in the variation of returns over time for a given portfolio. The proportion of the cross-sectional variation of portfolios' returns explained by portfolios' different asset allocations appears to be smaller but still very substantial.
- There are two major approaches to strategic asset allocation: asset-only and ALM. The asset-only approach does not take explicit account of the investor's liabilities, if any. The ALM approach involves explicitly modeling the investor's liabilities and adopting the asset allocation that is optimal in relation to funding liabilities.
- A dynamic approach to asset allocation has the advantage over a static approach in that it takes into account the links between the asset allocations chosen at different periods. The disadvantages of a dynamic approach are its greater cost and complexity.
- The specification of a numerical return objective should account for the costs of earning investment returns and inflation as well as their compound effects through time. A

multiplicative return objective takes compounding into account and is the most precise; an additive objective does not and thus will underestimate the return needed, despite providing a quick approximation. For instance, if the spending rate is 5 percent, the inflation rate 3 percent, and the costs of earning investment returns 0.30 percent, the multiplicative objective is $(1.05)(1.03)(1.003) - 1 = 0.0847$, or 8.47 percent; the corresponding additive objective is $0.05 + 0.03 + 0.003 = 0.083$, or 8.3 percent.

- The asset classes chosen for strategic asset allocation should satisfy the following five criteria: (1) Assets within an asset class should be relatively homogeneous, (2) asset classes should be mutually exclusive, (3) asset classes should be diversifying, (4) the asset classes as a group should make up a preponderance of world investable wealth, and (5) the asset class should have the capacity to absorb a significant fraction of the investor's portfolio without seriously affecting the portfolio's liquidity.
- After the preliminaries of specifying and listing investment policy statement (IPS)-permissible asset classes, asset allocation involves a series of steps on the capital markets side and the investor side. On the capital markets side, the steps are to (1) observe capital market conditions; (2) formulate a prediction procedure; and (3) obtain expected returns, risks, and correlations from the prediction procedure based on capital market conditions. On the investor side, the steps are to (1) observe the investor's assets, liabilities, net worth, and risk attitudes; (2) formulate the investor's risk tolerance function; and (3) obtain the investor's risk tolerance. The optimization approach (optimizer) is specified and the investor's asset mix is determined using the optimizer, using the investor's capital market expectations and risk tolerance as inputs. Finally, returns are observed, which provides feedback for the next asset allocation review.
- The mean–variance approach to asset allocation involves selecting the efficient portfolio that best satisfies the investor's risk and return objectives and constraints.
- Simulation and mean–variance analysis are used to develop the resampled efficient frontier. Because the procedure takes account of estimation error, the resampled efficient portfolios on the frontier may be more diversified and stable over time than conventional mean–variance efficient portfolios. The resampled efficient frontier is used as if it were a conventional efficient frontier to select the portfolio that best satisfies the investor's needs.
- The Black–Litterman approach with a constraint against short sales reverse-engineers the expected returns implicit in a diversified market portfolio; it combines those expected returns with the investor's own views (if any) in a systematic way that takes into account the investor's confidence in his or her views.
- Monte Carlo simulation is used to evaluate a proposed asset allocation's multiperiod performance. Important real-life complications such as cash inflows and outflows, taxes, and transaction costs can be modeled in a Monte Carlo simulation.
- The ALM approach to strategic asset allocation focuses on optimizing with respect to net worth or surplus (the value of assets minus the present value of liabilities). In its mean–variance implementation, ALM involves selecting a portfolio from the surplus efficient frontier; Monte Carlo simulation is helpful in evaluating the range of outcomes of a surplus efficient portfolio in funding liabilities over the investor's time horizon.
- Experience-based approaches include the ideas that a 60/40 stock/bond allocation is appropriate for the average investor; that the allocation to bonds should increase with the investor's risk aversion; that the allocation to stocks should increase with the investor's time horizon; and that younger investors should allocate more to stocks than older investors.
- In a mean–variance approach to asset allocation, a non-negativity constraint on asset-class weights is specified. A small number of portfolios called corner portfolios completely

describe the resulting efficient frontier. We can find the weights of any portfolio on the minimum-variance frontier (and efficient frontier) using the two corner portfolios that bracket it in terms of expected return. This result allows us to easily identify the composition of any efficient portfolio.

- Strategic asset allocation for individual investors should consider both their financial capital and their human capital (the present value of their expected future labor income). Human capital as a share of total capital tends to decline as an individual approaches retirement. Consequently, if an investor's human capital is risk free or low risk and uncorrelated with his financial capital, his optimal allocation to stocks tends to decline as he approaches retirement, all else equal. To the extent the investor's human capital is positively correlated with stocks, the investor's allocation to stocks will be less than otherwise. Individual investors have a focus on after-tax returns.
- Defined-benefit (DB) pension plans, life insurance companies, non–life insurance companies, and banks face high penalties for not meeting liabilities. Insurance companies and banks take an ALM approach to investing; DB pension plans frequently do also, or at least take ALM considerations into account. By contrast, foundations and endowments tend to take an asset-only approach to investing. Of the investors listed, life and non–life insurance companies and banks are taxable and have a focus on after-tax returns.

PROBLEMS

1. Paula Williams is chair of the Investment Committee of the Robinson Furniture Manufacturing (RFM) defined-benefit pension plan. The committee has established the strategic asset allocation given in Exhibit 5-1. The RFM pension liability can be modeled approximately as a short position in a long-term bond. The expected return on a long-term bond is 4.5 percent.

   A. Contrast the appropriateness of using indexed investments versus a single security to represent domestic and international equities in the RFM policy portfolio, given the economic role of strategic asset allocation.

EXHIBIT 5-1 RFM Policy Portfolio

	Asset Class	Target Allocation	Permissible Range
1	Domestic equities	40%	30–50%
2	International equities	10	5–15
3	Domestic long-term bonds	25	20–30
4	Inflation-protected bonds	25	20–30

EXHIBIT 5-2 Policy Portfolio: Statistics

Measure	
Expected return	8%
Standard deviation of return	12%
Sharpe ratio	0.40
Probability portfolio return is below 4.5% over one year	0.10

B. Discuss the effects of the following implementation choices on the measured importance of RFM's policy portfolio:

   i. Rebalancing to the policy mix.
   ii. Investing actively within an asset class or indexing to asset.
   iii. Adopting a policy portfolio that is much different from those of peers.

An institutional analyst makes a presentation to the Investment Committee showing promising past results from an investment program based on the following two variables, measured quarterly:

$X =$ (Earnings yield − Real short-term bond yield) − Past average difference

$Y =$ Change in OECD(Organization for Economic Cooperation and Development) leading indicators

The analyst proposes that the weightings of domestic and international equities be adjusted quarterly within a band of ± 10 percentage points of their target portfolio weights based on the values of X and Y.

C. Identify the type of investment program being suggested and critique the proposal.

The Investment Committee of RFM hears a second analyst presentation. This analyst recommends that the committee adopt a dynamic ALM approach to choosing its strategic asset allocation.

D. Justify the analyst's recommendation, explain the differences between a static and a dynamic ALM approach to asset allocation, and explain an advantage and a disadvantage of the dynamic approach.
E. Identify the risk-minimizing strategic asset allocation from an ALM perspective.

Use the data in Exhibit 5-3 to address Problems 2, 3, and 4.

EXHIBIT 5-3 Forecasts

	Investor's Forecasts	
Asset Allocation	Expected Return	Standard Deviation of Return
A	11.5%	18%
B	8	14
C	6	10

2. On the scale discussed in the text, Robert Langland's risk aversion (R_A) is 5. Recommend an asset allocation for him.
3. The Garrett Foundation would like to choose an asset allocation that minimizes the probability of returns below its annual spending rate of 3.5 percent. Recommend an asset allocation for the foundation.
4. William Ernst needs to spend 5 percent from his portfolio annually. He anticipates that inflation will be 2.4 percent annually. Ernst incurs expenses of 60 basis points a year in investing his portfolio. Which asset allocations satisfy Ernst's return requirement?
5. Critique the following specifications of asset classes:

   A. U.S. equities, world equities, U.S. bonds.
   B. Canadian equities, Canadian bonds, alternative assets.

C. Small-cap U.S. equities, large-cap U.S. equities, real estate, private equity, ex-U.S. developed market equities, emerging market equities, ex-U.S. bonds.

6. The Ingo Fund is a Swedish foundation currently invested in Swedish equities and government bonds. The portfolio has a Sharpe ratio of 0.40. The fund is considering adding U.S. real estate to its portfolio. U.S. real estate as represented by the NACREIF (National Council of Real Estate Investment Fiduciaries) Index has a predicted Sharpe ratio of 0.12; the predicted correlation with the existing portfolio is 0.35. Based solely on the above information, determine whether the Ingo Fund should add U.S. real estate to its portfolio.
7. Contrast the elements in the strategic asset allocation process that are relatively stable to those that frequently change.
8. Compare and contrast the global minimum variance portfolio with the minimum surplus variance portfolio.
9. Claudine Robert is treasurer and vice chair of the Investment Committee of Le Fonds de Recherche des Maladies du Coeur (FRMC), a French foundation with €95 million in assets that supports medical research relating to heart diseases and treatments. For the annual asset allocation review, Robert has prepared the set of capital market expectations shown in Exhibit 5-4.

   Based on these capital market expectations, Robert has developed the analysis shown in Exhibit 5-5.

   Robert also has noted the following facts:

   - FRMC's spending rate is 3.5 percent, the expected long-term inflation rate is 2.25 percent, and the cost of earning investment returns has averaged 43.6 basis points annually.

EXHIBIT 5-4 Capital Market Expectations

				Correlation			
	Asset Class	Expected Return	Standard Deviation	1	2	3	4
1	French equities	8.6%	20%	1.00			
2	Ex-France equities	6.7	15	0.65	1.00		
3	French bonds	4.1	10	0.34	0.25	1.00	
4	Real estate	5.0	12	0.50	0.35	0.17	1.00

EXHIBIT 5-5 Corner Portfolios

				Asset Class (Portfolio Weight)			
Portfolio	Expected Return	Standard Deviation	Sharpe Ratio	1	2	3	4
1	8.60%	20.00%	0.330	100.00%	0.00%	0.00%	0.00%
2	7.91	16.78	0.352	63.53	36.47	0.00	0.00
3	7.55	15.48	0.358	53.22	37.23	0.00	9.55
4	5.03	8.42	0.360	0.00	24.70	43.30	32.00
5	4.69	8.15	0.329	0.00	10.90	55.56	33.53

Note: Risk-free rate = 2 percent.

- FRMC has a multiplicative return requirement based on the spending rate, the expected inflation rate, and the cost of earning investment returns.

A. Describe how corner portfolios arise and explain how to use them in strategic asset allocation.
B. Compute FRMC's return requirement (in percent, to two decimal places) and contrast it to an additive return requirement based on the same inputs.
C. Recommend the strategic asset allocation that Robert should present for approval at the asset allocation review.

Use Exhibit 5-6 and Exhibit 5-7 to solve Problems 10 and 11.

- In Exhibit 5-6, plots are based on applying portfolio weights to true return parameters (mean returns, variances of returns, and correlations).
- In Exhibit 5-7, each of the three series of points (e.g., 1, 2, 3, 4, 5 is a series) represents one simulated efficient frontier from one simulation trial.

10. A. In Exhibit 5-6, if Frontier B is a mean–variance efficient frontier in which the efficient portfolios' portfolio weights reflect perfect knowledge of the true return parameters, discuss whether Frontier A could be

    i. the conventional mean–variance efficient frontier
    ii. the resampled efficient frontier

    B. Identify and explain the set of inputs to which mean–variance optimization is most sensitive.
11. A. Identify the scatter of points in Exhibit 5-7.
    B. Describe how to compute a resampled efficient frontier from the scatter of points shown in Exhibit 5-7.

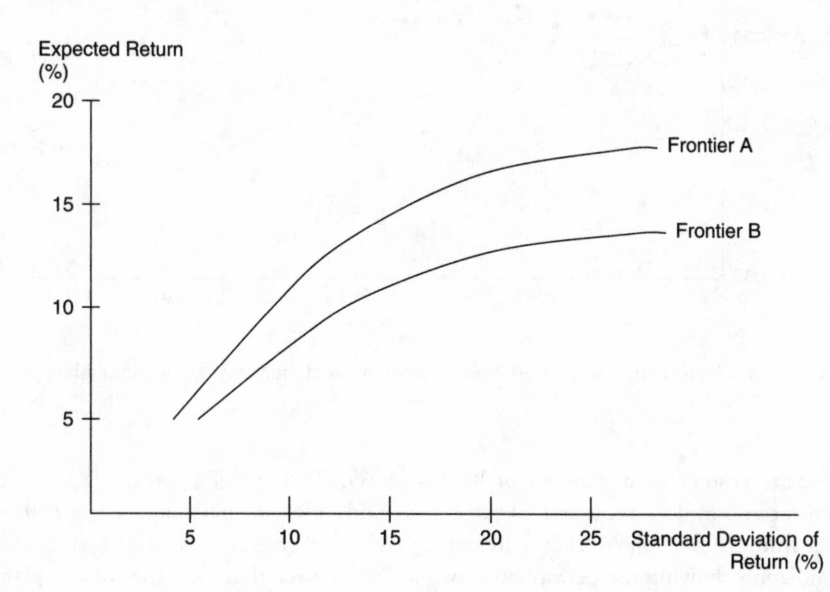

EXHIBIT 5-6 Efficient Frontiers

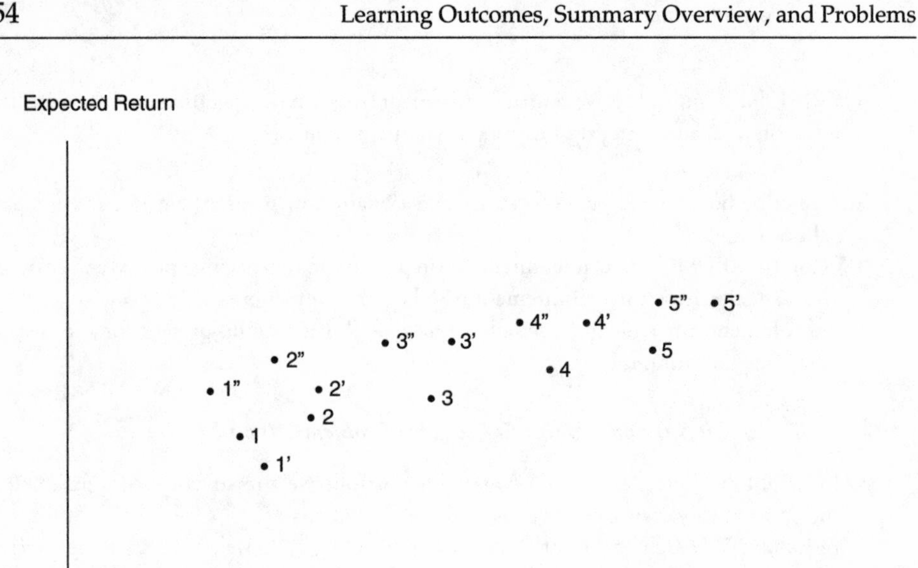

EXHIBIT 5-7 Simulated Efficient Frontiers

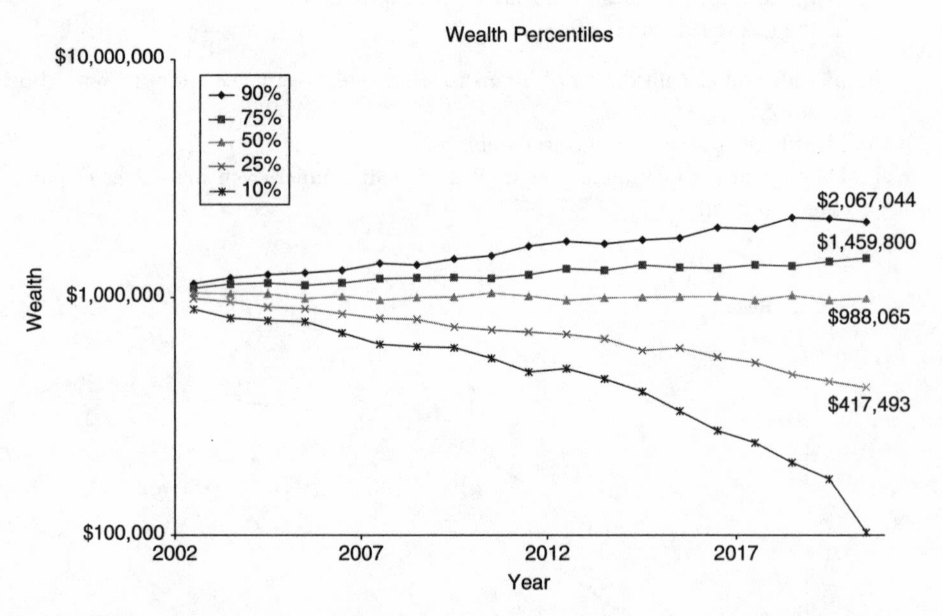

EXHIBIT 5-8 Performance of a 70/30 Asset Allocation based on Monte Carlo Simulation

12. John Stevenson retired at the end of 2002 at age 65. His $1 million portfolio is invested 70 percent in common stocks and 30 percent in bonds. He anticipates liquidating $50,000 a year from the portfolio during retirement. Exhibit 5-8 gives the results of a Monte Carlo simulation showing the performance of the 70/30 asset allocation (net of the planned liquidations) in real dollar terms given Stevenson's capital market expectations.

Stevenson wants his portfolio value (in real dollars) to be at least $630,000 when he turns 75 in 2012. He requires a 90 percent probability of meeting this goal. Determine whether Stevenson's current asset allocation promises to satisfy that requirement.

13. The Inner Life Insurance Company (ILIC) is considering the asset allocation shown in Exhibit 5-9 below. ILIC has risk aversion (R_A) of 5 using the scale presented in the text.

    A. Recommend an asset allocation for ILIC.
    B. Recommend a statistical method that ILIC should use to obtain information about a proposed asset allocation's performance over time, given its forecasts concerning liabilities and its capital market expectations.

14. For the following types of investors, appraise the importance of using the specified asset class for strategic asset allocation.

    A. Long-term bonds for a life insurer and for a young investor.
    B. Common stock for a bank and for a young investor.
    C. Domestic tax-exempt bonds for an endowment and for a mid-career professional.
    D. Private equity for a major foundation and for a young investor.

15. Exhibit 5-10 shows William Smith's financial and human capital in constant dollars terms at 30, 50, and 65 years of age.

    Smith's target asset allocation for total wealth is 60/40 stocks/bonds. Assume that his human capital is approximately risk free and uncorrelated with stock returns. Determine Smith's optimal asset allocation for stocks and bonds in his financial portfolio at the following ages:

    A. 30
    B. 50
    C. 65
    D. Discuss whether your conclusions in Parts A, B, and C are consistent with experience-based approaches to asset allocation.

EXHIBIT 5-9 Investor's Forecasts

Asset Allocation	Expected Surplus Return	Standard Deviation of Surplus Return
A	6.5%	14%
B	4	10
C	0	2

EXHIBIT 5-10 Financial and Human Capital

Age	Financial Capital	Human Capital
30	$ 100,000	$2,100,000
50	900,000	1,300,000
65	2,000,000	200,000

EXHIBIT 5-11 Expected Return for Asset Classes

Asset Class	Long-Term	Short-Term
Global Equities	*A*	*B*
U.S. equities	8%	14%
Ex-U.S. equities	10	10
Global Fixed Income	*C*	*D*
U.S. bonds	6%	8%
Ex-U.S. bonds	5	4

16. Wendy Willet is chief investment officer of the Allright University Endowment (AUE) based in the United States. The strategic asset allocation of AUE is as follows, where percentages refer to proportions of the total portfolio:

Global equities		60%
U.S. Equities	30%	
Ex-U.S. equities	30%	
Global fixed income		40%
U.S. bonds	30%	
Ex-U.S. bonds	10%	

Exhibit 5-11 gives Willet's expectations.

AUE runs a top-down global tactical asset allocation program that looks first at the overall allocation between global equities and global fixed income, then at the asset allocation within global equities and global fixed income. Assume that the asset classes' risk characteristics are constant.

A. Calculate the long-term and short-term expectations for global equities (*A* and *B*, respectively) and global fixed income (*C* and *D*, respectively).
B. Determine and justify the changes in portfolio weights (in relation to the policy portfolio target weights) that would result from a global tactical asset allocation program.

17. (Adapted from the 2000 CFA Level III Exam)

Hugh Donovan is chief financial officer (CFO) of LightSpeed Connections (LSC), a rapidly growing U.S technology company with a traditional defined-benefit pension plan. Because of LSC's young workforce, Donovan believes the pension plan has no liquidity needs and can thus invest aggressively to maximize pension assets. He also believes that Treasury bills and bonds, yielding 5.4 percent and 6.1 percent, respectively, have no place in a portfolio with such a long time horizon. His strategy, which has produced excellent returns for the past two years, is to invest the portfolio as follows:

- 50 percent in a concentrated pool (15 to 20 stocks) of initial public offerings (IPOs) in technology and Internet companies, managed internally by Donovan.
- 25 percent in a small-cap growth fund.
- 10 percent in a venture capital fund.
- 10 percent in an S&P 500 index fund.
- 5 percent in an international equity fund.

EXHIBIT 5-12 Alternative Asset Allocations and Current Portfolio

Asset	Portfolio A	Portfolio B	Portfolio C	Current Portfolio
S&P 500 Index	25%	16%	35%	10%
IPO/tech portfolio	20	40	10	50
Small-cap growth fund	26	10	19	25
International equity fund	0	16	15	5
Venture capital fund	10	5	5	10
Money market fund	7	7	2	0
Corporate bond fund	12	6	14	0
Total	100%	100%	100%	100%
Expected return	16.6%	22.1%	13.3%	26.2%
Standard deviation	26.7%	38.4%	19.8%	55.2%

Working with LSC's Investment Committee, the firm's president, Eileen Jeffries has produced a formal investment policy statement, which reads as follows:

The LSC Pension Plan's return objective should focus on real total returns that will fund its long-term obligations on an inflation-adjusted basis. The "time-to-maturity" of the corporate workforce is a key element for any defined pension plan; given our young workforce, LSC's Plan has a long investment horizon and more time available for wealth compounding to occur. Therefore, the Plan can pursue an aggressive investment course and focus on the higher return potential of capital growth. Under present U.S. tax laws, pension portfolio income and capital gains are not taxed. The portfolio should focus primarily on investments in businesses directly related to our main business to leverage our knowledge base.

Jeffries takes an asset-only approach to strategic asset allocation. She is considering three alternative allocations, shown in Exhibit 5-12 along with the portfolio's current asset allocation.

Select and justify the portfolio that is most appropriate for LSC's pension plan.

18. (Adapted from the 1995 CFA Level III Exam)

Bontemps International (BI) is a financially healthy, rapidly growing import/export company with a young workforce. Information regarding the company's Employee Retirement Income Security Act (ERISA)-qualified defined-benefit pension plan appears in Exhibits 5-13 and 5-14.

In accordance with BI policy, the plan discounts its liabilities at the market interest rate for bonds of the same duration.

Last year the surplus declined, although the actual investment return at 10 percent was 100 basis points more than the board's stated long-term objective. Anticipating the board's desire to avoid a repetition of last year's shrinkage in the surplus, BI's chief financial officer, Giselle Donovan, wants to recommend an alternative portfolio for board consideration. Donovan is considering the portfolios shown in Exhibit 5-15.

Recommend one of the portfolios (A through F) for the board's consideration and justify the choice.

19. (Adapted from the 1993 CFA Level III exam)

The Medical Research Foundation (MRF) has just learned that it will receive a $45 million cash gift in three months. The gift will greatly increase the size of the foundation's endowment from its current $10 million. The foundation's grant-making

EXHIBIT 5-13 Bontemps International Defined Benefit Pension Plan Portfolio Summary

Asset Class	Percent Allocation	Prior-Year Total Return
Large-cap U.S. equities	35%	10.0%
Small-cap U.S. equities	10	12.0
International equities	5	7.0
Total equities	50	
U.S. Treasury bills (1-year duration)	10	4.5
U.S. intermediate bonds and mortgage-backed securities (4-year duration)	39	1.0
U.S. long-term bonds (10-year duration)	1	19.0%[a]
Total fixed income	50%	
Total	100%	10.0%

[a]Income element 7.0%; gain element 12.0%.

EXHIBIT 5-14 Bontemps International Defined Benefit Pension Plan: Key Details

Present value of plan liabilities	$298 million
Market value of plan assets	$300 million
Surplus	$2 million
Duration of liabilities	10 years
Actuarial return assumption	7.0%
BI board's long-term total return objective	9.0%

EXHIBIT 5-15 Portfolio Alternatives

	Portfolio						
	A	B	C	D	E	F	Current Portfolio
Domestic large-cap equities	0%	25%	30%	0%	30%	30%	35%
Domestic small-cap equities	0	15	20	0	5	20	10
International equities	0	20	20	0	20	20	5
Subtotal equity	0%	60%	70%	0%	55%	70%	50%
Treasury bills (1-year duration)	100	20	5	0	0	0	10
Intermediate bonds (4-year duration)	0	20	20	0	0	0	39
Long bonds (10-year duration)	0	0	5	100	45	30	1
Subtotal fixed income	100%	40%	30%	100%	45%	30%	50%
Total	100%	100%	100%	100%	100%	100%	100%
Expected annual return	5.5%	9.4%	10.0%	7.1%	9.3%	10.2%	9.0%
Return volatility	0.0	10.3	13.0	0.0	10.3	14.0	10.0
Surplus volatility	11.0	7.0	11.0	0.0	5.5	7.5	8.0

EXHIBIT 5-16 Capital Markets Annualized Return Data

Asset	1926–1992 Average	1993–2000 Consensus Forecast
U.S. Treasury bills	3.7%	4.2%
Intermediate-term U.S. T-bonds	5.2	5.8
Long-term U.S. T-bonds	4.8	7.7
U.S. corporate bonds (AAA)	5.5	8.7
Non-U.S. bonds (AAA)	N/A	8.4
U.S. common stocks (large cap)	10.3	9.0
U.S. common stocks (small cap)	12.2	12.0
Non-U.S. common stocks (all)	N/A	10.1
Venture capital	N/A	15.5
Real estate	N/A	8.5
U.S. inflation	3.1%	3.5%

(spending) policy has been to pay out virtually all of its annual net investment income. Because MRF's investment approach has been conservative, the endowment portfolio now consists almost entirely of fixed-income assets. The finance committee understands that these actions are causing the real value of foundation assets and the real value of future grants to decline because of inflation effects. Until now, the finance committee has believed it had no alternative to these actions, given the large immediate cash needs of the research programs being funded and the size of the foundation's capital base. The foundation's annual grants must at least equal 5 percent of its assets' market value to maintain its U.S. tax-exempt status, a requirement that is expected to continue indefinitely. No additional gifts or fundraising activity are expected for the foreseeable future.

Given the change in circumstances that the cash gift will make, the finance committee wishes to develop new grant-making and investment policies. Annual spending must at least meet the 5 percent of market value requirement, but the committee is unsure how much higher spending can or should be. The committee wants to pay out as much as possible because of the critical nature of the research being funded; however, it understands that preserving the real value of the foundation's assets is equally important in order to preserve its future grant-making capabilities. You have been asked to assist the committee in developing appropriate policies. Exhibit 5-16 summarizes the capital markets data.

Recommend and justify a long-term asset allocation.

CHAPTER 6

FIXED-INCOME PORTFOLIO MANAGEMENT

H. Gifford Fong

Gifford Fong Associates
Lafayette, California

Larry D. Guin, CFA

Murray State University
Murray, Kentucky

LEARNING OUTCOMES

After completing this chapter, you will be able to do the following:

- Compare and contrast, with respect to investment objectives, the use of liabilities as a benchmark with the use of a bond index as a benchmark.
- Discuss the range of benchmark index–oriented bond investment strategies and compare and contrast pure bond indexing, enhanced indexing, and active investing with respect to the objectives, techniques, and advantages and disadvantages of each.
- Discuss criteria for selecting a benchmark bond index, and justify the selection of a benchmark index given a description of the investor's risk aversion, income needs, and liabilities.
- Review and justify the means (e.g., matching duration and key rate durations) by which an enhanced indexer may seek to align the risk exposures of the portfolio with those of the benchmark bond index.
- Contrast and illustrate total return and scenario analysis.
- Evaluate the effects of leverage on the rate of return on an investor's equity and discuss the use of repurchase agreements (repos) to finance bond purchases and the factors that affect the repo rate.
- Design a bond immunization strategy that will ensure funding of a predetermined liability and evaluate the strategy under various interest rate scenarios.
- Demonstrate the process of rebalancing a portfolio to reestablish the dollar duration of the portfolio to a desired level.

- Justify the importance of spread duration.
- Evaluate the extensions to classical immunization theory.
- Critique the risks associated with managing a portfolio against a liability structure (cap risk, contingent claim risk, and interest rate risk).
- Compare and contrast immunization strategies for a single liability, multiple liabilities, and general cash flows.
- Compare and contrast risk minimization with return maximization in immunized portfolios.
- Critique the following measures of portfolio risk: standard deviation, target semivariance, shortfall risk, and value at risk.
- Demonstrate the advantages of using futures instead of cash market instruments to alter portfolio risk.
- Formulate, construct, and evaluate an immunization strategy using interest rate futures.
- Discuss the types of credit options written on an underlying asset.
- Compare default risk, credit spread risk, and downgrade risk, and demonstrate which credit derivative instruments address each risk, including how they can be used in portfolio management.
- Evaluate the sources of excess return for an international bond portfolio.
- Analyze (1) the change in value of a foreign bond when domestic interest rates change, given the bond's duration and the country beta, and (2) the contribution of a foreign bond to a domestic portfolio's duration, given the duration of the foreign bond and the country beta.
- Recommend and justify whether to hedge an international bond investment.
- Illustrate how breakeven spread analysis can be used to evaluate the risk in seeking yield advantages across international bond markets.
- Discuss the advantages and risks in investing in emerging market debt.
- Discuss the selection of a fixed-income manager.

SUMMARY OVERVIEW

The management of fixed-income portfolios is a highly competitive field requiring skill in financial and economic analysis, market knowledge, and control of costs. Among the points that have been made are the following:

- Because a benchmark is the standard with which the portfolio's performance will be compared, it should always reflect the portfolio's objective. If a portfolio has liabilities that must be met, that need is the paramount objective and thus is the most appropriate benchmark. If a portfolio has no liabilities, the most relevant standard is a bond market index that very closely matches the portfolio's characteristics.
- Bond indexing is attractive because indexed portfolios have lower fees than actively managed portfolios and broadly based bond index portfolios provide excellent diversification.
- In selecting a benchmark index, the manager should choose an index with comparable market value risk, comparable income risk (comparable assured income stream), and minimal liability framework risk (minimal mismatch between the durations of assets and liabilities).
- For an indexed portfolio, the manager must carefully try to match the portfolio's characteristics to the benchmark's risk profile. The primary risk factors to match are the portfolio's

duration, key rate duration and cash flow distribution, sector and quality percentage, sector duration contribution, quality spread duration contribution, sector/coupon/maturity/cell weights, and issuer exposure.

- The indexing manager has a variety of strategies from which to choose ranging from a totally passive style to a very active style or points in between. The most popular of these strategies are pure bond indexing, enhanced indexing by matching primary risk factors, enhanced indexing by minor risk factor mismatches, active management by larger risk factor mismatches, and full-blown active management.
- Because a perfectly indexed portfolio will still underperform the benchmark by the amount of transactions costs, the manager may use a variety of techniques to enhance the return. These include lowering managerial and transactions costs, issue selection, yield curve positioning, sector and quality positioning, and call exposure positioning.
- Total return analysis and scenario analysis are methods of evaluating the impact of a trade given a change in interest rates and a range of changes in interest rates, respectively.
- The heart of a bond immunization strategy for a single liability is to match the average duration of the assets with the time horizon of the liability. However, this matching alone is not sufficient to immunize the portfolio, in general, because of the impact of twists and nonparallel changes in the yield curve. Care must be taken when designing the immunization strategy to ensure that the portfolio will remain immunized under a variety of different scenarios.
- In order to maintain the dollar duration of a portfolio, rebalancing may be necessary. Methods for achieving this include (1) investing new funds (if necessary), (2) changing the weight of a particular security to adjust the dollar duration, and (3) using derivatives. If new funds are invested to rebalance, after an interest rate change, calculate the new dollar duration of the portfolio, calculate the rebalancing ratio, then multiply the new market value of the portfolio by the desired percentage change.
- Spread duration is a measure of how the market value of a risky bond (portfolio) will change with respect to a parallel 100 bps change in its spread above the comparable benchmark security (portfolio). Spread duration is an important factor influencing a portfolio's total return because spreads do change frequently.
- Because parallel shifts in the yield curve are rare, classical immunization will not immunize the portfolio adequately. Extensions to classical immunization provide better results. These extensions include modifying the definition of duration (to multifunctional duration), overcoming the limitations of a fixed horizon, analyzing the risk and return trade-off for immunized portfolios, and integrating immunization strategies with elements of active bond market strategies.
- Three categories that describe the risk of not being able to pay a portfolio's liabilities are interest rate risk, contingent claim, and cap risk. A rising interest rate environment (interest rate risk) comprises the largest risk that a portfolio manager will face. When a security has a contingent claim provision, the manager may have lucrative coupon payments halted (as is the case with mortgage-backed securities) or a leveling off in the market value of a callable security. An asset that makes floating rate payments will typically have caps associated with the floating rate. The manager is at risk of the level of market rates rising while the asset returns are capped.
- Multiple liabilities immunization requires the portfolio payment stream to be decomposed so that each liability is separately immunized by one of the component streams, the composite duration of the portfolio must equal the composite duration of the liabilities, and the distribution of individual portfolio assets must have a wider range than the

distribution of the liabilities. For general cash flows, the expected cash contributions can be considered the payments on hypothetical securities that are part of the initial holdings. The actual initial investment can then be invested in such a way that the real and hypothetical holdings taken together represent an immunized portfolio.

- Risk minimization produces an immunized portfolio with a minimum exposure to any arbitrary interest rate change subject to the duration constraint. This objective may be too restrictive in certain situations however. If a substantial increase in the expected return can be accomplished with little effect on immunization risk, the higher-yielding portfolio may be preferred in spite of its higher risk.
- Standard deviation, target semivariance, shortfall risk, and value at risk have all been proposed as appropriate measures of risk for a portfolio. However, each has its own deficiency. For example, standard deviation (or variance) assumes that risk has a normal distribution (which may not be true). Semivariance often provides little extra information if returns are symmetric. Shortfall risk is expressed as a probability, not as a currency amount. Value at risk does not indicate the magnitude of the very worst possible outcomes.
- A repurchase agreement is subject to a variety of credit risks, including:

  a. *Quality of the collateral*. The higher the quality of the securities, the lower the repo rate will be.
  b. *Term of the repo*. Typically, the longer the maturity, the higher the rate will be.
  c. *Delivery requirement*. If physical delivery of the securities is required, the rate will be lower because of the lower credit risk.
  d. *Availability of collateral*. The buyer of the securities may be willing to accept a lower rate in order to obtain securities that are in short supply.
  e. *Prevailing interest rates in the economy*. As interest rates increase, the rates on repo transactions will generally increase.
  f. *Seasonal factors*. A seasonal effect may exist because some institutions' supply of funds varies by the season.

- The primary advantages to using futures to alter a portfolio's duration are increased liquidity and cost effectiveness.
- Futures contracts can be used to shorten or lengthen a portfolio's duration. The contracts may also be used to hedge or reduce an existing interest rate exposure. As such, they may be combined with traditional immunization techniques to improve the results.
- Unlike ordinary bond options that protect against interest rate risk, credit options are structured to offer protection against credit risk. Binary credit option and binary credit option based on a credit rating are the two types of credit options written on an underlying asset. The former pays the option buyer in the event of default; otherwise, nothing is paid. The latter pays the difference between the strike price and the market price when the specified credit rating event occurs and pays nothing if the event does not occur.
- Credit options are structured to offer protection against both default risk and credit spread risk, credit forwards offer protection again credit spread risk, and credit default swaps help in managing default risk.
- The sources of excess return for an international bond portfolio include bond market selection, currency selection, duration management/yield curve management, sector selection, credit analysis, and investing in markets outside the benchmark index.
- Emerging market debt (EMD) has matured as an asset class. The spread of EMD over risk-free rates has narrowed considerably as the quality of sovereign bonds has increased

to the point that they now have similar frequencies of default, recovery rates, and ratings transition probabilities compared with corporate bonds with similar ratings.

- Emerging market debt is still risky, however, and is characterized by high volatility and returns that exhibit significant negative skewness. Moreover, emerging market countries frequently do not offer the degree of transparency, court tested laws, and clear regulations found in established markets.
- For a change in domestic interest rates, the change in a foreign bond's value may be found by multiplying the duration of the foreign bond times the country beta. Because a portfolio's duration is a weighted average of the duration of the bonds in the portfolio, the contribution to the portfolio's duration is equal to the adjusted foreign bond duration multiplied by its weight in the portfolio.
- Breakeven spread analysis is used to estimate relative values between markets by quantifying the amount of spread widening required to reduce a foreign bond's yield advantage to zero. The breakeven spread can be found by dividing the yield advantage by the bond's duration.
- When funds are not managed entirely in-house, a search for outside managers must be conducted. The due diligence for selection of managers is satisfied primarily by investigating the managers' investment process, the types of trades the managers are making, and the organizational strengths.

PROBLEMS

1. The table below shows the active return for six periods for a bond portfolio. Calculate the portfolio's tracking risk for the six-period time frame.

Period	Portfolio Return	Benchmark Return	Active Return
1	14.10%	13.70%	0.400%
2	8.20	8.00	0.200
3	7.80	8.00	−0.200
4	3.20	3.50	−0.300
5	2.60	2.40	0.200
6	3.30	3.00	0.300

2. A portfolio manager decided to purchase corporate bonds with a market value of €5 million. To finance 60 percent of the purchase, the portfolio manager entered into a 30-day repurchase agreement with the bond dealer. The 30-day term repo rate was 4.6 percent per year. At the end of the 30 days, the bonds purchased by the portfolio manager have increased in value by 0.5 percent and the portfolio manager decided to sell the bonds. No coupons were received during the 30-day period.

   A. Compute the 30-day rate of return on the equity and borrowed components of the portfolio.
   B. Compute the 30-day portfolio rate of return.
   C. Compute the 30-day portfolio rate of return if the increase in value of the bonds was 0.3 percent instead of 0.5 percent.
   D. Use your answers to parts B and C above to comment on the effect of the use of leverage on the portfolio rate of return.

E. Discuss why the bond dealer in the above example faces a credit risk even if the bond dealer holds the collateral.

3. The table below shows the spread duration for a 70-bond portfolio and a benchmark index based on sectors. Determine whether the portfolio or the benchmark is more sensitive to changes in the sector spread by determining the spread duration for each. Given your answer, what is the effect on the portfolio's tracking risk?

	Portfolio		Benchmark	
Sector	% of Portfolio	Spread Duration	% of Portfolio	Spread Duration
Treasury	22.70	0.00	23.10	0.00
Agencies	12.20	4.56	6.54	4.41
Financial Institutions	6.23	3.23	5.89	3.35
Industrials	14.12	11.04	14.33	10.63
Utilities	6.49	2.10	6.28	2.58
Non-U.S. Credit	6.56	2.05	6.80	1.98
Mortgage	31.70	1.78	33.20	1.11
Asset Backed	—	2.40	1.57	3.34
CMBS	—	5.60	2.29	4.67
Total	100.00		100.00	

4. You are the manager of a portfolio consisting of three bonds in equal par amounts of $1 million each. The first table below shows the market value of the bonds and their durations. (The price includes accrued interest.) The second table contains the market value of the bonds and their durations one year later.

Initial Values				
Security	Price	Market Value	Duration	Dollar Duration
Bond #1	$106.110	$1,060,531	5.909	?
Bond #2	98.200	981,686	3.691	?
Bond #3	109.140	1,090,797	5.843	?
		Portfolio Dollar Duration =		?

After 1 year				
Security	Price	Market Value	Duration	Dollar Duration
Bond 1	$104.240	$1,042,043	5.177	?
Bond 2	98.084	980,461	2.817	?
Bond 3	106.931	1,068,319	5.125	?
		Portfolio Dollar Duration =		?

As manager, you would like to maintain the portfolio's dollar duration at the initial level by rebalancing the portfolio. You choose to rebalance using the existing security proportions of one-third each. Calculate:

A. The dollar durations of each of the bonds.
B. The rebalancing ratio necessary for the rebalancing.
C. The cash required for the rebalancing.

5. Your client has asked you to construct a £2 million bond portfolio. Some of the bonds that you are considering for this portfolio have embedded options. Your client has specified that he may withdraw £25,000 from the portfolio in six months to fund some expected expenses. He would like to be able to make this withdrawal without reducing the initial capital of £2 million.

   A. Would shortfall risk be an appropriate measure of risk while evaluating the portfolios for your client?
   B. What are some of the shortcomings of the use of shortfall risk?

6. The market value of the bond portfolio of a French investment fund is €75 million. The duration of the portfolio is 8.17. Based on the analysis provided by the in-house economists, the portfolio manager believes that the interest rates are likely to have an unexpected decrease over the next month. Based on this belief, the manager has decided to increase the duration of its entire bond portfolio to 10. The futures contract it would use is priced at €130,000 and has a duration of 9.35. Assume that the conversion factor for the futures contract is 1.06.

   A. Would the fund need to buy futures contracts or sell?
   B. Approximately, how many futures contracts would be needed to change the duration of the bond portfolio?

7. The trustees of a pension fund would like to examine the issue of protecting the bonds in the fund's portfolio against an increase in interest rates using options and futures. Before discussing this with their external bond fund manager, they decide to ask four consultants about their recommendations as to what should be done at this time. It turns out that each of them has a different recommendation. Consultant A suggests selling covered calls, Consultant B suggests doing nothing at all, Consultant C suggests selling interest rate futures, and Consultant D suggests buying puts. The reason for their different recommendations is that although all consultants understand the pension fund's objective of minimizing risk, they differ with one another in regards to their outlook on future interest rates. One of the consultants believes interest rates are headed downward, one has no opinion, one believes that the interest rates would not change much in either direction, and one believes that the interest rates are headed upward. Based on the consultants' recommendations, could you identify the outlook of each consultant?
8. The current credit spread on bonds issued by Great Foods Inc. is 300 bps. The manager of More Money Funds believes that Great Foods' credit situation will improve over the next few months, resulting in a smaller credit spread on its bonds. She decides to enter into a six-month credit spread forward contract, taking the position that the credit spread will decrease. The forward contract has the current spread as the contracted spread, a notional amount of $10 million, and a risk factor of 5.

A. On the settlement date six months later, the credit spread on Great Foods bonds is 250 bps. How much is the payoff to More Money Funds?
B. How much would be the payoff to More Money Funds if the credit spread on the settlement date is 350 bps?
C. How much is the maximum possible gain for More Money Funds?

9. Consider a collateralized debt obligation (CDO) that has a $250 million structure. The collateral consists of bonds that mature in seven years, and the coupon rate for these bonds is the seven-year Treasury rate plus 500 bps. The senior tranche comprises 70 percent of the structure and has a floating coupon of LIBOR plus 50 bps. There is only one junior tranche that comprises 20 percent of the structure and has a fixed coupon of seven-year Treasury rate plus 300 bps. Compute the rate of return earned by the equity tranche in this CDO if the seven-year Treasury rate is 6 percent and the London Interbank Offered Rate (LIBOR) is 7.5 percent. There are no defaults in the underlying collateral pool. Ignore the collateral manager's fees and any other expenses.
10. Assume that the rates shown in the table below accurately reflect current conditions in the financial markets.

Dollar/Euro Spot Rate	1.21
Dollar/Euro 1-Year Forward Rate	1.18
1-Year Deposit Rate:	
Euro	3%
U.S.	2%

In the table, the one-year forward dollar–euro exchange rate is mispriced, because it doesn't reflect the interest rate differentials between the United States and Europe.

A. Calculate the amount of the current forward exchange discount or premium.
B. Calculate the value that the forward rate would need to be in order to keep riskless arbitrage from occurring.

11. Assume that a U.S. bond investor has invested in Canadian government bonds. The duration of a 12-year Canadian government bond is 8.40, and the Canadian country beta is 0.63. Interest rates in the United States are expected to change by approximately 80 bps. How much can the U.S. investor expect the Canadian bond to change in value if U.S. rates change by 80 bps?
12. Assume that the spread between U.S. and German bonds is 300 bps, providing German investors who purchase a U.S. bond with an additional yield income of 75 bps per quarter. The duration of the German bond is 8.3. If German interest rates should decline, how much of a decline is required to completely wipe out the quarterly yield advantage for the German investor?
13. A portfolio manager of a Canadian fund that invests in the yen-denominated Japanese bonds is considering whether or not to hedge the portfolio's exposure to the Japanese yen using a forward contract. Assume that the short-term interest rates are 1.6 percent in Japan and 2.7 percent in Canada.

A. Based on the in-house analysis provided by the fund's currency specialists, the portfolio manager expects the Japanese yen to appreciate against the Canadian dollar by 1.5 percent. Should the portfolio manager hedge the currency risk using a forward contract?

B. What would be your answer if the portfolio manager expects the Japanese yen to appreciate against the Canadian dollar by only 0.5 percent?

14. A British fixed-income fund has substantial holdings in U.S. dollar–denominated bonds. The fund's portfolio manager is considering whether to leave the fund's exposure to the U.S. dollar unhedged or to hedge it using a U.K. pound–U.S. dollar forward contract. Assume that the short-term interest rates are 4.7 percent in the United Kingdom and 4 percent in the United States. The fund manager expects the U.S. dollar to appreciate against the pound by 0.4 percent. Assume interest rate parity (IRP) holds. Explain which alternative has the higher expected return based on the short-term interest rates and the manager's expectations about exchange rates.

CHAPTER 7

EQUITY PORTFOLIO MANAGEMENT

Gary L. Gastineau
ETF Consultants LLC
Summit, New Jersey

Andrew R. Olma, CFA
Barclays Global Investors
San Francisco, California

Robert G. Zielinski, CFA
Japan Advisory
Tokyo, Japan

LEARNING OUTCOMES

After completing this reading, you will be able to do the following:

- Discuss the role of equities in the overall portfolio.
- Discuss the rationales for passive, active, and semiactive (enhanced index) equity investment approaches and distinguish among those approaches with respect to expected active return and tracking risk.
- Recommend an equity investment approach based on an investor's investment policy statement (IPS) and beliefs concerning market efficiency.
- Distinguish among the predominant weighting schemes used in the construction of major equity share indices, evaluate the biases of each, and explain the composition of major equity share indices worldwide.
- Compare and contrast alternative methods for establishing a passive exposure to an equity market including indexed separate or pooled accounts, index mutual funds, exchange-traded funds, equity index futures, and equity total return swaps.
- Compare and contrast the full replication, stratified sampling, and optimization approaches to constructing an indexed portfolio, and recommend an approach given a description of the investment vehicle and the index to be tracked.

- Explain and illustrate equity investment styles, identify and explain the rationales and primary concerns of value investors and growth investors and the key risks of those styles, and demonstrate the difficulties in applying style definitions and distinguishing among styles.
- Discuss, compare, and contrast techniques for identifying investment styles and characterize the style of an investor given a description of the investor's security selection method, details on security holdings, or the results of a returns-based style analysis.
- Discuss, compare, and contrast the various methodologies used to construct equity style indices.
- Explain and interpret the equity style box and evaluate the effects of style drift.
- Explain the implementation of a socially responsible investing discipline.
- Compare and contrast long–short and long-only investment strategies, including their risks and potential alphas, and explain why pricing inefficiencies may exist on the short side.
- Explain the process of equitizing a long–short portfolio.
- Compare and contrast the selling disciplines of active investors.
- Contrast derivatives-based and stock-based enhanced indexing strategies, and demonstrate the fundamental law of active management, including its use to justify enhanced indexing.
- Explain and interpret a systematic approach to optimizing allocations to a group of managers.
- Compare and contrast the core-satellite and completeness fund approaches to managing a portfolio of active managers.
- Distinguish among the components of total active return ("true" active return and "misfit" active return), their associated risk measures ("true" active risk and "misfit" risk), and explain their relevance for evaluating a portfolio of managers.
- Explain alpha and beta separation as an approach to active management and demonstrate the use of portable alpha.
- Review the due diligence process of identifying, selecting, and contracting with equity managers, including the qualitative and quantitative factors in developing a universe of manager candidates (such as past performance information) and the use of equity manager questionnaires and fee schedules (ad valorem and performance based).
- Review the process of structuring equity research and security selection, including top-down and bottom-up security selection processes.

SUMMARY OVERVIEW

Equity portfolio management is not only challenging; for many investors, the skill applied to it can determine their long-term investment success. This chapter has provided a detailed introduction to the major concepts and tools that professional equity investors use.

- Equities play a growth role in investment portfolios.
- The major investment approaches are passive, active, and semiactive. The major passive approach is indexing, which is based on the rationale that after costs, the return on the average actively managed dollar should be less than the return on the average passively managed dollar. Active management is historically the dominant approach to investment and is based on the rationale that markets offer opportunities to beat a given equity benchmark. Semiactive or enhanced indexing is a growing discipline based on the rationale that markets offer opportunities to achieve a positive information ratio with limited risk relative to a benchmark.

- A successful active equity manager will have an expected active return of 2 percent or higher, but his tracking error is likely to be more than 4 percent. Hence, his information ratio will be 0.5 or lower. At the opposite end of the spectrum, an index fund will have minimal tracking risk and an expected active return of 0 percent, implying an information ratio of zero. Enhanced indexing strategies tend to have the highest information ratios, often in the range of 0.5 to 2.0.
- An indexer must choose the index that the portfolio will track and understand the details of the index's construction. The major types of index are:

  - *Price weighted.* In a price-weighted index, each stock in the index is weighted according to its absolute share price.
  - *Value weighted* (or *market-capitalization weighted*). In a value-weighted index, each stock in the index is weighted according to its market capitalization (share price multiplied by the number of shares outstanding). A subset of the value-weighted method is the float-weighted method, which adjusts value weights for the floating supply of shares (the fraction of shares outstanding that is actually available to investors).
  - *Equal weighted.* In an equal-weighted index, each stock in the index is weighted equally.

  A price-weighted index is biased toward shares with the highest price, and a value- or float-weighted index is biased toward the largest market cap companies, which may reflect positive valuation errors. An equal-weighted index is biased toward smaller-cap companies.
- Indexed separate or pooled accounts, index mutual funds, exchange-traded funds, equity index futures, and equity total return swaps are the major methods for implementing an indexing strategy. Indexed separate or pooled accounts are typically very low cost. Index mutual funds are a widely accessible alternative with a considerable range of cost structures. Exchange traded funds may have structural advantages compared with mutual funds and also permit short positions. Equity index futures are relatively low-cost vehicles for obtaining equity market exposure that require a rollover to maintain longer term. Equity total return swaps are a relatively low-cost way to obtain long-term exposure to an equity market that may offer tax advantages.
- Three methods of indexation include full replication (in which every index security is held in approximately the same weight in the fund as in the index), stratified sampling (which samples from the index's securities organized into representative cells), and optimization (which chooses a portfolio of securities that minimizes expected tracking risk relative to the index based on a multifactor model of index risk exposures). Full replication is the most common procedure for indices composed of highly liquid securities. Stratified sampling and optimization are applicable when full replication is not feasible or cost effective.
- All else being equal, value investors are more concerned about buying a stock that is deemed relatively cheap in terms of the purchase price of earnings or assets than about the company's future growth prospects. In contrast to value investors' focus on price, growth investors are more concerned with earnings growth. Value has substyles of low price-to-earnings ratio (P/E), contrarian, and high yield. Growth has substyles of consistent growth and earnings momentum.
- The main risk for a value investor is the potential for misinterpreting a stock's cheapness; it may be cheap for a very good economic reason that the investor does not fully appreciate. The major risk for growth investors is that the forecasted earnings per share (EPS) growth fails to materialize as expected. In that event, P/E multiples may contract at the same time as EPS, amplifying the investor's losses.

- Two major approaches to identifying style are returns-based style analysis, based on portfolio returns, and holdings-based style analysis based on analysis of security holdings. Returns-based style analysis is quickly executed, cost effective, and requires minimal information. Holdings-based style analysis requires detailed information on security holdings and can give an up-to-date and detailed picture of a manager's style. Most current style indices are constructed using a holdings-based approach.
- The style box is a means of visualizing a manager's style exposures, which is typically based on a holdings-based analysis. It may contain as many as nine cells representing a portfolio on value–market-oriented–growth and small–mid–large spectrums.
- Inconsistency in style, or style drift, is of concern to investors because (1) the investor may no longer have exposure to the particular style desired and (2) the manager may be operating outside her area of expertise.
- A long-only strategy can capture one overall alpha. With a long–short strategy, however, the value added can be equal to two alphas, one from the long position and one from the short position. A market-neutral strategy is constructed to have an overall zero beta. Long–short strategies may benefit from pricing inefficiencies on the short side (a greater supply of overvalued than undervalued securities).
- The Fundamental Law of Active Management states that $IR \approx IC\sqrt{Breadth}$, which implies that the information ratio approximately equals what the investor knows about the company multiplied by the square root of the number of independent active investment decisions made each year.
- The framework for optimizing allocations to a group of managers (in this context, equity managers within the equity allocation) involves maximizing active return for a given level of active risk determined by the investor's aversion to active risk.
- A core-satellite portfolio involves an indexed and/or enhanced indexed core portfolio and actively managed satellite portfolios.
- A completion fund may be used to neutralize unintended bets against the overall equity benchmark.
- Investment management contracts may involve an ad valorem fee schedule and/or an incentive fee schedule.
- Selecting and monitoring good managers is as complex a process as selecting and managing good investments.

PROBLEMS

1. Katrina Lowry works for the pension department of National Software. Her supervisor has asked her to evaluate the different style alternatives for a large-cap mandate and to highlight their differences.

   A. State the three main large-cap styles.
   B. Describe the basic premise and risks of each style identified in Part A.

2. Juan Varga is concerned about the performance and investment positions of an investment firm he hired five years ago. The firm, Galicia Investment Management, has been tasked with managing an active portfolio with a developed market mandate (MSCI World countries). Galicia is a well-known value manager. Varga performs some returns-based style analysis and finds the following results for the past two years (each quarterly snapshot is the result of a regression using the prior 36 months return data).

	MSCI World Value	MSCI World Growth	Other
1Q 2002	83%	16%	1%
2Q 2002	77%	20%	3%
3Q 2002	79%	19%	2%
4Q 2002	68%	29%	3%
1Q 2003	55%	40%	5%
2Q 2003	48%	45%	7%
3Q 2003	52%	45%	3%
4Q 2003	55%	43%	2%

What reasonable conclusions can Varga reach regarding the Galicia investment process?

3. David Burke is considering investing in a mutual fund that is classified generically under the term *growth and income.* In preparation for his CFA exams, Burke studied style investing. Using publicly available data sources, he gathered the following information about the mutual fund in question. How should he characterize the fund based on what he has learned in his CFA exam preparation?

	Fund	Market Benchmark
Number of stocks	80	600
Weighted-average market cap	$37 billion	$40 billion
Dividend yield	2.5%	2.1%
P/E	16	19
P/B	1.6	1.9
EPS growth (5-year projected)	11%	12%
Sector		
Consumer Discretionary	16%	10%
Consumer Staples	9	12
Energy	9	9
Finance	15	20
Health Care	9	7
Industrials	12	9
Information Technology	8	7
Materials	5	8
Telecommunications	7	10
Utilities	10	7

4. Phillipa Jenkins has been asked to manage internally a FTSE 100 index fund. Because the index's 10 largest stocks make up more than 50 percent of its weight, Jenkins is considering using optimization to build the portfolio using many fewer than 100 stocks. All 100 stocks in the index are considered liquid. Is optimizing the best approach?
5. Shawn Miller plans to use returns-based style analysis to analyze his global portfolio. He will use style indices as a proxy for style in the analysis and is debating whether to use indices like Dow Jones (which categorizes stocks as value, growth, or neutral) or like MSCI (which categorize stocks only as value or growth).

A. What are the benefits and drawbacks of each method?
B. Does it matter which type Miller chooses for a returns-based style analysis?

6. Explain the principal benefit of a market-neutral long–short portfolio. What risks are inherent in such a portfolio that a long-only equity portfolio lacks?
7. Simon Hayes is a long–short portfolio manager with Victoria Investment Management in London. His expertise lies in building market-neutral long–short strategies using U.K. equities. After meeting with his most important client, Hayes learns that the client is planning to hire an investment firm to manage a Japanese equity portfolio. How can Hayes satisfy this mandate using U.K. equities and no Japanese equities?
8. Yoko Suzuki manages an enhanced index portfolio benchmarked to the index for Kyushu Motors' pension fund. The strategy has a target alpha of 1.5 percent annually with an annualized active risk of 2 percent. Her client is quite pleased that the portfolio has met its stated objective for the past five years. Kyushu's other investment managers have not done so well against their objectives, however, and the pension fund now suffers from a large shortfall between its assets and liabilities. To make up this shortfall, Kyushu asks her to double the portfolio's active risk with the intention of doubling the alpha as well. How should Suzuki respond to this suggestion?
9. Mike Smith is a consultant evaluating a market neutral long–short strategy for his client. Based on the holdings data he receives from the client, Smith notices a small but persistent difference between the alphas generated on the long side and those generated on the short side. State which of the two alphas is more likely the larger one, and provide three reasons why that might be the case.
10. Karen Johnson is responsible for the U.S. equity portion of her company's pension plan. She is thinking about trying to boost the overall alpha in U.S. equities by using an enhanced index fund to replace her core index fund holding.

    A. The U.S. equity portion of the pension plan currently consists of three managers (one index, one value, and one growth) and is expected to produce a target annual alpha of 2.4 percent with a tracking risk of 2.75 percent. By replacing the index manager with an enhanced indexer the target alpha changes to 2.8 percent with a tracking risk of 2.9 percent. Does this change represent an improvement? Why?
    B. Johnson also needs to decide whether she prefers a stock-based or a synthetic enhanced index manager. What are the advantages and disadvantages of each?

11. Stephanie Whitmore is evaluating several alternatives for the U.S. equity portfolio of her company's pension plan, involving the following managers:

	Active Return	Active Risk (with Respect to Normal Benchmark)	Normal Benchmark
Index	0%	0%	Russell 3000
Semiactive	1	1.5	Russell 3000
Active A (Value)	3	5	Russell 1000 Value
Active B (Growth)	4	6	Russell 1000 Growth
Long–Short	6	6	Cash with Russell 1000 overlay

Active A's misfit risk is 7.13 percent. In all of the questions below, assume that the active returns are uncorrelated. The overall equity portfolio benchmark is the Russell 3000.

A. Whitmore has taken the information in the table above and used a mean variance optimizer to create an implementation efficient frontier. The highest risk point on the efficient frontier is a 100 percent allocation to the long–short manager with a 100 percent Russell 1000 overlay. The active risk of this portfolio is 6.1 percent. Why is the risk greater than 6 percent?
B. Calculate the total active risk for Active A.
C. Whitmore's current equity manager allocation is 30 percent Index and 70 percent Semiactive. Calculate this portfolio's current expected active return, active risk, and information ratio.
D. After determining the desired level of active risk, Whitmore selected the appropriate portfolio from the efficient frontier. The portfolio allocates 39 percent to the Index manager, 34 percent to the Semiactive manager, 7 percent to Active Manager A, 8 percent to Active Manager B, and 12 percent to the Long–Short manager. This portfolio has an expected active return of 1.59 percent and an expected active risk of 1.10 percent. Does this portfolio represent an improvement over the current allocation? If so, by how much?
E. Upon further investigation of the long–short manager, Whitmore learns that approximately 20 percent of the active return generated comes from equity positions in non-U.S. companies. Is this a concern? Why or why not?

CHAPTER 8

ALTERNATIVE INVESTMENTS PORTFOLIO MANAGEMENT

Jot K. Yau, CFA

Seattle University
Seattle, Washington
and
Strategic Options Investment Advisors Ltd
Hong Kong

Thomas Schneeweis

Alternative Investment Analytics
Amherst, Massachusetts

Thomas R. Robinson, CFA

TRRobinson and Associates
Coral Gables, Florida

Lisa R. Weiss, CFA

Black Knight Ventures, Inc.
Tampa, Florida

LEARNING OUTCOMES

After completing this chapter, you will be able to do the following:

- List and explain the major types of alternative investments.
- Characterize the common features of alternative investments and their markets and discuss how they may be grouped by the role they typically play in a portfolio.
- List, explain, and interpret the major due diligence checkpoints in selecting active managers of alternative investments.
- Explain and interpret the special issues that alternative investments raise for investment advisors of private wealth clients.
- Distinguish among the types of investments within alternative investment groups (real estate, private equity, commodity investments, hedge funds, managed futures, and distressed securities).
- Discuss the construction and interpretation of benchmarks, including biases, in alternative investment groups.
- Review the investment characteristics of the major types of investments within alternative investment groups, including risks and liquidity.
- Identify and evaluate, given relevant data, any return enhancement and/or risk-diversification effects of an alternative investment relative to a comparison portfolio (e.g., one invested in common equity and bonds) and justify any identified benefits in terms of characteristics and/or market opportunity exploited by the alternative investment.
- Identify and justify any special emphases in due diligence for a given alternative investment group.
- Review the advantages and disadvantages of direct equity investments in real estate.
- Identify the major issuers and buyers of venture capital, the stages through which private companies pass (seed stage through exit), the characteristic sources of financing at each stage, and the purposes of such financing.
- Compare and contrast venture capital funds and buyout funds.
- Discuss the use of convertible preferred stock in direct venture capital investment.
- Explain a typical structure of a private equity fund, including the compensation to the fund's sponsor (e.g., general partner) and typical timelines.
- State and discuss the issues that must be addressed in formulating a strategy for private equity investment.
- Discuss the rationales for indirect versus direct commodity investment.
- Calculate and interpret the components of the return to a commodity futures contract and predict the effects of the term structure of futures prices on the returns earned on a long futures position.
- Discuss the relationship between commodities and inflation, including distinctions among types of commodities.
- Identify and explain the style classification of a hedge fund, given a description of its investment strategy.
- Explain a typical structure of a hedge fund, including the compensation of the hedge fund managers and the rationale for high-water marks and other provisions.
- Explain the rationale and importance of hedge fund incentive fees and the concerns they may raise for hedge fund investors.
- Explain the advantages and disadvantages of fund-of-funds hedge funds.
- Discuss the limitations of using hedge fund indices in analyzing hedge fund performance.

- Discuss and illustrate the conventions and special issues involved in hedge fund performance evaluation and critique the use of the Sharpe ratio in hedge fund performance appraisal.
- Explain the characteristics of derivative markets that affect the investor's ability to earn a risk premium.
- Demonstrate and explain the major types of distressed securities investing strategies, including the possible reasons for each strategy's market opportunity.
- Explain event risk, market liquidity risk, market risk, and "J factor risk" as concerns for distressed securities investors.

SUMMARY OVERVIEW

Alternative investments have become a large portion of the portfolios of both individual and institutional investors. This chapter presented five groups of alternative investments: real estate, private equity, commodities, hedge funds, managed futures, and distressed securities.

- Common features of alternative investments include relative illiquidity, which tends to be associated with a return premium as compensation; diversifying potential relative to a portfolio of stocks and bonds; high due diligence costs; and the difficulty of performance evaluation.
- Checkpoints in due diligence for alternative investment selection should cover market opportunity, investment process, organization, people, terms and structure, service providers, documents, and write-up.
- Special concerns for advisers to private wealth clients include tax issues, determining suitability, communication with the client, decision risk (the risk of changing strategies at the point of maximum loss), and concentrated equity positions of the client in a closely held company.
- The physical real estate market is characterized by a relative lack of liquidity, large lot size, and high transaction costs.
- Real estate investments can be viewed in terms of direct ownership and indirect ownership. Direct ownership includes investment in residences, business real estate, and agricultural land. Indirect ownership includes vehicles such as real estate investment trusts (REITs).
- Advantages to real estate investment include tax benefits, the use of leverage, control over property, diversification, potential as an inflation hedge, and low volatility of returns.
- Disadvantages to real estate investment include the inability to subdivide real estate investments, high information costs, high commissions, maintenance and operating costs, location risk, and political risk related to tax deductions.
- Private equity investments are highly illiquid, and investors must be willing to hold these securities for long periods.
- Private equity investments include start-up companies, middle-market private companies, and private investment in public entities.
- Private equity investors include angel investors, venture capitalists, and larger companies in the same industry.
- There are two broad approaches to investing in commodities: direct and indirect. Direct commodity investment entails purchase of the physical commodities (e.g., agricultural products, metals, and crude oil). In contrast, indirect investment in commodities involves the acquisition of claims on commodities, such as in futures markets.

- Futures contract–based commodity indices have three separate components of return: price, collateral, and roll return.
- Price return derives from changes in commodity futures prices, which comes from the changes in the underlying spot prices via the cost-of-carry model. In other words, when the spot price goes up (down), so does the futures price, giving rise to a positive (negative) return to a long futures position.
- Collateral return is related to the assumption that when an investor invests in the commodity futures index, the full value of the underlying futures contracts is invested at a risk-free interest rate.
- Roll return or roll yield arises from rolling long futures positions forward through time and may capture a positive return when the term structure of futures prices is downward sloping.
- The inflation-hedging ability of commodity investing appears to differ according to the commodity.
- Hedge funds are skill-based investment strategies in various forms, including limited partnerships. The funds use different investment strategies and thus are often classified according to investment style. Within each style category, hedge funds are classified according to the underlying markets traded or the unique trading style—for example, relative value, event driven, hedged equity, and global macro.
- Within each style classification, there are a number of subgroups. For instance, within the hedge fund relative-value style classification, subgroups include market-neutral long–short equity, convertible hedging, and fixed-income arbitrage (or bond hedging).
- Hedge funds can provide return and diversification benefits, but the risks are not usually well represented by standard deviation.
- Distressed securities are securities of companies that are in financial distress or near bankruptcy. The securities could be equity, debt, trade, or other claims.
- Distressed securities investment exploits the fact that many investors are unable to hold below-investment-grade securities. Furthermore, few analysts cover the distressed market.
- Risks of distressed securities investing include event risk, "judge" factor risk, liquidity risk, market risk, and other risks.

PROBLEMS

1. Compare the relative liquidity characteristics of direct versus indirect investment in real estate. Discuss three factors that affect the liquidity of both forms of investment.

Problems 2 and 3 refer to Exhibit 8-1.

2. A. Summarize the major categories of direct and indirect investment in real estate.
   B. Using the data in Exhibit 8-1, evaluate the historical relative diversification benefits of both forms of investment when added to a 50 percent stock/50 percent bond portfolio. Use the National Council of Real Estate Investment Fiduciaries (NCREIF) Index unsmoothed to represent direct investment and the National Association of Real Estate Investment Trusts (NAREIT) Index to represent indirect investment.
3. The board trustees of Elite Corporation's US$50 million pension fund are meeting to discuss a presentation they recently received from their pension consultant, who is recommending that they diversify their current 50/50 stock/bond asset allocation to include a 10 percent allocation to real estate. Although the trustees would like to

EXHIBIT 8-1 Real Estate Performance 1990–2004

Measure	NAREIT Index	NAREIT Index Hedged	NCREIF Index	NCREIF Index Unsmoothed	S&P 500	Lehman Aggregate Bond Index
Annualized return	12.71%	8.96%	6.14%	7.27%	10.94%	7.70%
Annualized std. dev.	12.74%	11.93%	3.37%	8.95%	14.65%	3.91%
Sharpe ratio	0.66	0.39	0.55	0.33	0.45	0.87
Minimum quarterly return	−14.19%	−10.16%	−5.33%	−18.55%	−17.28%	−2.87%
Correlation w/NAREIT	1.00	0.94	−0.001	0.21	0.35	0.18
Correlation w/NAREIT hedged	0.94	1.00	0.00	0.24	0.00	0.14
Correlation w/NCREIF	0.00	0.00	1.00	0.71	0.01	−0.18
Correlation w/NCREIF unsmoothed	0.21	0.24	0.71	1.00	−0.01	−0.27

Source: CISDM (2005a).

reduce portfolio risk without sacrificing a significant amount of return, the trustees have previously been reluctant to change the asset allocation because they are concerned about "making a mistake we can't easily fix" if the economic environment changes.

One trustee, Maya Semyonova, makes reference to the table above and some notes that provide an overview of how the various indices are constructed. Semyonova states: "To address our stated risk and return objectives and given the superior historical benefits of direct investing in real estate, represented by the unsmoothed NCREIF Index, I recommend that we reallocate 10 percent from our bond investments indexed to the Lehman Aggregate to a direct real estate asset."

A second trustee, John Pearson, responds with a different recommendation: "I believe we should reallocate 10 percent from the 50 percent S&P 500 allocation to REITs to achieve our goals."

A. Critique Semyonova's recommendation with reference to the return, risk, diversification, and liquidity characteristics of the two asset classes to which Semyonova is referring.
B. Critique Pearson's recommendation with reference to the return, risk, diversification, and liquidity characteristics of the two asset classes that Pearson is referring to.
C. Of the reallocation scenarios suggested by Semyonova and Pearson, choose the one most appropriate for Elite Corporation's pension fund based on the trustees' objectives. Justify your choice with reference to returns, risks, and issues concerning construction of real estate and REIT indices.

4. Roger Guidry, chief investment officer (CIO) of a university endowment fund, is reviewing investment data related to the endowment's investment in energy commodities.

Year	GSCI Total Annual Return	GSCI Collateral Yield	GSCI Roll Yield	GSCI Spot Annual Return
1	29.1%	9.6%	?	6.1%
2	−30.5%	?	−14.2%	−24.3%

A. Calculate the roll yield for Year 1.
B. Calculate the collateral yield for Year 2.

Guidry notes that the collateral yield is positive in both scenarios, although the GSCI total annual return for Year 2 is −30.5 percent. He asks for an explanation with regard to the positive collateral yield.

C. Justify the positive collateral yield by discussing the concepts of margin and implied yield.

A consultant tells Guidry: "Commodities exhibit positive event risk."

D. Justify the consultant's statement by discussing the relationship between commodity prices and event risk.

5. Capital market analysts John Lake and Julie McCoy are reviewing the information in Exhibit 8-2. Lake and McCoy note that the Sharpe ratio for the GSCI is significantly lower than that of the S&P 500 and the Lehman Government/Corporate Bond indices. They also note that the minimum monthly returns for the GSCI and S&P 500 are similar.

   Lake states to McCoy: "Based on the historical record, I don't understand why we would invest in the GSCI when the annualized return for the GSCI is lower than that of the S&P 500 and Lehman Government/Corporate indices, the minimum monthly return is similar to that of the S&P 500, and the Sharpe ratio is significantly lower than either of the domestic equity or bond asset classes. The risk measure in the Sharpe ratio should completely capture a commodity index's risk."

   A. Critique Lake's statement.

   McCoy shows Lake in Exhibit 8-3 and suggests that these more recent data, which show a significant outperformance of commodity returns versus domestic

EXHIBIT 8-2 Commodity Index Performance 1990–2004

Measure	GSCI	S&P 500	Lehman Gov./Corp. Bond	MSCI World Equity	Lehman Global Bond
Annualized return	7.08%	10.94%	7.77%	7.08%	8.08%
Annualized Std. Dev.	19.26%	14.65%	4.46%	14.62%	5.23%
Sharpe ratio	0.15	0.45	0.78	0.19	0.72
Minimum monthly return	−14.41%	−14.46%	−4.19%	−13.32%	−3.66%
Correlation with GSCI	1.00	−0.08	0.03	−0.06	0.06

Source: CISDM (2005b).

EXHIBIT 8-3 Recent Commodity Index Performance 2000–2004

Measure	GSCI	S&P 500	Lehman Gov./Corp. Bond	MSCI World Equity	Lehman Global Bond
Annualized return	13.77%	−2.30%	8.00%	−2.05%	8.47%
Annualized std. dev.	22.10%	16.35%	4.76%	15.62%	6.02%
Sharpe ratio	0.50	−0.31	1.11	−0.30	0.96
Minimum monthly return	−14.41%	−10.87%	−4.19%	−10.98%	−3.66%
Correlation with GSCI	1.00	−0.05	0.05	0.00	0.10

Source: CISDM (2005b).

and international equities and bonds, make a much stronger case for investing in commodities. McCoy also states that the low correlations of commodities with the other asset classes indicate that inclusion of commodities will provide significant diversification benefits to the portfolio.

B. Judge the validity of McCoy's conclusions regarding returns and correlations of the various asset classes.

6. Explain the practical effects of the following possible characteristics of a hedge fund index:

   A. Survivorship bias
   B. Value weighting
   C. Stale price bias

7. Ian Parkinson, as chief pension officer of a large defined-benefit plan, is considering presenting a recommendation that the pension plan make its first investments in three different types of hedge funds: (1) market-neutral, (2) convertible arbitrage, and (3) global macro.

   An analyst who works for Parkinson comes by with Exhibit 8-4 below and makes the following comment: "The returns for global macro are very impressive. In fact, there are other strategies that have significantly outperformed the S&P 500, equity market-neutral, and convertible arbitrage over the past 15 years. I think that, based on their returns, we should focus specifically on the other strategies."

   A. Describe the three alternative strategies that Parkinson is considering, and evaluate each with respect to their level of market risk and credit risk. Interpret their correlations with the S&P 500 and the Lehman Government/Corporate Bond indices as presented in Exhibit 8-4.
   B. Critique the analyst's statement.

8. Interpret a "1 and 20" fee structure with reference to high-water marks and drawdowns.

EXHIBIT 8-4 Performance of Hedge Fund Strategies and Traditional Assets 1990–2004

Fund or Asset	Annual Return	Annual Standard Deviation	Sharpe Ratio	Minimum Monthly Return	Correlation with S&P 500	Correlation with Lehman Gov./Corp. Bond
HFCI	13.46%	5.71%	1.61	6.92%	0.59	0.17
Event driven	13.46%	5.59%	1.64	−9.37%	0.59	0.07
Equity hedge	15.90%	9.34%	1.24	−9.70%	0.64	0.10
Equity market neutral	9.24%	2.50%	1.98	−1.07%	0.09	0.24
Merger/risk arbitrage	9.07%	4.86%	0.99	−8.78%	0.48	0.10
Distressed	15.28%	6.07%	1.81	−9.71%	0.42	0.04
Fixed-income arbitrage	7.62%	3.61%	0.92	−6.61%	0.06	−0.06
Convertible arbitrage	10.23%	3.96%	1.50	−3.42%	0.19	0.13
Global macro	16.98%	8.38%	1.51	−5.41%	0.26	0.34
Short selling	−0.61%	19.39%	−0.25	−14.62%	−0.76	−0.01
S&P 500	10.94%	14.65%	0.45	−14.46%	1.00	0.13
Lehman Gov./Corp. Bond	7.77%	4.46%	0.78	−4.19%	0.13	1.00
MSCI World	7.08%	14.62%	0.19	−13.32%	0.86	0.09
Lehman Global Bond	8.09%	5.23%	0.73	−3.66%	0.11	0.74

Note: HFCI is the Hedge Fund Composite Index and was constructed by equally weighting the EACM 100, the HFR Fund Weighted Composite Index, and Credit Suisse/Tremont Hedge Fund Index.
Source: CISDM (2005c).

9. Susan DiMarco is evaluating a hedge fund that has a high level of portfolio turnover and a short investment record. The hedge fund makes a contractual stipulation with limited partners regarding a lock-up period that is quite common in the hedge fund industry. A colleague, Jane Farkas, who has reviewed the fund, makes the following statement to DiMarco: "Well, if we're unhappy with performance, we can always fire the hedge fund manager. If they trade frequently, as indicated by their high portfolio turnover, they must have high liquidity." Judge the validity of Carr's statement.
10. Jane Farkas tells Susan DiMarco that she has seen exciting data on the performance of market-neutral, convertible arbitrage, and global macro hedge funds. Farkas states: "The Sharpe ratios of all of these hedge fund strategies are much higher than for traditional equities or bonds, which means they have a great risk/return profile. We should definitely plan a major investment in hedge funds."

    DiMarco responds: "There are several reasons that the Sharpe ratio may be misleading."

A. Discuss the situations that could cause an upward bias in the calculation of the Sharpe ratio.
B. Evaluate the reasons that statistically indicate that the Sharpe ratio is not the most appropriate measure of risk for hedge funds.

For Problems 11 and 12, please refer to the following table of monthly returns for a hedge fund and an index portfolio. For the purpose of computation, the hurdle rate is the U.S. T-bill rate, assumed to be 5 percent per year.

Month	Hedge Fund Returns (%)	Index Returns (%)
January	3.50	−2.40
February	4.00	−4.00
March	−2.00	−1.60
April	−2.00	3.00
May	−1.00	−4.20
June	0.90	2.00
July	−1.00	2.50
August	1.70	−2.10
September	2.70	−2.00
October	3.70	0.50
November	0.40	3.10
December	−3.20	0.20

11. A. Calculate the average rolling returns for the hedge fund if the investor's investment horizon is nine months.
    B. Explain how rolling returns can provide additional information about the hedge fund's performance.
12. A. Compute the annualized downside deviations for the hedge fund and the index, and contrast them to the standard deviation. The annualized standard deviations for the hedge fund and the index are, respectively, 8.64 percent and 9.19 percent.
    B. Compute the Sortino ratio and, based on this statistic, evaluate the performance of the hedge fund against the performance of the index portfolio.
13. Andrew Cassano, CIO of a large charitable organization, is meeting with his senior analyst, Lori Wood, to discuss managed futures. Cassano believes that it would be beneficial to evaluate this alternative investment category before making a final decision with respect to hedge fund investment.

    Wood states: "Although managed futures are sometimes considered a subset of hedge funds, there are some differences that make them worthy of consideration."

    A. Determine which absolute-return hedge fund strategy to which managed futures are mostly closely related (i.e., managed futures are often considered a subgroup of this hedge fund strategy).
    B. Briefly discuss a primary similarity and a primary difference between managed futures and many other hedge fund strategies.
    C. Contrast the characteristics of two managed futures styles: systematic and discretionary.

14. Cassano asks: "If managed futures strategies are often momentum based, how do they achieve excess returns differently from traditional stock or bond investment vehicles?" Formulate an answer to Cassano's question.
15. List and discuss the sources of return available to managed futures programs through the use of derivative trading strategies.
16. Contrast "fallen angels" to high-yield debt.
17. Evaluate the role of investors in both the private equity and relative-value strategies—specifically, with respect to investing in distressed securities.
18. Formulate a description of the results of a prepackaged bankruptcy with reference to (a) "prebankruptcy" creditors of the company, (b) "prebankruptcy" shareholders, and (c) vulture investors.
19. Critique the following statement: "When the economy has been faltering and may be going into recession, it is typically a good time to invest in distressed securities."

CHAPTER 9

RISK MANAGEMENT

Don M.Chance, CFA

Louisiana State University
Baton Rouge, Louisiana

Kenneth Grant

Cheyne Capital
New York, New York

John Marsland, CFA

WMG Advisors LLP
London, England

LEARNING OUTCOMES

After completing this chapter, you will be able to do the following:

- Compare and contrast the main features of the risk management process, risk governance, risk reduction, and an enterprise risk management system.
- Recommend and justify the risk exposures an analyst should report as part of an enterprise risk management system, given a description of the company's business.
- Evaluate the strengths and weaknesses of a company's risk management processes.
- Evaluate possible responses to a risk management problem.
- Interpret value at risk (VaR) and its role in measuring overall and individual position market risk.
- Compare and contrast the analytical (variance–covariance), historical, and Monte Carlo methods for estimating VaR and discuss the advantages and disadvantages of each.
- Discuss the advantages and limitations of VaR and extension and supplements to it (e.g., cash flow at risk, earnings at risk, tail value at risk).
- Compare and contrast the various types of stress testing and discuss the advantages and disadvantages of each.
- Evaluate the results of stress tests.

- Evaluate a company's or a portfolio's exposures to market risk.
- Evaluate the credit risk of a position, including forward contract, swap, and option positions.
- Evaluate a company's or a portfolio's exposures to nonfinancial risk.
- Demonstrate the use of risk budgeting, position limits, and other methods for managing market risk.
- Demonstrate the use of the following methods of managing credit risk: limiting exposure, marking to market, using collateral, using netting arrangements, setting credit standards, and using credit derivatives.
- Compare and contrast the Sharpe ratio, risk-adjusted return on capital, return over maximum drawdown, and the Sortino ratio as measures of risk-adjusted performance.
- Demonstrate the use of VaR and stress testing in setting capital requirements.

SUMMARY OVERVIEW

Financial markets reward competence and knowledge in risk management and punish mistakes. Portfolio managers must therefore study and understand the discipline of successful risk management. In this chapter, we have introduced basic concepts and techniques of risk management and made the following points:

- Risk management is a process involving the identification of the exposures to risk, the establishment of appropriate ranges for exposures, the continuous measurement of these exposures, and the execution of appropriate adjustments to bring the actual level and desired level of risk into alignment. The process involves continuous monitoring of exposures and new policies, preferences, and information.
- Typically, risks should be minimized wherever and whenever companies lack comparative advantages in the associated markets, activities, or lines of business.
- Risk governance refers to the process of setting risk management policies and standards for an organization. Senior management, which is ultimately responsible for all organizational activities, must oversee the process.
- Enterprise risk management is a centralized risk management system whose distinguishing feature is a firmwide or across-enterprise perspective on risk.
- Financial risk refers to all risks derived from events in the external financial markets. Nonfinancial risk refers to all other forms of risk. Financial risk includes market risk (risk related to interest rates, exchange rates, stock prices, and commodity prices), credit risk, and liquidity risk. The primary sources of nonfinancial risk are operations risk, model risk, settlement risk, regulatory risk, legal risk, tax risk, and accounting risk.
- Traditional measures of market risk include linear approximations such as beta for stocks, duration for fixed income, and delta for options, as well as second-order estimation techniques such as convexity and gamma. For products with option-like characteristics, techniques exist to measure the impact of changes in volatility (vega) and the passage of time (theta). Sensitivity to movements in the correlation among assets is also relevant for certain types of instruments.
- VaR estimates the minimum loss that a party would expect to experience with a given probability over a specified period of time. Using the complementary probability (i.e., 100 percent minus the given probability stated as a percent), VaR can be expressed as a maximum loss at a given confidence level. VaR users must make decisions regarding appropriate time periods, confidence intervals, and specific VaR methodologies.

- The analytical or variance–covariance method can be used to determine VaR under the assumption that returns are normally distributed by subtracting a multiple of the standard deviation from the expected return, where the multiple is determined by the desired probability level. The advantage of the method is its simplicity. Its disadvantages are that returns are not normally distributed in any reliable sense and that the method does not work well when portfolios contain options and other derivatives.
- The historical method estimates VaR from data on a portfolio's performance during a historical period. The returns are ranked, and VaR is obtained by determining the return that is exceeded in a negative sense 5 percent or 1 percent (depending on the user's choice) of the time. The historical method has the advantage of being simple and not requiring the assumption of a normal distribution. Its disadvantage is that accurate historical time-series information is not always easily available, particularly for instruments such as bonds and options, which behave differently at different points in their life spans.
- Monte Carlo simulation estimates VaR by generating random returns and determining the 5 percent or 1 percent (depending on the user's choice) worst outcomes. It has the advantages that it does not require a normal distribution and can handle complex relationships among risks. Its disadvantage is that it can be very time consuming and costly to conduct the large number of simulations required for accuracy. It also requires the estimation of input values, which can be difficult.
- VaR can be difficult to estimate, can give a wide range of values, and can lead to a false sense of security that risk is accurately measured and under control. VaR for individual positions do not generally aggregate in a simple way to portfolio VaR. VaR also puts all emphasis on the negative outcomes, ignoring the positive outcomes. It can be difficult to calculate VaR for a large complex organization with many exposures. On the other hand, VaR is a simple and easy-to-understand risk measure that is widely accepted. It is also adaptable to a variety of uses, such as allocating capital.
- Incremental VaR measures the incremental effect of an asset on the VaR of a portfolio. Cash flow at risk and earnings at risk measure the risk to a company's cash flow or earnings instead of market value, as in the case of VaR. Tail value at risk is VaR plus the expected loss in excess of VaR, when such excess loss occurs. Stress testing is another important supplement to VaR.
- Credit risk has two dimensions, the probability of default and the associated recovery rate.
- Credit risk in a forward contract is assumed by the party to which the market value is positive. The market value represents the current value of the claim that one party has on the other. The actual payoff at expiration could differ, but the market value reflects the current value of that future claim.
- Credit risk in swaps is similar to credit risk in forward contracts. The market value represents the current value of the claim on the future payments. The party holding the positive market value assumes the credit risk at that time. For interest rate and equity swaps, credit risk is greatest near the middle of the life of the swap. For currency swaps with payment of notional principal, credit risk is greatest near the end of the life of the swap.
- Credit risk in options is one-sided. Because the seller is paid immediately and in full, she faces no credit risk. By contrast, the buyer faces the risk that the seller will not meet her obligations in the event of exercise. The market value of the option is the current value of the future claim the buyer has on the seller.
- VaR can be used to measure credit risk. The interpretation is the same as with standard VaR, but a credit-based VaR is more complex because it must interact with VaR based on market risk. Credit risk arises only when market risk results in gains to trading. Credit

VaR must take into account the complex interaction of market movements, the possibility of default, and recovery rates. Credit VaR is also difficult to aggregate across markets and counterparties.

- Risk budgeting is the process of establishing policies to allocate the finite resource of risk capacity to business units that must assume exposure in order to generate return. Risk budgeting has also been applied to allocation of funds to investment managers.
- The various methods of controlling credit risk include setting exposure limits for individual counterparties, exchanging cash values that reflect mark-to-market levels, posting collateral, netting, setting minimum credit, using special-purpose vehicles that have higher credit ratings than the companies that own them, and using credit derivatives.
- Among the measures of risk-adjusted performance that have been used in a portfolio context are the Sharpe ratio, risk-adjusted return on capital, return over maximum drawdown, and the Sortino ratio. The Sharpe ratio uses standard deviation, measuring total risk as the risk measure. Risk-adjusted return on capital accounts for risk using capital at risk. The Sortino ratio measures risk using downside deviation, which computes volatility using only rate-of-return data points below a minimum acceptable return. Return over maximum drawdown uses maximum drawdown as a risk measure.
- Methods for allocating capital include nominal position limits, VaR-based position limits, maximum loss limits, internal capital requirements, and regulatory capital requirements.

PROBLEMS

1. Discuss the difference between centralized and decentralized risk management systems, including the advantages and disadvantages of each.
2. Stewart Gilchrist follows the automotive industry, including Ford Motor Company. Based on Ford's 2003 annual report, Gilchrist writes the following summary:

   Ford Motor Company has businesses in several countries around the world. Ford frequently has expenditures and receipts denominated in non-U.S. currencies, including purchases and sales of finished vehicles and production parts, subsidiary dividends, investments in non-U.S. operations, etc. Ford uses a variety of commodities in the production of motor vehicles, such as nonferrous metals, precious metals, ferrous alloys, energy, and plastics/resins. Ford typically purchases these commodities from outside suppliers. To finance its operations, Ford uses a variety of funding sources, such as commercial paper, term debt, and lines of credit from major commercial banks. The company invests any surplus cash in securities of various types and maturities, the value of which are subject to fluctuations in interest rates. Ford has a credit division, which provides financing to customers wanting to purchase Ford's vehicles on credit. Overall, Ford faces several risks. To manage some of its risks, Ford invests in fixed-income instruments and derivative contracts. Some of these investments do not rely on a clearing house and instead effect settlement through the execution of bilateral agreements.

   Based on the above discussion, recommend and justify the risk exposures that should be reported as part of an Enterprise Risk Management System for Ford Motor Company.
3. NatWest Markets (NWM) was the investment banking arm of National Westminster Bank, one of the largest banks in the United Kingdom. On February 28, 1997, NWM revealed that a substantial loss had been uncovered in its trading books. During the 1990s, NatWest was engaged in trading interest rate options and swaptions on several underlying currencies. This trading required setting appropriate prices of the options by the traders

at NatWest. A key parameter in setting the price of an interest rate option is the implied volatility of the underlying asset—that is, the interest rate on a currency. In contrast to other option parameters that affect the option prices, such as duration to maturity and exercise price, implied volatility is not directly observable and must be estimated. Many option pricing models imply that the implied volatility should be the same for all options on the same underlying, irrespective of their exercise price or maturity. In practice, however, implied volatility is often observed to have a curvilinear relationship with the option's moneyness (i.e., whether the option is out of the money, at the money, or in the money), a relationship sometimes called the *volatility smile.* Implied volatility tended to be higher for out-of-the-money options than for at-the-money options on the same underlying.

NWM prices on certain contracts tended to consistently undercut market prices, as if the out-of-the money options were being quoted at implied volatilities that were too low. When trading losses mounted in an interest rate option contract, a trader undertook a series of off-market-price transactions between the options portfolio and a swaptions portfolio to transfer the losses to a type of contract where losses were easier to conceal. A subsequent investigation revealed that the back office did not independently value the trading positions in question and that lapses in trade reconciliation had occurred.

What type or types of risk were inadequately managed in the above case?

4. Sue Ellicott supervises the trading function at an asset management firm. In conducting an in-house risk management training session for traders, Ellicott elicits the following statements from traders:

   - Trader 1. "Liquidity risk is not a major concern for buyers of a security as opposed to sellers."
   - Trader 2: "In general, derivatives can be used to substantially reduce the liquidity risk of a security."

   Ellicott and the traders then discuss two recent cases of a similar risk exposure in an identical situation that one trader (Trader A) hedged and another trader (Trader B) assumed as a speculation. A participant in the discussion makes the following statement concerning the contrasting treatment:

   - Trader 3: "Our traders have considerable experience and expertise in analyzing the risk, and this risk is related to our business. Trader B was justified in speculating on the risk within the limits of his risk allocation."

   State and justify whether each trader's statement is correct or incorrect.

5. A large trader on the government bond desk of a major bank loses €20 million in a year, in the process reducing the desk's overall profit to €10 million. Senior management, on looking into the problem, determines that the trader repeatedly violated his position limits during the year. They also determine that the bulk of the loss took place in the last two weeks of the year, when the trader increased his position dramatically and experienced 80 percent of his negative performance. The bank dismisses both the trader and his desk manager. The bank has an asymmetric incentive compensation contract arrangement with its traders.

   A. Discuss the performance netting risk implications of this scenario.
   B. Are there any reasons why the timing of the loss is particularly significant?
   C. What mistakes did senior management make? Explain how these errors can be corrected.

6. Ford Credit is the branch of Ford Motor Company that provides financing to Ford's customers. For this purpose, it obtains funding from various sources. As a result of its interest rate risk management process, including derivatives, Ford Credit's debt reprices faster than its assets. This situation means that when interest rates are rising, the interest rates paid on Ford Credit's debt will increase more rapidly than the interest rates earned on assets, thereby initially reducing Ford Credit's pretax net interest income. The reverse will be true when interest rates decline.

   Ford's annual report provides a quantitative measure of the sensitivity of Ford Credit's pretax net interest income to changes in interest rates. For this purpose, it uses interest rate scenarios that assume a hypothetical, instantaneous increase or decrease in interest rates of 1 percentage point across all maturities. These scenarios are compared with a base case that assumes that interest rates remain constant at existing levels. The differences between the scenarios and the base case over a 12-month period represent an estimate of the sensitivity of Ford Credit's pretax net interest income. This sensitivity as of year-end 2003 and 2002 is as follows:

	Pretax net interest income impact given a 1 percentage point instantaneous *increase* in interest rates (in millions)	Pretax net interest income impact given a 1 percentage point instantaneous *decrease* in interest rates (in millions)
December 31, 2003	($179)	$179
December 31, 2002	($153)	$156

Source: Annual Report of Ford Motor Company, 2003.

   Describe the strengths and weaknesses of the interest rate risk analysis presented in the foregoing table.

7. A. An organization's risk management function has computed that a portfolio held in one business unit has a 1 percent weekly VaR of £4.25 million. Describe what is meant in terms of a minimum loss.
   B. The portfolio of another business unit has a 99 percent weekly VaR of £4.25 million (stated using a confidence limit approach). Describe what is meant in terms of a maximum loss.

8. Each of the following statements about VaR is true *except:*

   A. VaR is the loss that would be exceeded with a given probability over a specific time period.
   B. Establishing a VaR involves several decisions, such as the probability and time period over which the VaR will be measured and the technique to be used.
   C. VaR will be larger when it is measured at 5 percent probability than when it is measured at 1 percent probability.
   D. VaR will be larger when it is measured over a month than when it is measured over a day.

9. Suppose you are given the following sample probability distribution of annual returns on a portfolio with a market value of $10 million.

Return on Portfolio	Probability
Less than −50%	0.005
−50% to −40%	0.005
−40% to −30%	0.010
−30% to −20%	0.015
−20% to −10%	0.015
−10% to −5%	0.165
−5% to 0%	0.250
0% to 5%	0.250
5% to 10%	0.145
10% to 20%	0.075
20% to 30%	0.025
30% to 40%	0.020
40% to 50%	0.015
Greater than 50%	0.005
	1.000

Based on this probability distribution, determine the following.

A. 1 percent yearly VaR
B. 5 percent yearly VaR

10. An analyst would like to know the VaR for a portfolio consisting of two asset classes: long-term government bonds issued in the United States and long-term government bonds issued in the United Kingdom. The expected monthly return on U.S. bonds is 0.85 percent, and the standard deviation is 3.20 percent. The expected monthly return on U.K. bonds, in U.S. dollars, is 0.95 percent, and the standard deviation is 5.26 percent. The correlation between the U.S. dollar returns of U.K. and U.S. bonds is 0.35. The portfolio market value is $100 million and is equally weighted between the two asset classes. Using the analytical or variance–covariance method, compute the following:

A. 5 percent monthly VaR.
B. 1 percent monthly VaR.
C. 5 percent weekly VaR.
D. 1 percent weekly VaR.

11. You invested $25,000 in the stock of Dell Computer Corporation in early 2002. You have compiled the monthly returns on Dell's stock during the 1997–2001 period, as given below.

1997	1998	1999	2000	2001
0.2447	0.1838	0.3664	−0.2463	0.4982
0.0756	0.4067	−0.1988	0.0618	−0.1627
−0.0492	−0.0313	0.0203	0.3216	0.1743
0.2375	0.1919	0.0077	−0.0707	0.0215
0.3443	0.0205	−0.1639	−0.1397	−0.0717
0.0439	0.1263	0.0744	0.1435	0.0735

(continued)

(continued)

1997	1998	1999	2000	2001
0.4561	0.1700	0.1047	−0.1090	0.0298
−0.0402	−0.0791	0.1942	−0.0071	−0.2061
0.1805	0.3150	−0.1434	−0.2937	−0.1333
−0.1729	−0.0038	−0.0404	−0.0426	0.2941
0.0507	−0.0716	0.0717	−0.3475	0.1647
−0.0022	0.2035	0.1861	−0.0942	−0.0269

Using the historical method, compute the following:

A. 5 percent monthly VaR.
B. 1 percent monthly VaR.

12. Consider a $10 million portfolio of stocks. You perform a Monte Carlo simulation to estimate the VaR for this portfolio. You choose to perform this simulation using a normal distribution of returns for the portfolio, with an expected annual return of 14.8 percent and a standard deviation of 20.5 percent. You generate 700 random outcomes of annual return for this portfolio, of which the worst 40 outcomes are given below.

−0.400	−0.320	−0.295	−0.247
−0.398	−0.316	−0.282	−0.233
−0.397	−0.314	−0.277	−0.229
−0.390	−0.310	−0.273	−0.226
−0.355	−0.303	−0.273	−0.223
−0.350	−0.301	−0.261	−0.222
−0.347	−0.301	−0.259	−0.218
−0.344	−0.300	−0.253	−0.216
−0.343	−0.298	−0.251	−0.215
−0.333	−0.296	−0.248	−0.211

Using the above information, compute the following:

A. 5 percent annual VaR.
B. 1 percent annual VaR.

13. A. A firm runs an investment portfolio consisting of stocks as well as options on stocks. Management would like to determine the VaR for this portfolio and is thinking about which technique to use. Discuss a problem with using the analytical or variance–covariance method for determining the VaR of this portfolio.
B. Describe a situation in which an organization might logically select each of the three VaR methodologies.

14. An organization's 5 percent daily VaR shows a number fairly consistently around €3 million. A backtest of the calculation reveals that, as expected under the calculation, daily portfolio losses in excess of €3 million tend to occur about once a month. When such losses do occur, however, they typically are more than double the VaR estimate. The portfolio contains a very large short options position.

A. Is the VaR calculation accurate?
B. How can the VaR figure best be interpreted?

C. What additional measures might the organization take to increase the accuracy of its overall exposure assessments?

15. Indicate which of the following statements about credit risk is (are) false, and explain why:

 A. Because credit losses occur often, it is easy to assess the probability of a credit loss.
 B. One element of credit risk is the possibility that the counterparty to a contract will default on an obligation to another (i.e., third) party.
 C. Like the buyer of a European-style option, the buyer of an American-style option faces no current credit risk until the expiration of the option.

16. Ricardo Colón, an analyst in the investment management division of a financial services firm, is developing an earnings forecast for a local oil services company. The company's income is closely linked to the price of oil. Furthermore, the company derives the majority of its income from sales to the United States. The economy of the company's home country depends significantly on export oil sales to the United States. As a result, movements in world oil prices in U.S. dollar terms and the U.S. dollar value of the home country's currency are strongly positively correlated. A decline in oil prices would reduce the company's sales in U.S. dollar terms, all else being equal. On the other hand, the appreciation of the home country's currency relative to the U.S. dollar would reduce the company's sales in terms of the home currency.

 According to Colón's research, Raúl Rodriguez, the company's chief risk officer, has made the following statement:

 "The company has rejected hedging the market risk of a decline in oil prices by selling oil futures and hedging the currency risk of a depreciation of the U.S. dollar relative to our home currency by buying home currency futures in U.S. markets. We have decided that a more effective risk management strategy for our company is to not hedge either market risk or currency risk."

 A. State whether the company's decision to not hedge market risk was correct. Justify your answer with one reason.
 B. State whether the company's decision to not hedge currency risk was correct. Justify your answer with one reason.
 C. Critique the risk management strategy adopted.

17. Tony Smith believes that the price of a particular underlying, currently selling at $96, will increase substantially in the next six months, so he purchases a European call option expiring in six months on this underlying. The call option has an exercise price of $101 and sells for $6.

 A. How much is the current credit risk, if any?
 B. How much is the current value of the potential credit risk, if any?
 C. Which party bears the credit risk(s), Tony Smith or the seller?

18. Following are four methods for calculating risk-adjusted performance: the Sharpe ratio, risk-adjusted return on capital (RAROC), return over maximum drawdown (RoMAD), and the Sortino ratio. Compare and contrast the measure of risk that each method uses.

CHAPTER 10

EXECUTION OF PORTFOLIO DECISIONS

Ananth Madhavan
Barclays Global Investors
San Francisco, California

Jack L. Treynor
Treynor Capital Management, Inc.
Palos Verdes Estates, California

Wayne H. Wagner
Plexus Group, Inc.
Los Angeles, California

LEARNING OUTCOMES

After completing this chapter, you will be able to do the following:

- Compare and contrast market and limit orders, including the degree of execution uncertainty and price uncertainty associated with each.
- Calculate and interpret the effective spread of a market order and contrast it to the quoted bid–ask spread in measuring the cost of trading.
- Compare, contrast, and state examples of the following market structures: quote-driven (dealer) markets, order-driven markets (including electronic crossing networks, batch auctions, and automated auctions), brokered markets, and hybrid markets.
- Compare and contrast the roles of brokers and dealers.
- Explain the criteria of market quality and evaluate the quality of a market given a description of its characteristics.
- Review the components of execution costs, including explicit and implicit costs, and evaluate trades in terms of those costs.
- Calculate, interpret, and explain the importance of implementation shortfall as a measure of transaction costs.

- Contrast volume-weighted average price (VWAP) and implementation shortfall as measures of transaction costs.
- Explain the use of econometric methods in pretrade analysis to estimate implicit transaction costs.
- Discuss the major types of traders based on the motivation to trade, their time versus price preferences, and their preferred order types.
- Evaluate the uses, strengths, and weaknesses of major trading tactics, and recommend a trading tactic given a description of the motivation to trade, the size of the trade, and market characteristics.
- Explain the motivation for algorithmic trading and the classification of algorithmic trading strategies, including the objectives of simple logical participation and shortfall implementation strategies.
- Discuss the choice of an algorithmic trading strategy given a description of the size of the order, the average daily volume of the security, the current bid–ask spread, and the urgency of the order.
- Explain the meaning of best execution.
- Evaluate a firm's investment and trading procedures, including processes, disclosures, and record keeping, with respect to best execution.
- Discuss the role of ethics in trading.

SUMMARY OVERVIEW

The portfolio decision is not complete until securities are bought or sold. How well that last step is accomplished is a key factor affecting investment results. This chapter has made the following points.

- Market microstructure refers to the particular trading protocols that govern how a trader's latent demands are translated into executed trades. Knowledge of market microstructure helps investors understand how their trades will be executed and how market frictions may give rise to discrepancies between price and full-information expectations of value.
- Order-driven markets are those in which prices are established by public limit orders and include auction markets and electronic crossing networks (where trading occurs at prespecified points in time), as well as automated auctions (where trading takes place continuously). Quote-driven markets rely on market makers or dealers to establish prices at which securities can be bought and sold. Brokered markets are markets in which transactions are largely effected by brokers through a search mechanism. Hybrid markets are those, such as the NYSE, that incorporate features of more than one type of market.
- Execution services secured through a broker include the following: representing the order, finding the buyer, market information for the investor, discretion and secrecy, escrow, and support of the market mechanism. A trader's broker stands in an agency relationship to the trader, in contrast to dealers. Dealers provide bridge liquidity to buyers and sellers in that they take the other side of the trade when no other liquidity is present.
- The effective spread is two times the deviation of the price received or paid from the midpoint of the market at the time an order is entered to the actual execution price. The bid–ask spread is the difference between the bid and the ask prices. The effective spread is a better representation of the true cost of trading than the bid–ask spread because it captures both price improvement and price impact.

- Market quality is judged by the following criteria, which are positives for a market's liquidity: many buyers and sellers; diversity of opinion, information, and investment needs; a readily accessible location; continuous operation during convenient market hours; a reasonable cost of transacting; market integrity, in effect the honesty of market participants; assurity of the contract's integrity.
- Transaction costs include explicit costs and implicit costs. Explicit costs are the direct costs of trading and include broker commission costs, taxes, stamp duties, and fees. Implicit costs include indirect costs such as the impact of the trade on the price received.
- Implementation shortfall is an estimate of transaction costs that amounts to subtracting the all-in transaction costs from the market price at the time the decision was made to buy or sell the security.
- Econometric models for costs are useful for obtaining pretrade estimates of the costs of a trade. These models may use variables such as stock liquidity, risk, trade size relative to available liquidity, momentum, and trading style.
- The major types of traders are information-motivated traders (who trade on information with limited time value), value-motivated traders (who trade on valuation judgments), liquidity-motivated traders (who trade based on liquidity needs), and passive traders (who trade for indexed portfolios). Information-motivated and liquidity-motivated traders have very short trading time horizons and are more sensitive to time than price in execution. By contrast, value-motivated and passive traders have longer trading time horizons and are more sensitive to price than time in execution.
- The two major order types are market orders (for prompt execution in public markets at the best price available) and limit orders (specifying a price at which the order becomes executable). Market orders are among the order types preferred by information-motivated and liquidity-motivated traders because of their time preference. Limit orders are among the order types preferred by value-motivated and passive traders because they are sensitive to price.
- Major focuses influencing the choice of trading strategy include the following: liquidity needed at any cost, need trustworthy agent for possibly hazardous trading situation, costs are not important, advertise to draw liquidity, and low cost whatever the liquidity.
- Algorithmic trading refers to automated electronic trading subject to quantitative rules and user-specified benchmarks and constraints. Three broad categories of algorithmic trading strategies are logical participation strategies (which involve protocols for breaking up an order for execution over time), opportunistic strategies (which involve passive trading combined with the opportunistic seizing of liquidity), and specialized strategies (which cover a range of strategies that serve special purposes).

PROBLEMS

1. An analyst is estimating various measures of spread for Airnet Systems, Inc. (NYSE: ANS). On page 98 is a sample of quotes in ANS on the New York Stock Exchange on March 10, 2004, between 10:49:00 and 10:57:00.

   A buyer-initiated trade in ANS was entered at 10:50:06 and was executed at 10:50:07 at a price of $4.74. For this trade, answer the following:

   A. What is the quoted spread?
   B. What is the effective spread?
   C. When would the effective and quoted spreads be equal?

Time	Bid Price ($)	Ask Price ($)
10:49:44	4.69	4.74
10:50:06	4.69	4.75
10:50:11	4.69	4.76
10:50:14	4.70	4.76
10:54:57	4.70	4.75
10:56:32	4.70	4.75

Source: Trade and Quote (TAQ) database, NYSE.

2. In a report dated December 15, 2004, the Office of Economic Analysis of the U.S. Securities and Exchange Commission (SEC) compared trade execution quality on the NYSE and NASDAQ using a matched sample of 113 pairs of firms. The comparison is based on six months of data from January to June 2004. The results regarding which market has the better execution quality (NYSE or NASDAQ) vary across order size, firm size, and order type. The results below are for small market orders (100–499 shares) in shares of large market capitalization firms.

Spread (cents)	NASDAQ	NYSE
Quoted spread	2.737	2.791
Effective spread	2.650	2.490

Source: Office of Economic Analysis, SEC, December 15, 2004.

On the basis of the above results, address the following:

A. Determine whether dealers in NASDAQ shares and dealers ("specialists") in NYSE shares in the particular market being discussed provided price improvements.
B. Contrast the relative performance of dealers in the two markets with regard to any price improvements.

3. E-Crossnet is an electronic crossing network that operates in Europe. It runs a total of 14 crosses every day at half-hour intervals. After a cross is run, there are some stocks for which there are unmatched buy quantities and some stocks with unmatched sell quantities. Discuss whether E-Crossnet should disclose these unmatched quantities after a cross is run.
4. For each of the following, discuss which of the two orders in shares of Sunny Corporation will have a greater market impact. Assume that all other factors are the same.

A. i. An order to buy 5,000 shares placed by a trader on the NYSE.
   ii. An order to buy 50,000 shares placed by the same trader on the NYSE.
B. i. An order to buy 25,000 shares placed by a trader on the NYSE.
   ii. An order to buy 25,000 shares placed on the NYSE by another trader who is believed to represent informed investors in the stock.
C. i. An order to sell 20,000 shares placed by a trader on the NYSE.
   ii. An order to sell 20,000 shares placed by the same trader on POSIT, an electronic crossing network.

5. An investment manager placed a limit order to buy 500,000 shares of Alpha Corporation at $21.35 limit at the opening of trading on February 8. The closing market price of Alpha Corporation on February 7 was also $21.35. The limit order filled 40,000 shares, and the remaining 460,000 shares were never filled. Some good news came out about Alpha Corporation on February 8, and its price increased to $23.60 by the end of that day. However, by the close of trading on February 14, the price had declined to $21.74. The investment manager is analyzing the missed trade opportunity cost using the closing price on February 8 as the benchmark price.

   A. What is the estimate of the missed trade opportunity cost if it is measured at a one-day interval after the decision to trade?
   B. What is the estimate of the missed trade opportunity cost if it is measured at a one-week interval after the decision to trade?
   C. What are some of the problems in estimating the missed trade opportunity cost?

6. A portfolio manager would like to buy 5,000 shares of a very recent initial public offering (IPO) stock. However, he was not able to get any shares at the IPO price of £30. The portfolio manager would still like to have 5,000 shares, but not at a price above £45 per share. Should he place a market order or a limit order? What would be the advantage and disadvantage of each type of order, given his purposes?
7. An asset management firm wants to purchase 500,000 shares of a company. It decides to shop the order to various broker/dealer firms to see which firm can offer the best service and lowest cost. Discuss the potential negatives of shopping the order.
8. Able Energy, Inc., is a company listed on NASDAQ (symbol: ABLE). A trader sold 100 shares of this company on May 10, 2004 at 15:52:59 at a price of $2.66 per share. All the trades that occurred in Able Energy on that day are listed below.

Time	Trade Price ($)	Shares Traded
10:00:39	2.71	200
10:00:39	2.72	200
10:00:43	2.76	100
13:09:07	2.77	100
14:13:11	2.70	1100
15:52:59	2.66	100
15:53:01	2.65	100

Source: Trade and Quote (TAQ) database, NYSE.

The trader is analyzing the implicit costs of the trade, focusing on the bid–ask spread and market impact using specified price benchmarks.

   A. What would be the estimated implicit transaction costs using each of the following as the price benchmark?

      i. Opening price.
      ii. Closing price.
      iii. Volume-weighted average price (VWAP).

   B. Evaluate the effect on estimated implicit transaction costs of the choice of benchmark price.

9. A client of a broker evaluates the broker's performance by measuring transaction costs with a specified price benchmark. The broker has discretion over the timing of his trades for the client. Discuss what the broker could do to make his performance look good to the client (even though the broker's execution decisions may not be in the best interests of the client) if the price benchmark used by the client for evaluation is the:

   A. Opening price.
   B. Closing price.
   C. Volume-weighted average price (VWAP).

10. A trader decided to sell 30,000 shares of a company. At the time of this decision, the quoted price was €53.20 to €53.30. Because of the large size of the order, the trader decided to execute the sale in three equal orders of 10,000 shares spread over the course of the day. When she placed the first order, the quoted price was €53.20 to €53.30, and she sold the shares at €53.22. The trade had a market impact, and the quoted price had fallen to €53.05 to €53.15 when she placed the next order. Those shares were sold at €53.06. The quoted price had fallen to €52.87 to €52.98 when she placed the last order. Those shares were sold at €52.87. Suppose this was the market closing price of the shares that day. Answer the following questions, ignoring commissions.

    A. Estimate the total transaction cost of the sale of 30,000 shares if the closing price is used as the price benchmark.
    B. What is the implementation shortfall estimate of the total cost of executing the sale?
    C. Discuss and compare the answers to A and B above. Which of the two approaches is appropriate for the situation in this problem?

11. Suppose 1,000 shares of Acme Co. stock are ordered to be bought on Monday with a benchmark price of $10.00. On Monday, 600 shares are purchased at $10.02 per share. Commissions and fees are $20. On Tuesday, the benchmark price has fallen to $9.99 per share. On Tuesday, 100 more shares are purchased at $10.08 per share. Commissions and fees are $12. Shares for Acme close on Tuesday at $10.01 per share. The remaining shares are not purchased, and the order is canceled on Wednesday just as the market closes at $10.05 per share.

    A. Calculate the implementation shortfall for this trade.
    B. Calculate the components of the implementation shortfall for this trade.

12. Jane Smith manages an equity fund. She has decided to undertake a major portfolio restructuring by increasing the exposure of the fund to the telecommunications sector. The implementation of her decision would involve investing more than $2 million in the stocks of about 20 telecommunications companies. Contrast the use of a portfolio trade to the use of purchase orders for these stocks placed individually (stock by stock) in terms of the probable market impact of the two approaches.
13. Famed Investments has a C$25 million portfolio. It follows an active approach to investment management and, on average, turns the portfolio over twice a year. That is, it expects to trade 200 percent of the value of the portfolio over the next year. Every time Famed Investments buys or sells securities, it incurs execution costs of 75 basis points, on average. It expects an annual return before execution costs of 8 percent. What is the expected return net of execution costs?
14. Several British stocks trade on both the London Stock Exchange and the New York Stock Exchange. Due to the time difference between London and New York, these stocks trade

for six hours every day in London only, followed by the opening of the NYSE and a two-hour period when both markets are open before London closes. Werner and Kleidon (1996) found that the volatility of prices in London is much higher during the two-hour period when both markets are open than during the preceding six-hour period when only London is open. What could be an information-motivated reason for this finding? Assume that U.S. traders do not trade in London.

15. An employee retirement fund manager believes he has special information about a particular company. Based on this information, he believes the company is currently undervalued and decides to purchase 50,000 shares of the company. The manager decides that he will not place a large single order for 50,000 shares but will instead place several medium-sized orders of 2,500 to 5,000 shares spread over a period of time. Why do you think the manager chooses to follow this strategy?
16. Consider some stocks that trade in two markets, with a trader being able to trade in these stocks in either market. Suppose that the two markets are identical in all respects except that bid–ask spreads are lower and depths (the number of shares being offered at the bid and ask prices) are greater in one of the two markets. State in which market liquidity-motivated and information-motivated traders would prefer to transact. Justify your answer.
17. A trader has been given two trades to execute with the following characteristics. What tactics do you recommend?

Trade	Size (shares)	Average Daily Volume (ADV)	Price	Spread (%)	Urgency
A	200,000	6,000,000	10.00	0.03	High
B	150,000	200,000	10.00	0.60	High

18. A trader must rebalance a pension plan's actively managed $500 million U.S. small-cap equity portfolio to an S&P 500 indexed portfolio in order to effect a change in the plan's strategic asset allocation. He is told that his primary goal is to minimize explicit costs in this rebalance. What should his trading strategy be?

CHAPTER 11

MONITORING AND REBALANCING

Robert D. Arnott

First Quadrant, LP
Research Affiliates, LLC
Pasadena, California

Terence E. Burns, CFA

Campion Wealth Management LLC
Vienna, Virginia

Lisa Plaxco, CFA

First Quadrant, LP
Pasadena, California

Philip Moore

Pacific Investment Consultants, LLC
Stevenson Ranch, California

LEARNING OUTCOMES

After completing this chapter, you will be able to do the following:

- Explain and justify fiduciaries' responsibilities in monitoring.
- Contrast the monitoring of investor circumstances, market/economic conditions, and the portfolio, and interpret the effects on a client's portfolio of changes in each of those areas.
- Evaluate the need to revise an investor's investment policy statement and strategic asset allocation given altered investor circumstances (i.e., changes in wealth, time horizon,

liquidity requirements, tax concerns, and legal and regulatory factors) and recommend appropriate revisions.
- Discuss the benefits and costs of rebalancing a portfolio to the investor's strategic asset allocation.
- Contrast calendar rebalancing to percentage-of-portfolio rebalancing.
- Compare and contrast rebalancing an asset class to within the allowed range with rebalancing the asset class to its target portfolio weight.
- Evaluate the effects of the following factors on an asset class's optimal corridor width, assuming a percentage-of-portfolio rebalancing approach: transaction costs, risk tolerance, correlation, the asset class's volatility, and the volatility of the remainder of the portfolio.
- Distinguish among the payoffs in up, down, and nontrending markets of (1) rebalancing to a constant mix of equities and bills, (2) buying and holding equities, and (3) constant-proportion portfolio insurance (CPPI).
- Distinguish between linear, concave, and convex rebalancing strategies.
- Judge the appropriateness of constant mix, buy-and-hold, and CPPI rebalancing strategies given various investor risk tolerances and asset return expectations.

SUMMARY OVERVIEW

Even the most carefully constructed portfolios do not manage themselves. In this chapter we have discussed two ingredients to ensuring an investment program's continuing relevancy: monitoring and rebalancing.

- Portfolio managers need to monitor everything that is relevant to positioning a portfolio to satisfy the client's objectives and constraints. Three areas that the portfolio manager must monitor are changes in investor circumstances and wealth, market and economic changes, and the portfolio itself.
- Fiduciaries have an ethical and legal responsibility for adequate monitoring. Only by systematic monitoring can the fiduciary secure an informed view of the appropriateness and suitability of a portfolio for a particular client.
- Rebalancing to an investor's strategic asset allocation has benefits and costs. If the target asset class proportions of an investor's strategic asset allocation represent his optimum, any divergence from the target proportions represents an expected utility loss to the investor. The benefit in rebalancing equals the reduction in the present value of expected utility losses from not tracking the optimum. Rebalancing is a risk-control discipline that helps ensure an appropriate level of portfolio risk.
- The costs of rebalancing include transaction costs and, for taxable investors, tax costs (tax liabilities that are triggered by rebalancing trades).
- Calendar rebalancing involves rebalancing the portfolio to target weights on a periodic basis such as monthly, quarterly, semiannually, or annually. Calendar rebalancing is the simplest rebalancing discipline; it has the drawback of being unrelated to market performance. Yet it can suffice in ensuring that the actual portfolio does not drift far away from target for long periods of time if the rebalancing frequency is adequate given the portfolio's volatility.
- Percentage-of-portfolio rebalancing involves setting rebalancing thresholds (trigger points) that define a corridor or tolerance band for the value of that asset class such as 50% ± 5%. Compared with calendar rebalancing (particularly at lower frequencies such as

semiannually or annually), percentage-of-portfolio rebalancing can exercise tighter control on divergences from target proportions because it is directly related to market performance.
- In rebalancing, two disciplines are rebalancing to target weights and rebalancing to the allowed range. The former exercises tighter discipline on risk exposures, the latter allows for more control of costs and for tactical adjustment.
- Factors positively related to optimal corridor width for an asset class include transaction costs, risk tolerance, and correlation with the rest of the portfolio. The greater these factors, the wider the optimal corridor, in general.
- Factors negatively related to optimal corridor width for an asset class include the asset class's volatility and the volatility of the rest of the portfolio. The greater these factors, the narrower the optimal corridor, in general.
- Three contrasting strategies are buy and hold, constant mix (rebalancing to the strategic asset allocation), and constant proportion (which includes constant-proportion portfolio insurance).
- A buy-and-hold strategy is a passive strategy of buying an initial asset mix (e.g., 60/40 stocks/bills) and doing absolutely nothing subsequently. It is synonymous with a drifting asset mix. A constant-mix strategy involves rebalancing so that the investment in stocks is a constant fraction of portfolio value. A constant-proportion portfolio insurance strategy involves making trades so the investment in stocks represents a constant multiple of the cushion of portfolio value above a floor value.
- In strong bull markets, CPPI outperforms a buy-and-and hold strategy, while a buy-and-hold strategy outperforms a constant-mix strategy, in general. In strong bear markets, the same priority of performance holds. In a market characterized more by reversals than by trends, a constant-mix strategy tends to do best, followed by buy-and-hold and then CPPI strategies.

PROBLEMS

1. Evaluate the most likely effects of the following events on the investor's investment objectives, constraints, and financial plan.

   A. A childless working married couple in their late 20s adopts an infant for whom they hope to provide a college education.
   B. An individual decides to buy a house in one year. He estimates that he will need $102,000 at that time for the down payment and closing costs on the house. The portfolio from which those costs will be paid has a current value of $100,000 and no additions to it are anticipated.
   C. A foundation with a €150,000,000 portfolio invested 60 percent in equities, 25 percent in long-term bonds, and 15 percent in absolute return strategies has approved a grant totaling €15,000,000 for the construction of a radio telescope observatory. The foundation anticipates a new contribution from a director in the amount of €1,000,000 toward the funding of the grant.

2. (Adapted from the 2001 Level III examination)

   Duane Rogers, as chief investment officer (CIO) for the Summit PLC defined-benefit pension scheme, has developed an economic forecast for presentation to the plan's board of trustees. Rogers projects that U.K. inflation will be substantially higher over the next three years than the board's current forecast.

Rogers recommends that the board immediately take the following actions based on his forecast:

A. Revise the pension scheme's investment policy statement to account for a change in the U.K. inflation forecast.
B. Reallocate pension assets from domestic (U.K.) to international equities because he also expects inflation in the U.K. to be higher than in other countries.
C. Initiate a program to protect the pension scheme's financial strength from the effects of U.K. inflation by indexing benefits paid by the scheme.

State whether *each* recommended action is correct or incorrect. Justify *each* of your responses with *one* reason.

The following two interpretative monitoring problems are presented as two-part narratives: initial client circumstances, which comprise the gist of a client's investment policy statement (IPS) and the detailed information going into its formulation, followed by the changed client circumstances.

3. (Adapted from the 2002 CFA Level III examination)

Initial Client Circumstances

Claire Wisman, a vice president for Spencer Design, is a 42-year-old widow who lives in the United States. She has two children: a daughter, age 21, and a son, age 7. She has a $2.2 million portfolio; half of the portfolio is invested in Spencer Design, a publicly traded common stock, which has a cost basis of $350,000. Despite a substantial drop in the value of her portfolio over the last two years, her long-term annual total returns have averaged 7 percent before tax. The recent drop in value has caused her great anxiety, and she believes that she can no longer tolerate an annual decline greater than 10 percent.

Wisman intends to retire in 20 years, and her goals for the next 20 years, in order of priority, are as follows. The present values given are gross of taxes.

- Funding the cost of her daughter's upcoming final year of college, which has a present value of $26,000, and her son's future college costs, which have a present value of $130,000.
- Increasing the portfolio to a level that will fund her retirement living expenses, which she estimates to be $257,000 for the first year of her retirement.
- Building her "dream house" in five years, the cost of which (including land) has a present value of $535,000.
- Giving, if possible, each of her children $1 million when they reach age 40.

After subtracting the present value (before tax) of her children's education costs and her homebuilding costs, the present value of her portfolio is $1,509,000. With returns from income and gains taxable at 30 percent and with continued annual growth of 7 percent before tax (7% × (1 − 0.30) = 4.9% after taxes), the portfolio's value will be approximately $3,928,000 net of taxes at the end of 20 years.

Wisman's annual salary is $145,000, her annual living expenses are currently $100,000, and both are expected to increase at an inflation rate of 3 percent annually. Taxes on income and short-term capital gains (holding period one year or less) are substantially higher than taxes on long-term capital gains (holding period greater than one year). For planning purposes, however, Wisman wants to assume that her average tax rate on all income and gains is 30 percent. The inflation and tax rates are expected to remain constant. Currently,

Wisman rents a townhouse, has no debt, and adamantly intends to remain debt free. Spencer Design has no pension plan but provides company-paid medical insurance for executives for life and for their children to age 25. After taxes, Wisman's salary just covers her living expenses and thus does not allow her to make further meaningful capital contributions to her portfolio.

Wisman's current investment policy statement has the following elements:

Return requirement. A total return objective of 7 percent before tax is sufficient to meet Claire Wisman's educational, housing, and retirement goals. If the portfolio earns a total return of 7 percent annually, the value at retirement ($3.93 million) should be adequate to meet ongoing spending needs then ($\$257{,}000/\$\,3,928,000 = 6.5\%$ spending rate) and fund all Wisman's extraordinary needs (college and homebuilding costs) in the meantime. The million-dollar gifts to her children are unrealistic goals that she should be encouraged to modify or drop.

Risk tolerance. Wisman has explicitly stated her limited (below average) willingness to take risk. Wisman appears to have an average ability to take risk. Her portfolio has some flexibility, because her expected return objective of 7 percent will meet her goals of funding her children's education, building her "dream house," and funding her retirement. Overall, her risk tolerance is below average.

Time horizon. Her time horizon is multistage. The time horizon could be described as three-stage (the next 5 preretirement years defined by work/housing costs; the subsequent 15 preretirement years defined by work/college costs; and beyond 20 years postretirement).

Liquidity. Wisman has only a minor liquidity need ($26,000 in present value terms) to cover education expenses for her daughter next year. After that, she has no liquidity need for the next five years. Only then ($535,000 in present value terms, for home construction) and in Years 11 through 14 ($130,000 in present value terms, for her son's education) will significant liquidity concerns exist.

Taxes. Taxes are a critical concern because Wisman needs to fund outlays with after-tax dollars.

Unique circumstances. A significant unique circumstance is the large concentration (50 percent of her assets) in Spencer Design stock. Another factor is her desire to build a new home in five years yet incur no debt. Also, she would "like" to give each child $1 million, but this goal is unrealistic and should not drive portfolio decisions.

Wisman indicates that Spencer Design has a leading and growing market share. The company has shown steady fundamental growth trends, and Wisman intends to hold her Spencer Design stock, which is expected to return at least 9 percent annually before tax with a standard deviation of returns of 20 percent.

Changed Client Circumstances

Claire Wisman, now 47 years old, has recently married a coworker at Spencer Design. Wisman and her husband are buying their dream house at a total cost of $700,000, and they have decided to make an immediate down payment of $430,000 and finance the remainder over 15 years. Wisman also indicates that her son has contracted a rare disease, requiring major surgery; the disease will prevent him from attending college. Although Wisman and her husband have medical insurance that will pay her son's ongoing medical expenses, her son's surgery will cost an additional $214,000 immediately. The cost of medical expenditures is expected to grow at a rate exceeding the general inflation rate for the foreseeable future. Wisman has decided to quit work to care for her son, whose remaining life expectancy is 40 years. She also insists on the need to provide care for her son when she and her husband are no longer capable of doing so. Wisman's parents died one year ago, and her daughter is now financially independent. Wisman's husband intends to retire in 25 years.

Given these circumstances, the investment portfolio held by Wisman and her husband will need to provide an amount equal to $1,713,000 (present value) to meet their living expenses until his retirement. They also want their portfolio to grow enough to cover their living expenses at retirement, which they estimate to be $400,000 annually. They believe they will need a before-tax portfolio growth rate of approximately 8 to 10 percent annually to achieve this goal. Based on a retirement spending goal of $400,000, their corresponding effective postretirement spending rate will be approximately 6 to 7 percent annually before tax.

Wisman summarizes her new financial information in Exhibit 11-1. She indicates that her portfolio and her husband's portfolio should be considered as one. She further states that her husband has taken well above-average risk in the past, but he is now willing to leave the investment management decisions to her.

A. Indicate how *each* component of Wisman's investment policy statement should change as a result of Wisman's new circumstances. Justify *each* of your responses with *two* reasons based on Wisman's new circumstances.
B. Recommend whether the current allocation percentage (given in Exhibit 11-1) for *each* of the following assets should be decreased or increased as a result of Wisman's new circumstances. Justify *each* of your responses with *one* reason based on Wisman's new circumstances.

    i. Spencer Design common stock
    ii. Money market
    iii. Diversified bond fund

EXHIBIT 11-1 New Financial Information

	Claire Wisman	Husband	Combined	Current Allocation Percentage of Combined Portfolio
Salary	$ 0	$150,000	$ 150,000	–
Assets				
Money market	61,000	27,000	88,000	2.4%
Diversified bond fund	1,129,000	0	1,129,000	30.5%
Equities				
Large-capitalization equities	385,000	0	385,000	10.4%
Emerging market equities	0	407,000	407,000	11.0%
Spencer Design common stock	1,325,000	122,000	1,447,000	39.1%
Undeveloped commercial land	0	244,000	244,000	6.6%
Total portfolio	**$2,900,000**	**$800,000**	**$3,700,000**	**100.0%**

iv. Large-capitalization equities
v. Emerging market equities
vi. Undeveloped commercial land

4. (Adapted from the 2003 CFA Level III examination)

Initial Circumstances

Both parents of 12-year-old Andrew Campbell recently died in an accident. The parents had been supporting Andrew and his grandmother, Lisa Javier, age 77. The parents' accumulated assets prior to their death were $640,000 in a diversified common stock (both domestic and international) portfolio and $360,000 in the common stock of Newman Enterprises, a publicly traded company founded by Javier's husband. The parents' assets will now be held in a single U.S.-based trust—the Javier–Campbell Trust (the Trust)—to benefit both Javier and Campbell. In addition to these assets, the Trust received life insurance proceeds of $2 million.

Newman Enterprises will continue to provide medical coverage for Javier until her death. Campbell has government-provided health care until he reaches age 22. Campbell will attend college for four years beginning at age 18. In addition to normal living expenses, initial annual university costs are projected to be $38,000, rising 8 percent annually.

According to the provisions of the Trust document:

- The Trust should provide for Javier's and Campbell's annual living expenses, currently estimated to total $78,000 per year (after tax). The Trust portfolio should earn a return sufficient to cover the living expenses of Javier and Campbell, taking taxes into consideration and allowing for inflation (expected to be 2 percent annually). Income and capital gains are taxed at 30 percent, and this tax treatment is not expected to change.
- The Trust should limit shortfall risk (defined as expected total return minus two standard deviations) to no lower than a −10 percent return in any one year.
- Campbell is entitled to receive distributions from the Trust until he reaches age 32. At that point, the Trust will continue making distributions for Javier's living expenses.
- Upon Javier's death, the Trust's assets will go to Campbell, provided he is at least 32 years old. If Campbell is not yet aged 32 when Javier dies, the Trust will then distribute income and principal to Campbell until he reaches age 32, at which point the Trust will terminate and the assets will be distributed to Campbell.
- The Newman Enterprises common stock cannot be sold without Javier's approval for as long as she is alive. Javier has stated her strong desire to retain the Newman stock indefinitely, to fulfill a promise she made to her husband.
- The Trust must hold in cash equivalents an amount equal to nine months of living expenses (on a pretax basis) for Javier and Campbell.
- In the unlikely event that Campbell dies before Javier, distributions will continue for Javier's benefit until she dies, at which point any remaining Trust assets will be distributed to several charities.

As a result of poor financial advice, Javier lost all of her inheritance from her husband's estate. Because her assets are nearly depleted, she wants to minimize any future losses in the Trust portfolio; in fact, she has expressed serious concerns about the Trust's ability to meet Campbell's and her needs during her lifetime.

The risk tolerance and return requirement elements of the Javier–Campbell Trust's IPS are as follows:

Risk Tolerance

Ability. The Trust has average ability to assume risk, largely because of its substantial asset base in relation to its spending needs. Because the portfolio is Javier's only source of support, the Trust's ability to assume risk is lower than it might otherwise be.

Willingness. The Trust has below-average willingness to assume risk. The Trust document requires that the account be invested so that shortfall risk (defined as expected total return minus two standard deviations) is limited to a −10 percent return in any one year. This limitation implies that the Trust will be unwilling to tolerate any substantial volatility in portfolio returns.

Overall risk tolerance. The Trust has below-average risk tolerance and will continue to have it for many years, especially while Javier is alive.

Return Requirement

The return requirement reflects two major factors: the need to cover living expenses and the need to protect the portfolio from the adverse effects of inflation. Specifically, the Trust must generate a total before-tax return of at least 6.57 percent on an annual basis to meet these return requirements.

The living expenses, estimated at $78,000 per year, represent a $78,000/$3,000,000 = 2.6% spending rate in real, after-tax terms. However, because the Trust is taxed at 30 percent, it will need to earn a pretax return of (2.6% + 2%)/(1 − 0.30) = 6.57% to meet Javier and Campbell's living expenses.

Changed Client Circumstances

Ten years have now passed, and the Javier–Campbell Trust portfolio returns over the previous 10 years have failed to meet expectations. Lower returns, coupled with Lisa Javier's and Andrew Campbell's living expenses and Campbell's college costs, have combined to reduce the value of the Trust portfolio to $2 million.

Javier, now 87, recently moved to an assisted-living care facility. With her health failing, doctors have determined she will live no longer than three years and will require full-time care for the remaining time until her death. Javier's medical expenses are covered by insurance, but her care and living expenses now require $84,000 per year (after tax and adjusted for inflation) from the Trust. Inflation is expected to be 3 percent annually over the next several years. Javier has no other support and depends on the Trust to meet her financial needs. She has continued to express her concern that the Trust will not provide enough distributions to cover her expenses during her remaining lifetime. She still wishes to retain the Newman Enterprises common stock, which now constitutes 15 percent of the Trust portfolio and has an expected annual yield of 2 percent over the next several years. Legal constraints have not changed, and the Trust still requires nine months of living expenses (on a pretax basis) to be held in reserve.

Campbell, now 22, is a recent college graduate and has accepted a job with Elkhorn Consulting Partners. In the job offer, Elkhorn agreed to pay the cost of Campbell's MBA degree. Campbell also has the opportunity to buy a partnership stake in the company by making equal annual payments of $600,000 per year for five years. He will begin making those payments in 10 years. Campbell's starting salary is sufficient to cover his living expenses.

Although Campbell is concerned about providing for Javier, he believes that with the appropriate asset allocation, the Trust assets should be sufficient to take care of her expenditures until she dies and to provide the growth he needs to meet his partnership obligations. Campbell views growth from the Trust to be essential in meeting his long-term goals. Assuming that Campbell lives longer than Javier, the individual assets in the Trust will be distributed to Campbell upon termination of the Trust; the Trust portfolio will become Campbell's portfolio.

The trustee believes that circumstances have changed enough to warrant revising certain components of the investment policy statements for Campbell and the Trust.

Formulate revised statements about the Javier–Campbell Trust's willingness to take risk that reflect the changed circumstances of both Javier and Campbell. Your response should include appropriate supporting justification.

5. A foundation holds an equally weighted portfolio of domestic equities, international equities, private equity, and inflation-protected bonds.

   A. Critique a percentage-of-portfolio discipline that involves establishing a corridor of target percentage allocation $\pm$ 5 percent for each asset class in the foundation's portfolio.
   B. Evaluate the implications of the following sets of facts on the stated corridor, given an all-else-equal assumption in each case:

      i. The Foundation's risk tolerance has decreased. *Corridor for international equities.*
      ii. Transaction costs in international equities are one-half those for private equity. *Corridor for inflation-protected bonds.*
      iii. The correlation of private equity with the rest of the portfolio is lower than the correlation of domestic equities with the rest of the portfolio. *Corridor for private equity.*
      iv. The volatility of domestic equities is higher than that of inflation-protected bonds. *Corridor for domestic equities.*

6. A. Recommend an appropriate rebalancing discipline for an investor who cannot monitor portfolio values on a daily basis yet holds an above-average risk portfolio and low risk tolerance.
   B. How would the investment results of the recommended rebalancing discipline be affected if markets were nontrending?
7. (Adapted from the 2002 CFA Level III examination)

   Marvis University (MU) is a private, multiprogram U.S. university with a $2 billion endowment fund as of fiscal year-end May 31, 2002. With little government support, MU is heavily dependent on its endowment fund to support ongoing expenditures, especially because the university's enrollment growth and tuition revenue have not met expectations in recent years. The endowment fund must make a $126 million annual contribution, which is indexed to inflation, to MU's general operating budget. The U.S. Consumer Price Index is expected to rise 2.5 percent annually, and the U.S. higher education cost index is anticipated to rise 3 percent annually. The endowment has also budgeted $200 million due on January 31, 2003, representing the final payment for construction of a new main library.

   In a recent capital campaign, MU met its fundraising goal only with the help of one very successful alumna, Valerie Bremner, who donated $400 million of Bertocchi Oil and Gas common stock at fiscal year-end May 31, 2002. Bertocchi Oil and Gas is a large-capitalization, publicly traded U.S. company. Bremner donated the stock on the condition that no more than 25 percent of the initial number of shares may be sold in any fiscal year. No substantial additional donations are expected in the future.

Given the large contribution to and distributions from the endowment fund, the fund's investment committee has decided to revise its investment policy statement.

In the revised IPS, the endowment portfolio manager established that MU's return requirement is 10 percent. MU's average ability to take risk restrains its risk tolerance.

Five years have passed, and the Marvis University endowment fund's willingness and ability to assume risk have increased. The endowment fund's investment committee asks its consultant, James Chan, to discuss and recommend a rebalancing strategy to incorporate the new risk tolerance. Chan anticipates a bull market in growth assets over the next three to five years. He also believes that volatility will be below historical averages during that same time period. The investment committee directs Chan to incorporate his views into his recommendation. The committee also does not want the market value of the portfolio to decline more than 15 percent below its current market value.

A. Describe the following *three* primary rebalancing strategies:

  i. Buy and hold
  ii. Constant mix
  iii. Constant-proportion portfolio insurance

B. Determine which *one* of the three rebalancing strategies in Part A Chan should recommend for the Marvis University endowment fund. Justify your response with two reasons based on the circumstances described above.

CHAPTER 12

EVALUATING PORTFOLIO PERFORMANCE

Jeffery V. Bailey, CFA

Target Corporation
Minneapolis, Minnesota

Thomas M. Richards, CFA

Richards & Tierney, Inc.
Chicago, Illinois

David E. Tierney

Richards & Tierney, Inc.
Chicago, Illinois

LEARNING OUTCOMES

After completing this chapter, you will be able to do the following:

- Justify the importance of performance evaluation.
- Characterize and distinguish among the components of portfolio evaluation: performance measurement, performance attribution, and performance appraisal.
- Explain the calculation of return when an account receives an external cash flow (1) at the beginning of an evaluation period or (2) at the end of an evaluation period.
- Compute, compare, and contrast time-weighted and money-weighted rates of return.
- Evaluate the effect of external contributions and withdrawals in the calculation of time-weighted and money-weighted rates of return.
- Evaluate potential data quality issues as they relate to calculating rates of return.
- Demonstrate the analysis of portfolio returns into components due to the market, to style, and to active management.

- Identify and discuss the properties of a valid benchmark.
- Discuss the types of benchmarks and each type's advantages and disadvantages, and critique the appropriateness of each benchmark type for performance evaluation.
- Summarize the steps in constructing a custom security-based benchmark.
- Judge the validity of using manager universes as benchmarks.
- Evaluate benchmarks by applying tests of quality.
- Review hedge fund benchmarks and evaluate the effects of short positions on hedge fund performance measurement.
- Distinguish between macro and micro performance attribution.
- List and discuss the inputs that are necessary for a macro performance attribution.
- Demonstrate the incremental-return and incremental-value contributions to the ending value of the fund at the following attribution levels: net contributions, risk-free asset, asset category, benchmarks, investment managers, and allocation tactics.
- Demonstrate a performance attribution analysis, given data on the portfolio's and benchmark's sector weights and returns, and evaluate the impacts from pure sector allocation, within-sector selection, and allocation/selection interaction.
- Discuss fundamental factor model micro attribution.
- Compare and contrast the strengths and limitations of allocation/selection attribution and fundamental factor model attribution.
- Distinguish between the effect of the interest rate environment and the effect of active management on fixed-income portfolio returns.
- Explain the management factors contributing to a fixed-income portfolio's total return, and interpret the results of a fixed-income performance attribution analysis.
- Compute, compare, and contrast the following risk-adjusted performance appraisal measures in their ex post forms: ex post alpha, Treynor measure, Sharpe ratio, and M^2.
- Distinguish between the information ratio and the Sharpe ratio.
- Evaluate the risk-adjusted performance of one or more portfolios.
- Demonstrate the use of performance quality control charts in performance appraisal.
- Discuss the issues involved in manager continuation policy decisions, including the costs of hiring and firing investment managers.
- Contrast Type I and Type II errors in manager continuation decisions.

SUMMARY OVERVIEW

Performance evaluation is as important as it is challenging. Decisions reached concerning manager skill can affect the attainment of investment objectives. It therefore benefits investors and their advisers to be up to date in their knowledge of this field.

- From the fund sponsor's perspective, performance evaluation serves as a feedback mechanism to a fund's investment policy. It identifies strengths and weaknesses, attributes results to key decisions, and focuses attention on poor performance. It provides evidence to fund trustees on whether the investment program is being conducted effectively. From the investment manager's perspective, performance evaluation permits an investigation of the effectiveness of various elements of the investment process and the contributions of those elements to investment results.
- Performance evaluation is composed of three parts: (1) performance measurement, (2) performance attribution, and (3) performance appraisal.

- The rate of return on an asset is typically defined as the investment-related growth in the asset's value over the evaluation period. When there are intraperiod cash flows, the rate of return can be measured as the growth rate applied to a single dollar invested at the start of the period (time-weighted rate of return, or TWR) or to an "average" amount of dollars invested over the evaluation period (money-weighted rate of return, or MWR). The MWR is sensitive to the size and timing of cash flows, but the TWR is not. Because investment managers rarely have control over the size or timing of cash flows, the TWR is the most commonly used performance measure.
- When the investment manager has control over the size and timing of cash flows into an account, the MWR may be an appropriate performance measure.
- When the MWR is calculated over reasonably frequent time periods and those returns are chain-linked over the entire evaluation period, which could be of any length, an approximation of the TWR for the period, called the linked internal rate of return (LIRR), is obtained.
- If external funds are added to an account prior to a period of strong performance, the MWR will give a higher rate of return than the TWR. If a large amount is withdrawn prior to a period of strong performance, the MWR will yield a lower rate of return than the TWR. The opposite effect is experienced during periods of weak performance.
- Data quality is important in determining the accuracy of rates of return. Rates of return for large-capitalization securities are likely to be more accurate than those for illiquid and infrequently priced assets.
- A valid benchmark should meet the following criteria: It should be unambiguous, investable, measurable, and appropriate for the manager's style and area of expertise; reflect current investment opinions; be specified in advance; and exhibit ownership by the investment manager.
- The types of benchmarks in common use are: absolute return, manager universes, broad market indexes, style indexes, factor model–based, returns-based, and custom security-based. A custom security–based benchmark meets all fundamental and quality-based benchmark criteria, making it the most appropriate benchmark to use.
- The median manager or median fund, though intuitively appealing, lacks the following desirable benchmark properties: It is not specified in advance, it is not investable, and it cannot serve as a passive investment.
- Steps in creating a custom security-based benchmark are: Identify prominent aspects of the manager's investment process; select securities consistent with that investment process; devise a weighting scheme for the benchmark securities, including a cash position; review the preliminary benchmark and make modifications; and rebalance the benchmark portfolio on a predetermined schedule.
- Good benchmarks should generally display the following characteristics: minimal systematic bias between the account and the benchmark, less tracking error of the account relative to the benchmark when compared to alternative benchmarks, strong correspondence between the manager's universe of potential securities and the benchmark, and low turnover.
- When a factor model is used as a benchmark, an analysis of past portfolios gives a sense of typical exposures (betas) to various systematic sources of return. A "normal" portfolio is one in which the factor sensitivities are set to these "normal" betas.
- Performance attribution compares account and benchmark performance and identifies and quantifies sources of differential returns. It requires an appropriate framework for decomposing an account's returns relative to those of the benchmark.

- A manager has two basic avenues for superior performance relative to the benchmark: (1) selecting superior (or avoiding inferior) performing assets and (2) owning the superior (inferior) assets in greater (lesser) proportions than are held in the benchmark.
- Performance attribution conducted at the fund sponsor level is called macro attribution. It has three sets of inputs: (1) policy allocations to asset categories within the fund and to individual managers within asset categories; (2) benchmark portfolio returns; and (3) account returns, valuations, and external cash flows.
- Several decision-making levels can be of interest when evaluating a fund sponsor's decision-making process. These decision levels include: net contributions, the risk-free asset, asset categories, investment style, investment managers, and allocation effects.
- Micro attribution is concerned with the investment results of individual portfolios rather than the entire fund. Over a given period, the difference between the portfolio return and the benchmark return is the manager's value-added return, or active return. Because security-by-security micro attribution is unwieldy, a more productive method uses a factor model of returns to assign value-added return to sources of systematic returns.
- The common stock manager's value-added can be expressed as the difference between the weighted average return on the economic/industry sectors in the portfolio and the benchmark. This value-added return can be further divided into (1) a pure sector allocation component, (2) a within-sector selection component, and (3) an allocation/selection interaction.
- For common stocks, fundamental factors such as company size, industry, and growth characteristics seem to have a systematic impact on account performance. These factors can be combined with economic sector factors to conduct micro attribution.
- Fixed-income portfolio returns may be decomposed to show the contributions from the external interest rate environment, on one hand, and the management effect, on the other.
- The widely accepted tenet that investors are risk averse leads to risk-adjusted performance appraisal methods which compare returns with an account's corresponding risk. Two types of risk measures are typically used: the account's systematic risk (beta) and the account's standard deviation of returns.
- There are several measures of the return relative to the risk of a portfolio. The *ex post* alpha measures the account's excess return over the risk-free rate relative to the excess return of the market proxy over the risk-free rate scaled by the account's beta. The intercept, or alpha, from the estimating regression is a measure of the manager's skill. The Treynor measure is similar to the *ex post* alpha measure and will always give the same assessment of investment skill. It is the account's average return less the average risk-free rate divided by the account's beta. Unlike the *ex post* alpha and Treynor measures, which compare returns on an account relative to its systematic risk, the Sharpe ratio measures returns relative to the account's standard deviation of returns. The Sharpe ratio is an account's average return less the average risk-free rate divided by the account's standard deviation. The M^2 measure is equal to the Sharpe measure multiplied by the standard deviation of the market index and then added to the average risk-free rate.
- The Sharpe ratio can be generalized to directly compare the performance of an account to that of a specific benchmark. In this general form, the Sharpe ratio is called the information ratio and is defined as the excess return of the account over the benchmark, divided by the standard deviation of the excess returns.
- Roll's critique is a major issue when using methods based on the capital asset pricing model (CAPM) to evaluate performance. Slight changes in the market portfolio surrogate can yield significantly different performance appraisal answers.

- Quality control charts are an effective way of illustrating performance appraisal data. In simple terms, a quality control chart plots a portfolio manager's performance over time and relative to a benchmark within a statistically derived confidence band. The confidence band indicates whether the manager's performance was statistically different from that of the benchmark.
- Fund sponsors adopt manager continuation policies (MCPs) to guide their manager evaluations. An MCP seeks to develop consistent procedures designed to retain good managers and remove inferior ones based on both quantitative and qualitative information.
- If we begin with the null hypothesis that all managers under evaluation are zero-value-added managers (have no investment skill) and our goal is to identify and separate positive-value-added managers from those without skill, then two types of error can occur. A Type I error results when we keep or hire managers because we believe they are superior when in fact they are not. A Type II error causes us to not reject the null hypothesis when it is incorrect, thus firing or not hiring skillful managers.

PROBLEMS

1. Paul Joubert retired from his firm. He has continued to hold his private retirement investments in a portfolio of common stocks and bonds. At the beginning of 2002, when he retired, his account was valued at €453,000. By the end of 2002, the value of his account was €523,500. Joubert made no contributions to or withdrawals from the portfolio during 2002. What rate of return did Joubert earn on his portfolio during 2002?
2. Frederic Smith works for the Swanson Manufacturing Company and participates in the savings plan at work. He began the month with a balance in his account of £42,000. When he got paid on the last day of the month, the company deposited 10 percent of his gross salary into his savings plan account (£5,000 gross salary). The ending balance in his account at the end of the month was £42,300.

   A. What was the rate of return for the month in Smith's savings plan?
   B. What would be the rate of return for the month if Swanson had paid Smith and deposited 10 percent of his salary on the first rather than the last day of the month, holding all else constant?

3. Mary Nesbitt has an investment account with a local firm, and she makes contributions to her account as funds become available. Self-employed, Mary receives money from her clients on an irregular basis. She began the month of September with a balance in her account of $100,000. She received funds in the amount of $3,000 and made a deposit into her account on September 14. Next, she received a payment of $2,500 on September 21 and made another contribution. The value of her account after the first contribution was $105,000, and the account value was $108,000 after the second contribution. The account was valued at $110,000 at the end of the month. Mary believes that it will be difficult, if not impossible, to determine an accurate rate of return for her account, since her cash flows do not occur on a regular basis.

   A. State and justify whether an accurate rate of return can be calculated.
   B. If an accurate rate of return can be calculated, determine that rate of return.

4. An investment manager has time-weighted returns for the first six months of the year as follows:

January:	1.25%
February:	3.47%
March:	−2.36%
April:	1.89%
May:	−2.67%
June:	2.57%

   A. Calculate a time-weighted rate of return for the investment manager by chain-linking the monthly time-weighted returns.
   B. Compare and contrast the time-weighted rate of return with a calculation involving adding the monthly rates of return.

5. Compare and contrast the time-weighted rate of return with the money-weighted rate of return. In general terms, how is each calculated? Are there certain situations that would cause the two methods to have drastic differences in the calculated rates of return?
6. A pension portfolio manager is about to upgrade his performance calculation software. Currently, his performance software will only calculate his performance on a quarterly basis. For the year 2005, the quarterly performance numbers are as shown below:

Quarter 1:	5.35%
Quarter 2:	−2.34%
Quarter 3:	4.62%
Quarter 4:	1.25%

   These values were calculated on a money-weighted rate-of-return basis.

   A. Explain how you would approximate a time-weighted rate of return for the entire year (2005).
   B. Determine the approximate time-weighted rate of return.

7. Swennson, who manages a domestic equities portfolio of Swedish shares, has had fairly volatile returns for the last five years. Nevertheless, Swennson claims that his returns over the long run are good. Another Swedish equity manager, Mattsson, has had less volatile returns. Their records are as follows:

Year	Swennson	Mattsson
1	27.5%	5.7%
2	−18.9%	4.9%
3	14.6%	7.8%
4	−32.4%	−6.7%
5	12.3%	5.3%

Assume no interim cash flows.

A. Calculate the annualized rates of return for Swennson and Mattsson.
B. State which manager achieved a higher return over the five-year period.

8. A U.S. large-cap value portfolio run by Anderson Investment Management returned 18.9 percent during the first three quarters of 2003. During the same time period, the Russell 1000 Value Index had returns of 21.7 percent and the Wilshire 5000 returned 25.2 percent.

A. What is the return due to style?
B. What is the return due to active management?
C. Discuss the implications of your answers to Parts A and B for assessing Anderson's performance relative to the benchmark and relative to the market.

9. You have selected a U.S. domestic equity manager for a small-cap mandate. Your consultant has suggested that you use the Russell 2000® Index as a benchmark. You find the following information on the Russell/Mellon web site (www.russellmellon.com):

Russell 3000® Index

The Russell 3000 Index offers investors access to the broad U.S. equity universe representing approximately 98 percent of the U.S. market. The Russell 3000 is constructed to provide a comprehensive, unbiased, and stable barometer of the broad market and is completely reconstituted annually to ensure new and growing equities are reflected.

Russell 2000® Index

The Russell 2000 Index offers investors access to the small-cap segment of the U.S. equity universe. The Russell 2000 is constructed to provide a comprehensive and unbiased small-cap barometer and is completely reconstituted annually to ensure larger stocks do not distort the performance and characteristics of the true small-cap opportunity set. The Russell 2000 includes the smallest 2000 securities in the Russell 3000.

As of the latest reconstitution, the average market capitalization was approximately $607.1 million; the median market capitalization was approximately $496 million. The index had a total market-capitalization range of approximately $1.6 billion to $175.8 million.

What analysis could you conduct to verify that the Russell 2000® index is appropriate for the small-cap manager?

10. The information in Exhibit 12-1 pertains to a New Zealand pension plan sponsor.

Based on the information given in the table, address the following:

A. Which asset classes and managers have done relatively well and which have done relatively poorly as judged by returns alone?
B. Characterize the overall performance of the pension plan sponsor.
C. Assuming that relative outperformance or underperformance as indicated in the table is representative of performance over a substantial time period, would you recommend any changes? If so, what changes would you consider?

11. Briefly discuss the properties that a valid benchmark should have.
12. Kim Lee Ltd., an investment management firm in Singapore managing portfolios of Pacific Rim equities, tells you that its benchmark for performance is to be in the top quartile of its peer group (Singapore managers running portfolios of Pacific Rim equities) over the previous calendar year. Is this a valid benchmark? Why or why not?

EXHIBIT 12-1 New Zealand Pension Plan Sponsor Account Valuations and Returns Year of 2002 (All values shown in NZ$ net-of-fees)

Asset Category	Beginning Value	Ending Value	Actual Return	Benchmark Return
Domestic Equities	143,295,254	149,799,531	4.54%	4.04%
Equity Mgr A	93,045,008	97,473,950	4.76	4.61
Equity Mgr B	50,250,246	52,325,581	4.13	4.31
International Equities	35,762,987	38,049,834	6.39	5.96
Int'l Equity Mgr A	20,453,512	21,791,172	6.54	5.82
Int'l Equity Mgr B	15,309,475	16,258,662	6.20	6.02
Domestic Fixed Income	43,124,151	43,961,750	2.16	2.56
Fixed-Income Mgr A	24,900,250	25,298,654	1.60	1.99
Fixed-Income Mgr B	18,223,900	18,663,096	2.41	2.55
Total Fund	444,364,783	463,622,230	4.33	4.22

13. Susan Jones is a U.S. domestic equities investor. Her portfolio has a zero-factor value of 0.5 and a beta of 1.15 at the beginning of the investment period. During the first quarter of 2003, the return on the Wilshire 5000, a broad U.S. equity market index, was 5.9 percent.

    Jones has just been hired by a large plan sponsor. The sponsor is sophisticated in its use of benchmarks. It has developed a custom benchmark for her portfolio. This benchmark has a zero-factor value of 1.5 and a beta of 0.95.

    Calculate the expected return on the portfolio and the benchmark. What is the incremental expected return of the portfolio versus the benchmark? If the portfolio actually returned 8.13 percent during the period, what is the total differential return, and how much of this can be attributed to the value-added investment skill of Jones?
14. A plan sponsor is considering two U.K. investment managers, Manchester Asset Management and Oakleaf Equities, for the same mandate. Manchester will produce on average an annual value-added return of 1.5 percent over the benchmark, with variability of the excess returns of 2.24 percent. Oakleaf is expected to produce a higher annual value-added return of 4 percent, but with variability of excess returns around 10 percent. Using the information in Exhibit 12-2, determine which manager has a larger chance of underperforming the benchmark over periods of 1, 5, and 10 years. Explain the factor(s) causing the manager you identify to have a larger chance of underperforming for a given time period.

EXHIBIT 12-2 Probability of a Manager Outperforming a Benchmark Given Various Levels of Investment Skill

	Information Ratio					
Years	0.20	0.30	0.40	0.67	0.80	1.00
1.0	57.93	61.79	65.54	74.75	78.81	84.03
5.0	67.26	74.88	81.45	93.20	96.32	98.73
10.0	73.65	82.86	89.70	98.25	99.43	99.92
20.0	81.70	91.01	96.32	99.86	99.98	99.99

15. You are a plan sponsor trying to decide between two equity portfolio managers. As you review the information you have gathered during your search, you notice that the two managers have similar investment styles and similar returns for the equity portion of their portfolios. However, the first manager, Acorn Asset Management, keeps its cash level very low, typically around 1 percent of assets. But the second manager, Zebra Investments, has much more cash in the portfolio and usually keeps approximately 10 percent in cash for clients' accounts.

    Contrast Zebra and Acorn in terms of cash level in the accounts relative to overall portfolio performance. Are there time periods when higher or lower cash levels could be beneficial to an equity portfolio?
16. Briefly explain the challenges inherent in performance measurement and performance evaluation for a long–short hedge fund. If traditional performance measurement and evaluation are not appropriate in a long–short environment, are there other options that may be useful?
17. Compare and contrast macro attribution with micro attribution. What is the difference between using a return metric and using a dollar metric? Briefly discuss the inputs and methodology that could be used with a macro analysis.

CHAPTER 13

GLOBAL INVESTMENT PERFORMANCE STANDARDS

Philip Lawton, CFA
CFA Institute
Charlottesville, Virginia

W. Bruce Remington, CFA
Wells Fargo
Lincoln, Nebraska

LEARNING OUTCOMES

After completing this chapter, you will be able to do the following:

- Summarize the reasons for the creation of the Global Investment Performance Standards (GIPS® standards), the standards' evolution, and their benefits to an investment firm's managers and prospective clients.
- Formulate the objectives, key characteristics, and scope of the GIPS standards.
- Discuss the fundamentals of compliance with the GIPS standards, including the definition of the firm, the conditions under which an investment management firm can claim compliance, and the correct wording of the prescribed GIPS compliance statement.
- Formulate the requirements and recommendations of the GIPS standards with respect to input data, including accounting policies related to asset valuation and performance measurement.
- Summarize and justify the requirements of the GIPS standards with respect to return calculations including the treatment of large external cash flows, and calculate a time-weighted total return consistent with those standards.

- Formulate the requirements and recommendations of the GIPS standards with respect to composite return calculations, including methods for asset-weighting portfolio returns.
- Demonstrate the meaning of "discretionary" in the context of composite construction and evaluate whether a portfolio is discretionary given a description of the relevant facts.
- Discuss the role of investment strategies or styles in the construction of composites.
- Formulate the requirements and recommendations of the GIPS standards with respect to composite construction, including switching portfolios among composites and the timing of including new portfolios in composites and excluding terminated portfolios from composites.
- Formulate the requirements and recommendations of the GIPS standards for: asset class segments carved out of multiasset class portfolios; fees; the use of leverage and derivatives; conformity with local laws and regulations that conflict with the GIPS standards; and noncompliant performance records.
- Formulate the requirements of the GIPS standards with respect to presentation and reporting, including the required timeframe of compliant performance records, annual returns, composite market values, and benchmarks.
- Discuss the conditions under which the performance record of a past firm or affiliation must be linked to or used to represent the historical record of a new firm or new affiliation.
- Evaluate the relative merits of high/low, interquartile range, and standard deviation as measures of the dispersion of portfolio returns within a composite.
- Discuss the recommendations of the GIPS standards with respect to presentation and reporting.
- Explain the types of investments that are subject to the GIPS standards for real estate and private equity.
- Explain the requirements of the GIPS standards with respect to reporting total return, income return, and capital return for real estate assets.
- Summarize the performance presentation requirements and recommendations for private equity.
- Discuss the purpose and scope of verification.
- Formulate the requirements for compliance with the GIPS Advertising Guidelines.
- Discuss approaches to after-tax benchmark selection and contrast the preliquidation and mark-to-liquidation methods for calculating after-tax performance.
- Identify the items in a performance report that are not compliant with GIPS standards and revise the report to bring it into compliance.

SUMMARY OVERVIEW

The Global Investment Performance Standards meet the need for consistent, globally accepted standards for investment management firms in calculating and presenting their results to clients and potential clients. This chapter has made the following points:

- The GIPS standards are ethical standards that promote fair representation and full disclosure of an investment firm's performance history. The GIPS standards were created and funded by CFA Institute (formerly known as the Association for Investment Management and Research, or AIMR) with the participation of many experts and local sponsorship from numerous industry groups. The Investment Performance Council is the governance body responsible for developing and interpreting the GIPS standards.

- The objectives of the GIPS standards are to obtain worldwide acceptance of a common standard for calculating and presenting investment performance; to ensure accurate and consistent performance data; to promote fair, global competition for all markets; and to foster the notion of industry self-regulation.
- Only investment management firms can claim compliance with the GIPS standards. A firm may claim compliance only when it has satisfied all the requirements of the GIPS standards.
- Portfolio valuations must be based on market values (not cost basis or book values). Accrual accounting must be used for all assets that accrue interest income, and for periods beginning January 1, 2005, trade-date accounting must be used.
- Under the GIPS provisions for return-calculation methodology, firms must calculate time-weighted total returns. For periods beginning January 1, 2005, if a firm uses approximated rates of return, it must adjust them for daily weighted cash flows. For periods beginning January 1, 2010, firms must value portfolios on the date of all large external cash flows.
- Large external cash flows can significantly distort the accuracy of estimated returns when markets are volatile. The GIPS standards require firms to document composite-specific policies for the treatment of external cash flows and to adhere to those policies consistently.
- Total return calculations must include returns from cash and cash equivalents and must be reduced by actual trading expenses.
- Composite returns must be calculated by asset-weighting the individual portfolio returns using beginning-of-period values or a method that reflects both beginning-of-period values and external cash flows.
- All actual, fee-paying, discretionary portfolios must be included in at least one composite. Portfolios are discretionary if client-imposed restrictions do not prevent the firm from implementing the intended investment strategy.
- Composites must be defined according to their investment objectives or strategies.
- Firms must include new portfolios in composites on a timely and consistent basis. Terminated portfolios must be included in the historical record of the appropriate composite up to the last full measurement period they were under management. A firm cannot switch portfolios from one composite to another unless documented changes in client guidelines make switching appropriate or the composite is redefined.
- When a single asset class (e.g., equities) is carved out of a multiple asset class portfolio (e.g., a balanced account invested in equity and fixed-income securities) and the returns are presented as part of a single-asset-class composite, cash must be allocated to the carve-out returns in a timely and consistent manner. Beginning January 1, 2010, carve-out returns are not permitted to be included in single asset class composite returns unless the carved-out segment is actually managed separately with its own cash balance.
- The GIPS standards include detailed disclosure requirements related to the firm, performance calculations and benchmarks, fees, composites, and composite performance presentations, among other items. Additional disclosures are recommended.
- The GIPS provisions for presentation and reporting require that at least five years of GIPS-compliant performance must be shown (or from inception if the firm or composite has been existence for a shorter period). The GIPS-compliant performance record must then be extended each year until 10 years of results are presented.
- The GIPS standards specify required elements of composite performance presentations, including annual composite and benchmark returns for all years presented, the number of portfolios in the composite (if five or more), the amount of assets in the composite, either the percentage of the firm's total assets represented by the composite or the

amount of total firm assets at the end of each period, and a measure of dispersion of individual portfolio returns within the composite. Additional presentation elements are recommended.

- Acceptable measures of dispersion include but are not limited to high/low, the interquartile range, and standard deviation.
- Performance track records of a past firm or affiliation must be linked to or used to represent the historical record of a new firm or affiliation if all the following conditions are met: substantially all the investment decision makers are employed by the new firm; the staff and decision-making process remain intact and independent within the new firm; and the new firm has records that document and support the reported performance. The new firm must disclose that the performance results from the past firm are linked to the performance record of the new firm.
- If a firm uses a custom benchmark, it must describe the benchmark creation and rebalancing process. The frequency of rebalancing can affect the reported benchmark return.
- The main GIPS standards also apply to real estate and private equity; however, specific provisions exist for these two asset classes.
- Real estate investments must be valued at market value at least once every 12 months (for periods beginning January 1, 2008, at least quarterly). Real estate investments must be valued at least every 36 months by an external professionally designated, certified or licensed commercial property valuer or appraiser.
- In addition to total return for real estate, a firm must show the income and capital appreciation component returns and disclose the calculation methodology for component returns. The GIPS provisions for real estate also recommend that firms present the since-inception internal rate of return (SI-IRR) for the composite.
- Private equity investments must be valued according to the GIPS Private Equity Valuation Principles, which recommend fair value valuations. Firms must calculate the annualized SI-IRR using either daily or monthly cash flows and the period-end valuation of the remaining holdings.
- Performance presentations for private equity must include the annualized gross-of-fees and net-of-fees SI-IRR of the composite and of the benchmark, if any, for each year since inception. Paid-in capital, invested capital, and cumulative distributions must be presented for each period. The investment multiple (the ratio of total value to paid-in capital, or TVPI), the realization multiple (the ration of cumulative distributions to paid-in capital, or DPI), the ratio of paid-in capital to committed capital (PIC), and the ratio of residual value to paid-in capital (RVPI) must also be presented for each period.
- Verification is the review of a firm's performance measurement processes and procedures by a qualified, independent third party. Verification tests whether the firm has complied with all the composite construction requirements on a firmwide basis and whether the firm's processes and procedures are designed to calculate and present performance in compliance with the GIPS standards. A single verification report is issued for the entire firm; verification cannot be carried out for an individual composite. Firms that have been verified may choose to have a further in-depth examination of a specific composite presentation, but they cannot make any claim to the effect that a composite has been verified.
- The GIPS Advertising Guidelines allow a firm to claim compliance with the GIPS standards in an advertisement. All advertisements stating a claim of compliance following the GIPS Advertising Guidelines must use the prescribed wording for the claim. Advertisements that state a claim of compliance and show performance results must present additional information taken from a GIPS-compliant performance presentation.

- The GIPS standards do not require firms to present after-tax returns. For a conceptual framework, the former AIMR Performance Presentation Standards included provisions for after-tax return calculations. Preliquidation after-tax returns reflect the impact of taxes realized during the measurement period. Mark-to-liquidation methods calculate the after-tax returns that would be earned if unrealized gains held in the portfolio were immediately realized. After-tax returns should be calculated using the client's anticipated tax rate or the highest applicable tax rate. Supplemental information may include returns adjusted to compensate for the tax impact of nondiscretionary asset sales, information about the benefits of tax loss harvesting during the measurement period, and various tax efficiency measures.

PROBLEMS

1. Walker, Pierce Corporation is a global financial services company. In addition to its London headquarters, the company has subsidiaries in New York, Frankfurt, and Hong Kong. Walker, Pierce Corporation has decided not to implement the GIPS standards. However, the head of marketing for its continental European subsidiary, Walker, Pierce & Company of Frankfurt, believes that the division would benefit by implementing the GIPS standards. Is it possible for Walker, Pierce & Company of Frankfurt to become GIPS-compliant even if Walker, Pierce Corporation does not implement the GIPS standards companywide?
2. Larson Dynamic Management claims to comply with the GIPS standards. At the time the firm first achieved compliance, trade-date accounting was recommended but settlement date accounting was acceptable. On January 1, 2005, trade-date accounting became mandatory. Larson Dynamic Management has been unable to reprogram its accounting system to produce statements on a trade-date basis. Larson Dynamic Management includes the following statement with composite performance presentations covering periods that began after January 1, 2005: "Larson Dynamic Management has prepared and presented this report in compliance with the Global Investment Performance Standards (GIPS®), except that settlement date accounting has been used as an acceptable alternative." Is this compliance statement allowable?
3. The Dennett Electronics Pension Plan had the following quarterly returns during the last two years:

1Q Year 1:	+4.76%
2Q Year 1:	+12.08%
3Q Year 1:	−4.88%
4Q Year 1:	+7.14%
1Q Year 2:	−13.57%
2Q Year 2:	+17.65%
3Q Year 2:	+1.08%
4Q Year 2:	+0.97%

Calculate the following:

A. Annual performance for Year 1.
B. Annual performance for Year 2.

C. Cumulative performance for the two-year period.
D. Annualized compound performance for the two-year period.

4. Smith & Jones Asset Management has been managing equity, fixed-income, and balanced accounts since 1986. Senior management has decided that to remain competitive and fairly present performance to prospective clients, the firm must adopt the GIPS standards companywide. After compiling performance data, management discovers that prior to 1999, the market values of fixed-income securities excluded accrued income. In addition, some accounts used derivative securities for hedging. Is it possible for Smith & Jones to incorporate pre-1999 performance into a GIPS-compliant performance presentation?
5. In March 1997, Smith & Jones Asset Management, a GIPS-compliant firm, introduced a new technical analysis model that management believed would be a powerful tool in tactical asset allocation. After extensive back-testing, Smith & Jones began to use the model to manage actual "live" portfolios in June 1997, and managers constructed a composite composed of actual, fee-paying, discretionary portfolios managed in accordance with the model. In 2000, after three very successful years of managing client funds in this way, management decided that because the actual performance of live portfolios validated the performance of the model, it should present the simulated performance of the model through the back-testing period to prospective clients. Smith & Jones proceeded to link the backtested returns to the actual performance of the composite and presents 3-, 5- and 10-year performance as a continuous record to prospects. Does this practice comply with the GIPS standards?
6. Barry, Smith Investment Management specializes in balanced account management for midsize pension plans. On March 12, 2006, a contribution of $2,265,000 is made to Dennett Electronics' Pension Plan, which is included in Barry Smith's Balanced Tax-Exempt Composite. Barry, Smith invests the contribution on March 12. The pension plan's portfolio had a market value of $16,575,000 at the beginning of March. For the purpose of calculating portfolio performance, how should Barry, Smith handle the external cash flow?
7. Use the following input data on the Dennett portfolio for the month of March 2006 to answer questions A through C.

Market value 28 February	$16,575,000
Cash contribution 12 March	2,265,000
Market value March 12[a]	19,550,000
Market value March 31	19,250,000

[a]Includes cash contribution of $2,265,000 received and available for investment on 12 March

A. Calculate the approximate time-weighted return for March using the Modified Dietz formula.
B. Calculate the true time-weighted rate of return for March.
C. What accounts for the difference between the approximate and the true return?

8. How must the firm treat trading expenses when calculating performance that adheres to the requirements of the GIPS standards? What is the rationale for the required treatment?
9. A European equity composite contains three portfolios. Use the data given in Exhibit 13-1 to answer parts A through C.

EXHIBIT 13-1 European Equity Composite

		Portfolio (€ Millions)		
	Cash Flow Weighting Factor	A	B	C
Market value as of July 31		74.9	127.6	110.4
External cash flows				
August 8	0.742		−15	
August 12	0.613	7.5		
August 19	0.387		−5	15
Market value as of August 31		85.3	109.8	128.4

A. Calculate the returns of Portfolio A, Portfolio B, and Portfolio C for the month of August using the Modified Dietz formula. For convenience, the cash flow–weighting factors are presented above.
B. Calculate the August composite return by asset-weighting the individual portfolio returns using beginning-of-period values.
C. Calculate the August composite return by asset-weighting the individual portfolio returns using a method that reflects both beginning-of-period values and external cash flows.

10. Explain how the concept of discretion is used to determine whether or not an account should be included in a composite.
11. Midwest National Bank manages a domestic equity portfolio for the Springfield Municipal Employees' Retirement Fund (SMERF), a mature defined-benefit pension plan. The SMERF portfolio belongs to Midwest's Institutional Equity composite. The composite description states, "Portfolios included in the Institutional Equity composite are actively managed for long-term capital appreciation." SMERF's investment policy statement includes the following provisions:

    - All security transactions must be approved in advance by the SMERF Investment Committee.
    - SMERF anticipates making regular net withdrawals in substantial amounts from the portfolio to meet pension liabilities. SMERF staff will prepare a schedule of withdrawals at the beginning of each fiscal year. The portfolio manager must manage liquidity so as to disburse funds in accordance with the withdrawal schedule.

    In view of these restrictions, discuss whether Midwest National Bank can justify including the SMERF portfolio in the composite.
12. The GIPS standards require that a firm's composites must be defined according to similar objectives, strategies, or styles. State the guiding principles for composite definition, and explain the suggested hierarchy for defining composites.
13. Smith & Jones Asset Management manages numerous balanced accounts in addition to equity and fixed-income accounts. Discuss an approach for defining balanced account composites in accordance with the GIPS standards.
14. When should a new client's portfolio be added to an existing composite?
15. Under what conditions may a portfolio be switched from one composite to another? How must the historical record of the portfolio be treated?
16. What is the minimum number of portfolios that a composite must contain to comply with the GIPS standards? Must a firm disclose the number of portfolios in a composite?

17. The performance of the equity composites presented by Shelbourne Capital Company declines after seven members of the equity investment management group leave the small firm in April 2006. The head of performance measurement informs senior management that the GIPS standards require firms to disclose all significant events that help a prospective client interpret the performance record. The chief investment officer, who heads Shelbourne's Investment Strategy Committee, responds that it is the firm's investment decision process, not the talent of individual employees, that produces returns and that the recent underperformance was caused by factors other than employee turnover. Should Shelbourne Capital Company disclose the departure of the equity managers in its equity performance presentations?
18. Smith & Jones wants to include the performance and assets of the equity and fixed-income portions of its balanced accounts in separate composites. Management recognizes that the GIPS standards require cash to be allocated to carve-out segments. Data on a balanced account composite with an 80/20 strategic asset allocation appear below.

	Market Value as of June 30	Strategic Mix	July Return
Stocks	96,425,706	80%	0.79%
Bonds	20,777,934	20%	0.44%
Cash	8,514,010	0%	0.21%
Total balanced composite assets	125,717,650	100%	0.69%

A. Calculate the return for the month of July of the equity segment, including cash allocated in accordance with the beginning-of-period allocation method.
B. Calculate the July return of the equity segment, including cash allocated in accordance with the strategic asset allocation method.

19. Claiborne and Jackson, recognizing that its equity performance was poor, terminates some of its investment professionals and hires a new team of equity portfolio managers from a rival firm, Shelbourne Capital Company, in 2006. The new employees of Claiborne and Jackson include two members of the former firm's five-member Investment Strategy Committee, and these individuals maintain that they were responsible for Shelbourne Capital's enviable performance track record in equities. All the former Shelbourne Capital employees were compelled in a court of law to return records they had taken when they left the firm, including client lists and historical performance data. Claiborne and Jackson sees that linking the returns of the Shelbourne Capital composites to its own composites would improve its ability to compete for new business, and it does not consider such treatment misleading because prospective clients will have the benefit of the same investment expertise that produced the historical returns. Can Claiborne and Jackson link the composite returns its new employees achieved during their affiliation with another firm to its existing composites?
20. Because Smith & Jones Asset Management's net-of-fees performance record is superb, management has chosen to present performance (calculated monthly using the Modified Dietz method) net of investment management fees. The firm's fees are not bundled. What are the GIPS standards' requirements and recommendations regarding the presentation of net-of-fees returns?
21. Bentwood Institutional Asset Management has been managing equity, fixed-income, and balanced accounts since 1986. The firm became GIPS-compliant on January 1, 2001, and

prepared composite performance presentations for the 1996–2000 period. Fixed-income performance was poor prior to 2001, when a new team of managers was brought on board. When Christopher Cooper joins Bentwood as marketing director in June 2006, he suggests showing performance starting with calendar 2001, the first year that performance started to improve. He proposes to show composites with returns for the five calendar years 2001 through 2005. Does this course of action comply with the GIPS standards?

22. Larson Dynamic Management, a GIPS-compliant firm, has specialized in equity investment management for more than 20 years. Employing a large-cap growth style of equity management, the company has compiled a mediocre track record during the last decade and has slipped below its benchmark during the last three years. The benchmark is a capital market index that is widely used to gauge investment results in the large-cap growth style. Several of Larson's portfolio managers have informed Chief Investment Officer Russ Larson that clients are complaining about performance shortfalls versus the benchmark and are threatening to leave the firm. In addition, the head of marketing has reported that the firm's investment performance record compared with the benchmark is an impediment to winning new business. Larson believes that performance has been reasonable, given the risk taken in most of the accounts, and counters that perhaps a different benchmark is in order. He instructs the head of performance measurement to conduct research on other commercially available large-cap growth indices, with attention to how the indices are constructed and how their historical returns compare to those of Larson Dynamic Management's existing benchmark. What do the GIPS standards say about selecting and changing composite benchmarks?
23. Renner, Williams & Woods specializes in management of equity and balanced individual, personal accounts with an emphasis on income generation. Because most of its clients are elderly and care little about performance as long as they receive a steady, monthly income stream, Renner, Williams & Woods decides that there is no reason to show a benchmark when presenting composite investment performance. Is this decision permissible under the GIPS standards?
24. A performance analyst determines that an asset-weighted composite return for one year is 2.59 percent and the mean return of the portfolios in the composite is 2.57 percent. She calculates the following dispersion measures for the portfolios that were in the composite for the full year:

High	3.65%
Low	1.92%
High/low range	1.73%
Interquartile range	0.82%
Equal-weighted standard deviation	0.55%

Explain what these measures mean and evaluate their relative advantages and disadvantages.

25. Bronson Growth Property is a real estate development organization that raises funds from wealthy individuals and rehabilitates blighted commercial buildings for sale. Second-quarter financial information about one of Bronson's funds, called Rehab XI, appears in Exhibit 13-2.

    A. Using the data in Exhibit 13-2, calculate the capital return for the second quarter.
    B. Using the data in Exhibit 13-2, calculate the income return for the second quarter.
    C. Calculate the total return for the second quarter.

EXHIBIT 13-2 Rehab XI Second Quarter

Beginning capital as of March 31	8,000,000
Capital contribution May 15 (weight: 0.51)	1,000,000
Portfolio market value as of March 31	7,450,000
Portfolio market value as of June 30	8,375,000
Capital expenditures	1,750,000
Sale proceeds	2,250,000
Accrued investment income	75,000
Nonrecoverable expenses	200,000
Interest expense on debt	137,500
Property taxes paid	20,000

26. Renner, Williams & Woods decides to have its equity and balanced composites verified. Because the firm has only a handful of fixed-income accounts and does not present fixed-income management results in marketing materials shown to prospects, management decides that it would be a waste of time and money to hire a verification firm to verify such a small composite. Is it possible for Renner, Williams & Woods to obtain a firmwide verification that covers only the equity and balanced composites?
27. Bristol Capital Management manages an equity portfolio on a tax-aware basis for Martin Flemington, a high-net-worth individual. Flemington's tax accountant advises Bristol that Flemington's expected federal income tax rate is 17.2 percent, his expected state income tax rate is 4.3 percent, and his expected city income tax rate is 2.1 percent. State and city income taxes are deductible from the federal income tax liability. Dividend income and short-term capital gains are taxable at the income tax rates. Flemington's expected long-term capital gains tax rate is 15.0 percent. Information about the Flemington portfolio in the month of April is given in Exhibit 13-3.

    A. Calculate Flemington's anticipated combined federal, state, and city income tax rate to one decimal place (XX.X%).
    B. Assuming that investment income is included in the ending market value, calculate the approximate pretax time-weighted return for April.
    C. Using the Modified Dietz formula, calculate the after-tax return on a preliquidation basis.
    D. Calculate the preliquidation after-tax return adjusted for the impact of nondiscretionary capital gains.

EXHIBIT 13-3 Flemington Portfolio

Market value as of March 31	127,945,000
Cost as of March 31	92,120,400
Withdrawal on April 17	(8,950,000)
Market value as of April 30	123,159,825
Cost as of April 30	85,676,400
Dividend income in April	533,105
Net short-term capital gains realized in April	975,000
Net long-term capital gains realized in April	12,545,000

EXHIBIT 13-4 Bristol Capital Management Performance Results: Intermediate Global Fixed-Income Composite January 1, 2002 through March 31, 2007

Year	Gross-of-Fees Return (percent)	Benchmark Return (percent)	No. of Portfolios	Composite Dispersion (percent)	Total Assets at End of Period ($million)	Percent of Firm Assets ($million)	Total Firm Assets ($million)
2002	12.7	10.7	8	6.6	512	21	$2,438
2003	9.5	7.2	12	4.7	780	23	3,391
2004	2.1	1.5	22	6.5	1,250	27	4,629
2005	14.2	14.1	25	3.0	1,425	32	4,453
2006	4.9	6.1	29	1.9	1,712	32	4,891
1Q 2007	7.1	5.9	34	4.4	1,994	37	5,389

(Returns for 1Q 2007 are annualized)

Bristol Capital Management has prepared and presented this report in compliance with the Global Investment Performance Standards (GIPS®), except for the use of cash-basis accounting for the recognition of interest income.

Notes

1. Bristol Capital Management is an independent investment management firm founded in November 1995.
2. Performance results are presented before investment management and custodial fees.
3. Portfolio valuations are computed quarterly and are denominated in U.S. dollars.
4. Bristol Capital Management uses derivative products to enhance portfolio returns.
5. All accounts worth more than $1 million that are invested in the Intermediate Global Fixed Income strategy are included in the composite at the beginning of the first full quarter under management.
6. The Intermediate Global Fixed Income composite includes several non-fee-paying accounts.
7. Allied Verification, Ltd. has verified the Bristol Capital Management Intermediate Global Fixed Income Composite.

28. (Adapted from the 2002 CFA Level III examination)

It is 2007. Bristol Capital Management is the intermediate global fixed-income manager for the Jarvis University endowment fund. Bristol has prepared the performance report shown in Exhibit 13-4. James Chan, consultant to Jarvis University, reviews the report and tells the fund's investment committee that the report does not meet the minimum requirements of the GIPS standards.

Identify *four* omissions that prevent the Bristol Capital Management performance report from being in compliance with GIPS standards. Also identify *four* items included in the Bristol Capital Management performance report (other than omissions) that do not comply with GIPS standards.

PART II

SOLUTIONS

CHAPTER 1

THE PORTFOLIO MANAGEMENT PROCESS AND THE INVESTMENT POLICY STATEMENT

SOLUTIONS

1. A. The liquidity requirement for this individual is her need for cash in excess of her savings during the coming year. Therefore, her liquidity requirement is €95,000 – €50,000 = €45,000.

   B. The Wilson-Fowler Endowment's anticipated liquidity requirement is $600,000, calculated as $1 million (the planned contribution to the construction of the new dormitory) minus $400,000 (the anticipated amount of new contributions to the endowment). Note that the amount of 4% × $75 million = $3 million, as provided for in the spending rule, is fully committed to budgetary support; thus this amount is not available to help meet the endowment's planned contribution to the building project.

2. The Judd Endowment's risk tolerance is limited by its ability and willingness to accept risk. Risk tolerance is *not* a function of a need for higher returns. The return objective should be consistent with risk tolerance, so an appropriate return objective for the Judd Endowment is 7 percent. A spending rate of 6 percent is too high for this endowment; raising the return objective to 9 percent would only compound the problem created by a 6 percent spending rate, which is inappropriately high for this endowment.

3. A. The country allocation strategy as described mixes elements of active and passive investment approaches. The portfolio weights are actively determined and differ from benchmark weights, within limits. However, the investments in individual countries are passive, indexed investments.

   B. Overall, we can classify the country allocation strategy as a semiactive or controlled-active investment approach.

4. A. This is an absolute return objective because it does not reference a comparison to the performance of another portfolio but rather is stated in terms of a fixed number (an 8 percent annual return).

B. This is an absolute risk objective because it does not reference a comparison to the performance of another portfolio but rather is stated in terms of a fixed number (a standard deviation of return of 20 percent a year).

C. This is a relative return objective because it references a comparison to the performance of other portfolios.

D. This is an absolute risk objective because it addresses the risk that a portfolio's return will fall below a minimum acceptable level over a stated time horizon.

E. This is a relative risk objective because it references a comparison to the performance of another portfolio, the benchmark.

5. D is correct. The IPS identifies pertinent investment objectives and constraints for a *particular* investor. Clearly identified objectives and constraints ensure that the policy statement is accurate and relevant to the investor's specific situation and desires. The result should be an optimal balance between return and risk for that investor. The IPS provides a long-term plan for an investor and a basis for making disciplined investment decisions over time. The absence of an investment policy statement reduces decision making to an individual-event basis and often leads to pursuing short-term opportunities that may not contribute to, or may even detract from, reaching long-term goals.
6. B is correct. An investor's ability to take risk puts an upper limit on a reasonable return objective.
7. D is correct. Even though Stephenson describes his risk tolerance as "average," his present investment portfolio and his desire for large returns indicate an above-average willingness to take risk. His financial situation (large asset base, ample income to cover expenses, lack of need for liquidity, and long time horizon) indicates an above-average ability to accept risk.
8. B is correct. Stephenson has adequate income to cover his living expenses and has no major outlays for which he needs cash, so his liquidity needs are minimal. He is not a tax-exempt investor (both income and capital gains are taxed at 30 percent), so taxes should play a considerable role in his investment decisions.
9. D is correct. Stephenson's time horizon is long—he is currently only 55 years old. The time horizon consists of two stages: the first stage extends to his retirement in 15 years; the second stage may last for 20 years or more and extends from retirement until his death.
10. D is correct.

Risk. Stephenson has an above-average risk tolerance based on both his ability and willingness to assume above-average risk. His large asset base, long time horizon, ample income to cover expenses, and lack of need for liquidity or cash flow indicate an above-average ability to assume risk. His concentration in U.S. small-capitalization stocks and his desire for high returns indicate substantial willingness to assume risk.

Return. Stephenson's financial circumstances (long time horizon, sizable asset base, ample income, and low liquidity needs) and his risk tolerance warrant an above-average total return objective. His expressed desire for a continued return of 20 percent, however, is unrealistic. Coppa should counsel Stephenson on what level of returns to reasonably expect from the financial markets over long periods of time and to define an achievable return objective.

11. James Stephenson

1. Underline the word at right that best describes the client's:

A. *Willingness to accept risk*	Below average	Above average Explanation in 2A below
B. *Ability to accept risk*	Below average	Above average Explanation in 2A below
C. *Risk tolerance*	Below average	Above average Explanation in 2A below
D. *Liquidity requirement*	Significant	Not significant $70,000 can be met by expected annual saving of $\$350{,}000 \times (1 - 0.3) - \$150{,}000 = \$95{,}000$
E. *Time horizon*	Single stage	Multistage Stage 1: Pre-retirement Stage 2: Retirement
F. *Overall time horizon*	Short to intermediate term	Long term Overall time horizon could be 20 to 30 years or more
G. *Tax concerns*	Significant Taxed at 30% rate	Not significant

2. Discuss appropriate client objectives:

A. *Risk.* Stephenson has an above-average risk tolerance based on both his ability and willingness to assume above-average risk. His large asset base, long time horizon, ample income to cover expenses, and lack of need for liquidity or cash flow indicate an above-average ability to assume risk. His concentration in U.S. small-capitalization stocks and his desire for high returns indicate substantial willingness to assume risk.

B. *Return.* Stephenson's financial circumstances (long time horizon, sizable asset base, ample income, and low liquidity needs) and his risk tolerance warrant an above-average total return objective. His expressed desire for a return 10 percentage points above the average return on U.S. small capitalization stocks, however, is unrealistic. The portfolio manager should counsel Stephenson on what level of returns to reasonably expect from the financial markets over long periods of time and to define an achievable return objective.

12. Foothill College Endowment Fund

1. Underline the word at right that best describes the client's:

A. *Risk tolerance*	Below average	Above average Explanation in 2A below
B. *Liquidity requirement*	Significant	Not significant Budgeted support at 4% × $1 billion exceeds scholarship needs of $39.5 million

C. *Time horizon*	Single stage	Multistage
D. *Overall time horizon*	Short to intermediate term	Long term Provide support in perpetuity
E. *Tax concerns*	Significant	Not significant Tax exempt

2. Discuss appropriate client objectives:

A. *Risk.* The endowment fund, with a large asset base and very long time horizon, has an above-average risk tolerance.

B. *Return.* An estimate for the endowment's required annual return is the sum of the spending rate (4 percent) plus the expected annual college tuition inflation rate (3 percent) for a total of 7 percent.
The endowment's objective is to maintain the long-term purchasing power of its assets while providing a stable flow of funds for scholarships.

13. Vincenzo Donadoni

1. Underline the word at right that best describes the client's:

A. *Willingness to accept risk*	Below average	Above average Explanation in 2A below
B. *Ability to accept risk*	Below average	Above average Explanation in 2A below
C. *Risk tolerance*	Below average	Above average Explanation in 2A below
D. *Liquidity requirement*	Significant CHF 1.5 million needed now CHF 2 million due in nine months	Not significant
E. *Time horizon*	Single stage	Multistage *Three stages:* First nine months Next 20 to 30 years Life of trust
F. *Overall time horizon*	Short to intermediate term	Long term Overall time horizon is approximately 20 to 30 years

2. Discuss appropriate client objectives:

A. *Risk.* Donadoni has an above-average risk tolerance based on both his willingness and ability to accept above-average risk. He is a risk taker with a long time horizon, a relatively low need for income, and a large asset base.

B. *Return.* To meet his long-term goal of a leaving a CHF 15.0 million trust fund for his three children, Donadoni must also achieve growth of his current assets. In accordance with his above-average risk tolerance and his goal of leaving the trust, Donadoni should adopt an above-average total real return objective.

Donadoni has a minimal need for additional cash flow given his current expenses, income, and asset base: (250,000 − 125,000)/(13 million − 1.5 million) = 1.1%. In nine months, his need will grow due to inflation of his expenses, his reduction in income, and his reduced asset base:

(250,000 − 0)/(13 million − 1.5 million − 2 million in taxes) = 2.6 percent return. As a long-run average, a 2.6 percent real return should be achievable.

CHAPTER 2

MANAGING INDIVIDUAL INVESTOR PORTFOLIOS

SOLUTIONS

1. Need for cash:

Ongoing expenses	€132,500/year
Emergency reserve	€132,500
Anticipated income	€50,000/year art sales
€82,500/year expected total return on portfolio (subject to risk)	
€1,020,000 after taxes from sale of IngerMarine	

   The after-tax proceeds from the imminent sale of IngerMarine well exceed her anticipated needs for cash for the coming year (2 × €132,500 = €265,000). Thus, Christa's liquidity needs are currently met. Because portfolio returns are risky and her anticipated annual income of €132,500 just covers her annual cash needs, however, Christa may face a challenge in the form of liquidity requirements at some point in the future.

2. After the sale of IngerMarine, Christa's portfolio will have a market value of roughly €1,120,000, taking account of the after-tax proceeds from the sale of IngerMarine (€1,020,000), her balanced mutual funds (€75,000), and her money market fund (€25,000). Her expected portfolio return is €82,500, equal to a 7.4 percent rate of return. Her required real return, if she reduces her spending by combining her apartment and studio, is €50,000 (art sales of €50,000 less €100,000 expenses), or 4.5 percent as a rate of return on her portfolio.

   Because the portfolio's expected return of 7.4 percent translates to a real return of approximately 4.4 percent (7.4 percent less 3 percent inflation), the portfolio is *not* expected to meet the return requirement of 4.5 percent.

3. Portfolio guidelines and investment policy should be reviewed whenever a significant change occurs in the underlying assumptions of the policy statement. At Christa's portfolio performance reviews, the need for an interim reevaluation of the policy statement should always be considered. Possible triggers for a policy statement review might include the following:

   - A change in personal circumstances affecting risk–return objectives or portfolio constraints. Examples could include an increase in expected income from nonportfolio sources, uninsured health problems, or marriage.

- A change in market conditions affecting long-term risk–return relationships among asset classes. Examples could include a shift in outlook for inflation and global political changes.
- New investment markets or vehicles. Examples could include markets made accessible through commingled investment funds and retirement saving accounts.
- A change in tax laws. An example could be elimination of the capital gains tax.
- A severe performance shortfall, sufficient to jeopardize the portfolio's ability to meet expense needs in excess of income from other sources.

4. Hans's reckless actions will significantly reduce his portfolio. Hopefully, this incident will make him aware of his financial vulnerability and the long-term consequences of his actions. The potential costs of the accident have created an immediate need for liquidity. Currently, Hans has a diversified equity portfolio valued at €200,000 and cash of €100,000. If he has not already done so, he should immediately use the cash to retain an attorney for his upcoming legal challenges. He should also make his financial advisor aware of his situation and instruct him or her to establish a high level of portfolio liquidity. Hans may need to convert a portion of his IngerMarine holdings to cash, if he can, and should notify his father of this possibility. Alternatively, Hans may be able to obtain a loan using IngerMarine shares as collateral. If the IngerMarine holdings cannot be monetized, Hans may be able to borrow against the equity in his home.
5. In light of the auto accident, Hans must reassess his investment portfolio. Assuming that the legal challenges against him are successful, he stands to lose €1,000,000 in savings (after insurance). In addition, his legal fees may be large, resulting in a further decline in net worth. His salary has not been reduced, but depending on the outcome of his legal troubles, he may face job termination. His investment personality profile classified Hans as a spontaneous risk taker, and his propensity to engage in riskier investing will have to be reevaluated. Even though Hans is young, his ability to take risk has been severely curtailed by the recent incident. His net worth may be reduced by as much as half, and he faces the potential loss of his current income. Hans will now need to consider rebuilding his life, engaging in lower-risk investing until his contingent liabilities are settled.
6. Peter and Hilda are subject to a flat tax of 25 percent on all income and a capital gains tax of 15 percent. The analysis below presents comparative after-tax returns. Even though the High Growth Stock Fund maintains high portfolio turnover, its return is high enough to provide superior after-tax performance. Of course, a complete investment evaluation should also address the relative risk of each investment alternative. The High Growth Stock Fund is quite likely to have high portfolio volatility, and this factor must also be considered before a final decision is made.

After-Tax Investment Evaluation

Investment Vehicle	High-Growth Stock Fund	Equity Value Fund	Municipal Bond Fund
Investment	€1,000,000	€1,000,000	€1,000,000
Projected income	20,000	25,000	50,000
Projected price appreciation	120,000	100,000	20,000
Projected income tax liability	(5,000)	(6,250)	0
Projected capital gains tax liability[a]	(13,500)	(3,750)	(450)
Net investment gains	**€ 121,500**	**€ 115,000**	**€ 69,550**

[a]Gains tax liability = Price appreciation × 15% × Turnover rate.

7. Remaining investment portfolio:

Stocks	€ 750,000
Bonds	1,000,000
Cash	1,000,000
Gold	500,000
	€3,250,000

Additional resources:

Hilda's trust distribution	€ 75,000/year
House	1,200,000
Peter's RSA	50,000

The goal of replacing Peter's €500,000 salary has become a "desired" portfolio return that is clearly not realistic. Peter and Hilda must now reconsider the return that they will "require" in order to meet their basic financial goals. The required return must be reconcilable with their new investment constraints and ability to assume risk. Before reaching an achievable return objective, Peter and Hilda will have to address some difficult decisions regarding their future lifestyle and long-term goals. Possible changes might include the following:

- Postpone retirement.
- Attempt to rebuild IngerMarine.
- Return to the workforce as consultants or salaried employees.
- Sell home.
- Curtail gifting programs.
- Cancel plans for second home.
- Cancel investment in *Exteriors* magazine.
- Liquidate Hilda's design company.

8. Portfolio Constraints

- *Liquidity.* The Ingers' short-term liquidity needs have clearly increased. Because spending commitments are sometimes difficult to curtail, Peter and Hilda may need to withdraw as much as €500,000 in the coming year from their remaining assets, to pay for expenses previously covered by Peter's salary. Fortunately, the Ingers have an emergency reserve of cash and bullion equivalent to approximately three years' salary.

  The Ingers must ultimately reconcile their ongoing liquidity needs, as well as targeted liquidity events, with their remaining net worth. Left unchanged, the increased liquidity requirements will require an increasing allocation to investments with lower volatility and lower return. At the same time, withdrawals will begin to outstrip returns, leaving the Ingers' portfolio in a deteriorating situation.
- *Time horizon.* Peter and Hilda's investment time horizon has been shortened, as the increased need to secure their own financial future has left them less able to approach portfolio risk from a multigenerational perspective. Their joint life expectancy, however, would reasonably warrant a portfolio time horizon that is still long term (20 to 25 years or more).

- *Taxes.* Tax rates remain unchanged for the Ingers, although their tax burden will decline with the loss of Peter's income. Their business loss from IngerMarine may be available to offset future investment gains.
- *Regulatory environment.* The regulatory environment is unchanged.
- *Unique circumstances.* It would be appropriate to note the bankruptcy of IngerMarine and any consequences it might have for portfolio management, such as the allocation of portfolio assets to build a new family business.

9. A. i. *Return objective.* Stephenson's expressed desire for 20 percent average annual return is unrealistic. Coppa should counsel Stephenson on the level of returns he can reasonably expect from the financial markets over long time periods and to define an achievable return objective. Nevertheless, Stephenson's circumstances support an above-average return objective that emphasizes capital appreciation. This formulation is justified by the following:

   - Because Stephenson has a sizable asset base and ample income to cover his current spending, focus should be on growing the portfolio.
   - Stephenson's low liquidity needs and long time horizon support a long-term capital appreciation approach.
   - Stephenson is in the consolidation phase of his life cycle and does not rely on the portfolio to meet living expenses.

   Stephenson stated that he wants a return in excess of 5.0 percent for the remainder of the year. This short-term goal needs to be considered to the extent possible but should not be a significant factor in the IPS, which focuses on the client's long-term return objective.

   To maintain his lifestyle after retirement, Stephenson needs approximately \$234,000 in inflation-adjusted after-tax income annually when he retires in 15 years [$\$150{,}000 \times (1.03)^{15} = \$233{,}695$]. Assuming he can achieve a 7 percent return (3% inflation + 4% real return = 7%), Stephenson will have \$5,500,000 in 15 years [$\$2{,}000{,}000 \times (1.07)^{15} = \$5{,}520{,}000$]. Generating \$234,000 from a \$5,520,000 asset base requires a 4.2% after-tax return.

   ii. *Risk tolerance.* Stephenson has an above-average risk tolerance.

   - Although Stephenson describes his risk tolerance as "average," his current investment portfolio indicates an apparent above-average willingness to take risk.
   - His financial situation (large current asset base, ample income to cover expenses, lack of need for liquidity or cash flow, and long time horizon) indicates an above-average ability to assume risk.

   iii. *Liquidity requirements.* Stephenson's liquidity needs are low.

   - Stephenson has no regular cash flow needs from the portfolio because the income from his medical practice meets all current spending needs.
   - No large, one-time cash needs are stated. It would be appropriate, however, to keep a small cash reserve for emergencies.

   iv. *Time horizon.* Stephenson's time horizon is long term and consists of two stages:

   - Time until retirement, which he expects to be 15 years.
   - His lifetime following retirement, which could range from 15 to 20 years.

B. Fund D represents the single best addition to complement Stephenson's current portfolio, given his selection criteria. First, Fund D's expected return (14.0 percent) has the potential to increase the portfolio's return somewhat. Second, Fund D's relatively low correlation coefficient with his current portfolio (+0.65) indicates that it will provide larger diversification benefits than any of the other alternatives except Fund B. The result of adding Fund D should be a portfolio with about the same expected return and somewhat lower volatility compared with the original portfolio.

The three other funds have shortcomings in either expected return enhancement or volatility reduction through diversification benefits:

- Fund A offers the potential for increasing the portfolio's return but is too highly correlated to provide substantial volatility reduction benefits through diversification.
- Fund B provides substantial volatility reduction through diversification benefits but is expected to generate a return well below the current portfolio's return.
- Fund C has the greatest potential to increase the portfolio's return but is too highly correlated to provide substantial volatility reduction benefits through diversification.

10. A. i. The IPS's *return objective* section is inadequate.

- Although Wheeler accurately indicates Taylor's personal income requirement, she has not recognized the need to support Renee.
- Wheeler does not indicate the need to protect Taylor's purchasing power by increasing income by at least the rate of inflation over time.
- Wheeler does not indicate the impact of income taxes on the return requirement.
- Wheeler calculates required return based on assets of $900,000, appropriately excluding Taylor's imminent $300,000 liquidity need (house purchase) from investable funds. However, Taylor may invest $100,000 in his son's business. If he does, Taylor insists this asset be excluded from his plan. In that eventuality, Taylor's asset base for purposes of Wheeler's analysis would be $800,000.
- Assuming a $900,000 capital base, Wheeler's total return estimate of 2.7 percent is lower than the actual required after-tax real return of 5.3 percent ($48,000/ $900,000).

ii. The *risk tolerance* section is inappropriate.

- Wheeler fails to consider Taylor's below-average willingness to assume risk as exemplified by his aversion to loss, his consistent preference for conservative investments, his adverse experience with creditors, and his desire not to work again.
- Wheeler fails to consider Taylor's below-average ability to assume risk, which is based on his recent life changes, the size of his capital base, high personal expenses versus income, and expenses related to his mother's care.
- Wheeler's policy statement implies that Taylor has a greater willingness and ability to accept volatility (higher risk tolerance) than is actually the case. Based on Taylor's need for an after-tax return of 5.3 percent, a balanced approach with both a fixed-income and growth component is more appropriate than an aggressive growth strategy.

iii. The *time horizon* section is partially appropriate.

- Wheeler accurately addresses the long-term time horizon based only on Taylor's age and life expectancy.

- Wheeler fails to consider that Taylor's investment time horizon is multistage. Stage 1 represents Renee's life expectancy, during which time Taylor will supplement her income. Stage 2 begins at Renee's death, concluding Taylor's need to supplement her income, and ends with Taylor's death.

iv. The *liquidity* section is partially appropriate.

- Wheeler addresses potential liquidity events.
- Wheeler fails to specifically consider ongoing expenses ($2,000/month for Taylor's living expenses and $2,000/month to support his mother) relative to expected portfolio returns.
- The reference to a "normal, ongoing cash reserve" is vague. The reserve's purpose and size should be specified.

B. Allocation B is most appropriate for Taylor. Taylor's nominal annual return requirement is 6.3 percent, based on his cash flow (income) needs ($50,400 annually), to be generated from a current asset base of $800,000. After adjusting for expected annual inflation of 1.0 percent, the real return requirement becomes 7.3 percent. To grow to $808,000 ($\$800,000 \times 1.01$), the portfolio must generate $58,400 ($\$50,400 + \$8,000$) in the first year ($\$58,400/\$800,000 = 7.3\%$).

Allocation B meets Taylor's minimum return requirement. Of the possible allocations that provide the required minimum real return, Allocation B also has the lowest standard deviation of returns (i.e., the least volatility risk) and by far the best Sharpe ratio. In addition, Allocation B offers a balance of high current income and stability with moderate growth prospects.

Allocation A has the lowest standard deviation and best Sharpe ratio but does not meet the minimum return requirement when inflation is included in that requirement. Allocation A also has very low growth prospects.

Allocation C meets the minimum return requirement and has moderate growth prospects but has a higher risk level (standard deviation) and a lower Sharpe ratio, as well as less potential for stability, than Allocation B.

11. A. The Muellers' investment policy statement should include the following objectives and constraints.

i. *Return objective.* The Muellers' return objective should reflect a total return approach that combines capital appreciation and capital preservation. After retirement, they will need approximately $75,000 (adjusted for inflation) annually to maintain their current standard of living. Given the Muellers' limited needs and asset base, preserving their financial position on an inflation-adjusted basis may be a sufficient objective. Their long life expectancy and undetermined retirement needs, however, lead to the likely requirement for some asset growth over time, at least to counter any effects of inflation.

Although the Muellers wish to exclude the future trust distribution from their current planning, that distribution will substantially increase their capital base and dramatically alter the return objective of their future IPS, primarily by reducing their needed return level.

ii. *Risk tolerance.* The Muellers are in the middle stage of the investor life cycle. Their income (relative to expenses), total financial resources, and long time horizon give them the ability to assume at least an average, if not an above-average, level of investment risk. Their stated preference of "minimal volatility" investments, however, apparently indicates a below-average willingness to assume risk. The large realized losses they incurred in previous investments may contribute to their desire for safety. Also, their need for continuing cash outflow to meet their daughter's college expenses may temporarily and slightly reduce their risk-taking ability. In sum, the Muellers' risk tolerance is average.

Two other issues affect the Muellers' ability to take risk. First, the holding of Andrea's company stock represents a large percentage of the Mueller's total investable assets and thus is an important risk factor for their portfolio. Reducing the size of this holding or otherwise reducing the risk associated with a single large holding should be a priority for the Muellers. Second, the future trust distribution will substantially increase their capital base and thus increase their ability to assume risk.

iii. *Time horizon.* Overall, the Muellers' ages and long life expectancies indicate a long time horizon. They face a multistage horizon, however, because of their changing cash flow and resource circumstances. Their time horizon can be viewed as having three distinct stages: the next five years from now (some assets, negative cash flow because of their daughter's college expenses), the following five years (some assets, positive cash flow), and beyond 10 years (increased assets from a sizable trust distribution, decreased income because they plan to retire).

iv. *Liquidity.* The Muellers need $50,000 now to contribute to the college's endowment fund. Alternatively, they may be able to contribute $50,000 of Andrea's low-cost-basis stock to meet the endowment obligation. In addition, they expect the regular annual college expenses ($40,000) to exceed their normal annual savings ($25,000) by $15,000 for each of the next five years. This relatively low cash flow requirement of 2.7 percent ($15,000/$550,000 asset base after $50,000 contribution) can be substantially met through income generation from their portfolio, further reducing the need for sizable cash reserves. Once their daughter completes college, the Muellers' liquidity needs should be minimal until retirement because their income more than adequately covers their living expenses.

v. *Tax concerns.* The Muellers are subject to a 30 percent marginal tax rate for ordinary income and a 20 percent rate for realized capital gains. The difference in the rates makes investment returns in the form of capital gains preferable to equivalent amounts of taxable dividends and interest.

Although taxes on capital gains would normally be a concern to investors with low-cost-basis stock, this is not a major concern for the Muellers because they have a tax loss carryforward of $100,000. The Muellers can offset up to $100,000 in realized gains with the available tax loss carryforward without experiencing any cash outflow or any reduction in asset base.

vi. *Unique circumstances.* The large holding of the low-basis stock in Andrea's company, a "technology company with a highly uncertain future," is a key factor to be included in the evaluation of the risk level of the Muellers' portfolio and the future management of their assets. In particular, the family should systematically reduce the size of the investment in this single stock. Because of the existence of the tax loss carryforward, the stock position can be reduced by at least 50 percent (perhaps more depending on the exact cost basis of the stock) without reducing the asset base to pay a tax obligation.

In addition, the trust distribution in 10 years presents special circumstances for the Muellers, although they prefer to ignore these future assets in their current planning. The trust will provide significant assets to help meet their long-term return needs and objectives. Any long-term investment policy for the family must consider this circumstance, and any recommended investment strategy must be adjusted before the distribution takes place.

B. *Personal portfolio.* Portfolio A is the most appropriate portfolio for the Muellers. Because their pension income will not cover their annual expenditures, the shortfall will not likely be met by the return on their investments, so the 10 percent cash reserve is appropriate. As the portfolio is depleted over time, it may be prudent to allocate more than 10 percent to cash equivalents. The income deficit will be met each year by a combination of investment return and capital invasion.

Now that their daughter is financially independent, the Mueller's sole objective for their personal portfolio is to provide for their own living expenses. Their willingness and need to accept risk is fairly low. Clearly, there is no need to expose the Muellers to the possibility of a large loss. Also, their health situation has considerably shortened their time horizon. Therefore, a 70 percent allocation to intermediate-term high-grade fixed-income securities is warranted.

The income deficit will rise each year as the Muellers' expenses rise with inflation, but their pension income remains constant. The conservative 20 percent allocation to equities should provide diversification benefits and some protection against unanticipated inflation over the expected maximum 10-year time horizon.

Portfolio B, the second-best portfolio, has no cash reserves, so it could not meet the Muellers' liquidity needs. Also, although it has a higher expected return, Portfolio B's asset allocation results in a somewhat higher standard deviation of returns than Portfolio A.

Portfolios C and D offer higher expected returns but at markedly higher levels of risk and with relatively lower levels of current income. The Muellers' large income requirements and low risk tolerance preclude the use of Portfolios C and D.

C. *Trust distribution portfolio.* Portfolio B is the most appropriate for the trust assets. Portfolio B's expected return of 5.8 percent exceeds the required return of 5.4 percent, and the required return will actually decline if the surviving spouse lives longer than five years. The portfolio's time horizon is relatively short, ranging from a minimum of 5 years to a maximum of 10 years. The Muellers' sole objective for this money is to adequately fund the building addition. The portfolio's growth requirements are modest, and the Muellers have below-average willingness to accept risk. The portfolio would be unlikely to achieve its objective if large, even short-term losses were absorbed during the minimum five-year time horizon. Except for taxes, no principal or income disbursements are expected for at least five years; therefore, only a minimal or even zero cash reserve is required. Accordingly, an allocation of 40 percent to equities to provide some growth and 60 percent to intermediate-term fixed-income to provide stability and capital preservation is appropriate.

There is no second-best portfolio. Portfolio A's cash level is higher than necessary, and the portfolio's expected return is insufficient to achieve the $2.6 million value within the minimum value in five years. Portfolio C has a sufficient expected return, but it has a higher cash level than is necessary and, more importantly, a standard deviation of return that is too high given the Muellers' below-average risk tolerance. Portfolio D has a sufficient return and an appropriate cash level but a clearly excessive risk (standard deviation) level. Portfolios C and D share the flaw of having excessive equity allocations that fail to recognize the relatively short time horizon and that generate risk levels much higher than necessary or warranted.

12. A. To prepare an appropriate IPS, a manager should address the Smiths' return objective, risk tolerance, and constraints.

Return objective. To achieve its objectives, the Family Portfolio must provide for after-tax distributions equal to the difference between the Smiths' expenses and their fixed income payments. To maintain its real value, the portfolio must also grow at a rate that offsets inflation's impact on the Smiths' total expenses, including those currently covered by the fixed pension and Gift Fund payments.

A secondary objective is the gifting of $1 million to the Smiths' granddaughter. Because the Family Portfolio will be worth $1 million after the renovation of their house, the Smiths need no further capital growth to reach their nominal goal. To maintain its real value, the portfolio must have growth at least equal to the rate of inflation.

Risk tolerance. The Smiths are in a relatively late stage of the investor life cycle, and their comments suggest a conservative bias or below-average willingness to accept risk. In light of their long-term goals and current financial security, however, the Smiths have the ability to accommodate moderate portfolio volatility.

In the short term, the consequences of an adverse investment outcome are limited; the Smiths could use principal from the Family Portfolio to cover occasional performance shortfalls. They are thus able to accommodate some measure of short-term volatility in return for greater long-term expected returns. In extreme circumstances, the Smiths could modify or forgo their secondary objective of leaving $1 million to their granddaughter.

The consequences of an adverse portfolio outcome in the long term, however, could be serious. Depending on the length of their remaining lifetimes and the growth rate of their expenses, the Smiths could seriously deplete the corpus of the Family Portfolio and jeopardize their financial security.

The Smiths' comments imply that they have spent a lifetime saving and building a "safe" collection of income-oriented investments. Their desire to preserve market value and the WealthMax Financial Consultants (WFC) policy statement's emphasis on secure investments suggest that they may fall, at least partially, into the "cautious" category, a group with below-average risk tolerance.

Time horizon. The Family Portfolio should have an intermediate to slightly longer-term investment horizon.

The Smiths' joint life expectancy, at 65 years of age, is still substantial. Because their objective of financial security is well provided for in the short term (see discussion of risk tolerance), the Smiths can afford to focus more on the long-term aspects of that objective.

To the extent that the Smiths emphasize the objective of leaving $1 million to their granddaughter in their planning, a longer-term time horizon would be warranted.

Liquidity requirements. The Smiths' current annual living costs ($150,000 after taxes) are being met, which allows them to address longer-term growth objectives. The Smiths must plan for the upcoming expense of renovating their home. Their Family Portfolio should anticipate the renovation costs by holding a reserve of at least $200,000 in highly liquid, short-term funds

Laws and regulations. No special legal or regulatory problems are apparent.

Tax concerns. The Smiths must pay a higher tax on dividends and interest than on capital gains. All else being equal, therefore, they prefer portfolio returns in the form of capital gains rather than equivalent amounts of taxable investment income.

Unique circumstances. Establishment of the Gift Fund has increased the Smiths' dependence on fixed payments. As a consequence of this increased exposure to the eroding effects of inflation, the Smith's long-term financial security is significantly reduced.

Synopsis: The Smiths may not fully appreciate the impact of inflation and taxes on their financial security. The Family Portfolio can meet their immediate needs, but it is unlikely to grow at the same rate as disbursements. Depending on how long the Smiths live, the secondary objective of giving $1 million to their granddaughter may not be fully attainable, even in nominal terms.

B. Rather than a true policy statement, the WFC statement is a compendium of opinions and assertions that may or may not be supportable by evidence and may or may not be appropriate to the Smiths' specific situation. WFC's statement fails to:

- Identify specific return requirement.
- Consider inflation.
- Consider the Smiths' willingness and ability to accept risk.
- Consider the Smiths' investment time horizon.
- Specify the Smiths' liquidity requirements.
- Address the possibility of legal and regulatory constraints.
- Consider tax concerns.
- Consider possible unique circumstances.

C. i. Portfolio B is an appropriate recommendation based on three portfolio characteristics other than expected return and yield: diversification, efficiency (Sharpe ratio), and risk.

- Diversification across asset classes contributes to portfolio efficiency and is a desirable portfolio characteristic. Portfolio B appears to be the most broadly diversified.
- Efficiency, as measured by return for each unit of risk (Sharpe ratio), is a desirable portfolio characteristic. Portfolio B dominates the other portfolios on this criterion.
- Risk is an attribute that must be constrained to fit the Smiths' fiscal and psychological tolerance levels. The 85 percent allocation to equities and venture capital in Portfolio C entails relatively high risk. Portfolio B, which is more balanced between fixed-income and equity markets, is better suited to the Smiths' below-average risk profile.

ii. Meeting the Smiths' return objectives in the first year will require an after-tax total return of 7.5 percent on the $1 million remaining in the Family Portfolio after their house renovation. The Family Portfolio must accommodate a disbursement of $45,000 and grow at a rate that offsets the impact of inflation:

Expenses		($150,000)
Sources of funds		
Pension (after tax)	65,000	
Gift Fund (after tax)	40,000	105,000
Family Portfolio disbursement (after tax)		45,000
		$150,000

Required return	
Disbursement ($45,000)	4.50%
Inflation	3.00%
Total	7.50%

Subsequent distributions from the Family Portfolio will increase at a rate substantially higher than inflation (to offset the lack of growth in $105,000 of fixed pension and Gift Fund payments):

	Year 1	**Year 2**	**Change**
Expenses (3% growth)	$150,000	$154,500	3%
Portfolio distribution	$ 45,000	$ 49,500	10%

Portfolios B and C both have expected returns that meet the Smiths' projected disbursements in Year 1. Portfolio C's expected return is closer to that necessary to meet their objective over a longer time frame. However, Portfolio C's level of risk is too high given the Smiths' risk tolerance. Although Portfolio C should allow the Smiths to both fund their lifetime real income needs and leave $1 million to their grandchild, the risk in Portfolio C may endanger both their income and the bequest.

The Smiths' adviser should select Portfolio B based on its appropriate risk level and conformity with the Smiths' constraints. As a consequence of Portfolio B's probable inability to meet the Smiths' long-term spending needs, however, principal invasion may be necessary, and the secondary objective of giving $1 million, even in nominal terms, to their granddaughter may be forfeited.

13. A. i. The Maclins' overall risk objective must consider both willingness and ability to take risk:

Willingness. The Maclins have a below-average willingness to take risk, based on their unhappiness with the portfolio volatility they have experienced in recent years and their desire not to experience a loss in portfolio value in excess of 12 percent in any one year.

Ability. The Maclins have an average ability to take risk. Although their fairly large asset base and long time horizon in isolation would suggest an above-average ability to take risk, their living expenses of £74,000 are significantly higher than Christopher's after-tax salary of £80,000 (1 − 0.40) = £48,000 causing them to be very dependent on projected portfolio returns to cover the difference and thereby reducing their ability to take risk.

Overall. The Maclins' overall risk tolerance is below average, as their below-average willingness to take risk dominates their average ability to take risk in determining their overall risk tolerance.

ii. The Maclins' return objective is to grow the portfolio to meet their educational and retirement needs as well as to provide for ongoing net expenses. The Maclins will require annual after-tax cash flows of £26,000 (calculated below) to cover ongoing net expenses and will need £2 million in 18 years to fund their children's education and their retirement. To meet this objective, the Maclins' pretax required return is 7.38 percent which is determined below.

The after-tax return required to accumulate £2 million in 18 years beginning with an investable asset base of £1,235,000 (calculated below) and with annual outflows of £26,000 is 4.427 percent, which when adjusted for the 40 percent tax rate, results in a 7.38 percent pretax return (4.427%/(1 − 0.40) = 7.38%).

Christopher's annual salary	£80,000
Less: taxes (40%)	−32,000
Living expenses	−74,000
Net annual cash flow	−£26,000
Inheritance	900,000
Barnett Co. common stock	220,000
Stocks and bonds	160,000
Cash	5,000
Subtotal	£1,285,000
Less one-time needs:	
Down payment on house	−30,000
Charitable donation	−20,000
Investable asset base	£1,235,000

Note: No inflation adjustment is required in the return calculation because increases in living expenses will be offset by increases in Christopher's salary.

B. The Maclins' investment policy statement should include the following constraints:

i. *Time horizon.* The Maclins have a two-stage time horizon, because of their changing cash flow and resource needs. The first stage is the next 18 years. The second stage begins with their retirement and the university education years for their children.

ii. *Liquidity requirements.* The Maclins have one-time immediate expenses totaling £50,000 that include the deposit on the house they are purchasing and the charitable donation in honor of Louise's father.

iii. *Tax concerns.* A 40 percent tax rate applies to both ordinary income and capital gains.

iv. *Unique circumstances.* The large holding of the Barnett Co. common stock represents almost 18 percent of the Maclins' investable asset base. The concentrated holding in Barnett Co. stock is a key risk factor of the Maclins' portfolio and achieving better diversification will be a factor in the future management of the Maclins' assets.

The Maclins' desire not to invest in alcohol and tobacco stocks is another constraint on investment.

CHAPTER 3

MANAGING INSTITUTIONAL INVESTOR PORTFOLIOS

SOLUTIONS

1. Worden Technology, Inc.

   IPS Y and IPS X offer different components that are appropriate for Worden Technology's pension plan:

   i. *Return requirement.* IPS Y has the appropriate return requirement for Worden's pension plan. Because the plan is currently underfunded, the manager's primary objective should be to make it financially stronger. The risk inherent in attempting to maximize total returns would be inappropriate.
   ii. *Risk tolerance.* IPS Y has the appropriate risk tolerance for Worden's plan. Because of its underfunded status, the plan has a limited risk tolerance; a substantial loss in the fund could further jeopardize payments to beneficiaries.
   iii. *Time horizon.* IPS Y has the appropriate time horizon for Worden's plan. Although going-concern pension plans usually have long time horizons, the Worden plan has a comparatively short time horizon because of the company's reduced retirement age and relatively high median age of its workforce.
   iv. *Liquidity.* IPS X has the appropriate liquidity constraint for Worden's plan. Because of the early retirement feature starting next month and the age of the workforce (which indicates an increasing number of retirees in the near future), the plan needs a moderate level of liquidity to fund monthly payments.

2. LightSpeed Connections

   A. i. Concentrating LSC's pension assets as Donovan has done subjects the plan beneficiaries to an extraordinarily high level of risk because of the high correlation between the market values of the portfolio and LSC's business results.
      ii. By concentrating the pension assets heavily in technology and Internet companies, Donovan has increased the company's risk as the pension plan's sponsor. LightSpeed now faces the prospect of having to provide additional funding to the pension plan at a time when the company's own cash flow and/or earnings position may be weakened. A more prudent approach would be to invest in assets expected to be less highly correlated with the company's market value, so in the event additional

funding for the pension plan becomes necessary, it will be less likely to occur when LSC is in a weakened financial position.

B. i. The IPS drafted by Jeffries and the investment committee correctly identifies that the return requirement should be total return, with a need for inflation protection that is sufficient to fund the plan's long-term obligations. The IPS is weak in that it neglects to state a specific return requirement.

ii. The IPS fails to address the pension plan's risk tolerance, one of the two main objectives of a complete investment policy statement. Consequently, the IPS does not provide the guidance on risk tolerance that would highlight the potential risk to the beneficiaries and the company of LSC's current aggressive investment strategy.

iii. The IPS correctly addresses the time horizon constraint by stating that the assets are long-term in nature, both because of LSC's young workforce and the normal long-term nature of pension investing.

iv. The IPS fails to address the liquidity constraint; although liquidity is a minimal concern in this case, the IPS should nonetheless address that fact.

3. Gwartney International

A. The amount of surplus will decline when the present value of plan liabilities rises faster than the market value of the assets. According to the information provided, GI's liabilities have a duration of 10 years, the same as U.S. long-term bonds which returned a total of 19 percent for the previous year (7 percent income, 12 percent from capital gains associated with a decline in interest rates for the period). The decline in interest rates for long-term bonds translates into a lower discount rate for the plan's liabilities. The 12 percent gain in bonds implies that the plan's liabilities would have increased by the same amount. The combination of a 12 percent gain in liabilities and a 10 percent return on assets resulted in a decrease in the pension plan's surplus.

B. Investment time horizon is a primary determinant of an investor's risk tolerance. GI has a young workforce with many years until retirement, indicating a long time horizon. GI should thus adopt a long investment horizon, allowing investment in higher-risk, higher-expected-return asset classes.

C. The plan's risk tolerance embodies the plan sponsor's ability and willingness to absorb the consequences of adverse investment outcomes and/or prolonged subpar investment performance (i.e., its sensitivity to the possibility of being required to increase contributions at unpredictable times and intervals). The less risk an investor can tolerate, the less return will be achieved in the long run.

GI is financially healthy and growing. Given its financial health, the company has the ability to increase contributions when necessary. Because of GI's young workforce, the pension plan has a long time horizon, allowing for investment in riskier assets. The plan is also currently fully funded, and GI is financially strong. All these considerations point to GI having an above-average risk tolerance.

4. Food Processors Inc. (FPI)

A. In the United States, every Employee Retirement Income Security Act (ERISA)-qualified defined-benefit pension plan has a projected benefit obligation, which represents the discounted present value of the retirement benefits that the plan is obligated by law to make, given certain assumptions about future rates of pay and workforce factors. If the plan assets at fair market value exceed the projected benefit obligation (PBO), the plan is said to be overfunded. Conversely, if the value of the plan assets falls short of the PBO, the plan is said to be underfunded. Given that FPI's plan is underfunded by $200 million and its assets total $750 million, its PBO must be $950 million.

B. FPI faces a dilemma. On the one hand, it needs to improve returns in order to "catch up" on its underfunding; this necessity implies that more risk should be taken. On the other hand, FPI cannot afford to have the underfunding become worse, which it would if FPI incurs more risk that does not produce higher returns in the short run. Alternatively, the company might be tempted, as the chair suggests, to raise the actuarial assumption of what future return levels will be, thereby making the asset base automatically more productive simply by declaring it to be so. Future returns, however, are generated not by actuaries or other individuals but by markets, by asset-class exposures within markets, and by long-term relationships between economic and market factors—all taking place in the context of funding, allocation, and payout decisions unique to FPI's pension plan.

Of primary importance is that the return expected must be consistent with the return the various alternative investment instruments available to the plan can reasonably offer in the long term.

C. A U.S. pension plan's discount rate is the rate applied in determining the present value of its pension obligations. Because pension liabilities are typically long term, the discount rate should bear some rational relationship to the long-term interest rates in the marketplace at the time of the calculation. The usual model for the discount rate is the rate at which high-quality, long-term bonds such as the long Treasury bond are quoted, reflecting consensus expectations of long-run inflation plus a real rate of return. Thus, a manager may decide to reduce the discount rate based on capital market conditions reflecting a decline in long-term interest rates, as seen in Exhibit 3-4. Based on the consensus forecasts for long-term Treasury bonds and inflation shown in Exhibit 3-4, a discount rate of 6 to 7 percent would be reasonable. FPI is currently using an 8 percent discount rate, which is out of line with current capital market conditions. FPI should thus consider adopting a lower discount rate.

D. Reducing the discount rate applied to FPI's PBO would have the effect of increasing the present value of FPI's pension benefit obligations. Because the market value of the assets available to liquidate this obligation remains unchanged, the underfunded situation would be made worse by a reduction in the discount rate. The size of the gap between the PBO and the value of the assets, now $200 million, would increase.

5. Medical Research Foundation

A. Key elements that should determine the foundation's grant-making (spending) policy are as follows:

- Average expected inflation over a long horizon.
- Average expected nominal return on the endowment portfolio over the same long horizon.
- The 5 percent of asset value payout requirement imposed by the tax authorities as a condition for ongoing tax exemption.

To preserve the real value of its assets and to maintain its spending in real terms, the foundation cannot pay out more, on average over time, than the average real return it earns from its portfolio net of investment management expenses. The portion of the total return representing the inflation rate must be retained and reinvested if the foundation's principal is to grow with inflation. Because of the minimum 5 percent spending policy mandated by tax considerations, the real return of the portfolio will have to equal or exceed 5 percent plus the cost of earning investment returns in order to preserve the foundation's tax-exempt status and maintain its real value of principal and future payouts.

B. The new IPS should include the following components:

- *Return objective.* A total return approach is recommended to meet the foundation's objective of maintaining real value after grants. The required annual return shall be the sum of the spending rate plus the expected inflation rate.[1]
- *Risk tolerance.* The adoption of a clear-cut spending policy will permit cash flows to be planned with some precision, adding stability to annual budgeting and reducing the need for liquidity. Based on its long time horizon, low liquidity needs, and (now) ample assets, the foundation's risk tolerance is above average.
- *Liquidity requirements.* Based on asset size and the predictable nature of cash payouts, liquidity needs are low.
- *Time horizon.* The Foundation, with an unlimited lifespan, has a very long time horizon.
- *Tax considerations.* The foundation is tax-exempt under present U.S. law as long as the annual minimum payout of 5 percent is met.
- *Legal and regulatory constraints.* The foundation is governed by the Uniform Management of Institutional Funds Act (UMIFA) as well as IRS regulations.
- *Unique circumstances.* None apply, other than those previously discussed.

6. James Children's Hospital

A. The current spending request of \$1.6 million represents \$1.6 million/\$20million = 0.08 or 8 percent of the value of the endowment. This level of spending is high given the endowment's long-term expected total return of 8.6 percent per year (in nominal terms) and expected 4 percent inflation rate for medical equipment prices. If such spending is permitted, the current beneficiaries of the JCHE (for example, the patients of JCH) may receive benefits at the expense of future beneficiaries, because the endowment is unlikely to be able to maintain its value in inflation-adjusted terms.

B. JCHE has a perpetual time horizon; it can thus tolerate a higher risk level (in terms of volatility of returns) than a fund with a shorter time horizon. The higher risk tolerance results from the longer period available to make up for any market downturns. With a higher risk tolerance, JCHE can target a higher expected return.

C. JCHE's long-term spending policy should balance the needs of current and future beneficiaries. Its spending policy should balance income needs and the need to build the payout stream to preserve purchasing power. JCHE balances these conflicting objectives only when future beneficiaries receive the same inflation-adjusted distribution that current beneficiaries receive. With zero real growth, intergenerational neutrality exists. Because market returns are variable, JCHE should use a smoothing mechanism that will apply the spending rate to a moving average of market value:

[1]This additive return objective is easy to understand; as discussed in the text, a multiplicative return objective would be more precise.

Expected total return	8.6%
− Inflation	−4.0
Real expected return	4.6
− Spending rate	−4.6
Expected real growth	0.0%
Recommended spending rate	4.6%

7. Donner Life Insurance

Leighton made both incorrect and correct statements about life insurance and endowment portfolios:

1. *Both endowments and life insurance companies have aggressive return requirements* is an inaccurate statement. The return requirements of life insurance companies are first and foremost liability driven, matching assets with fixed obligations, and must be consistent with their conservative stance toward risk. Life insurance companies' return requirements also include as an objective the earning of a competitive return on the assets that fund surplus.

   The return requirements of endowments, although subject to a range of risk tolerances, are driven by the endowment's spending rate, the need to preserve purchasing power, and the need to provide a growing financial contribution to the endowed organization.
2. *Endowments are less willing to assume risk than life insurance companies because of donor concerns about volatility and loss of principal* is an inaccurate statement. Life insurance companies tend to have a lower tolerance for risk than endowments do. Confidence in a life insurance company's ability to pay its benefits (obligations) as they come due is a crucial element in the industry's financial viability. Life insurance companies thus are sensitive to the risk of any significant chance of principal loss or any significant interruption of investment income.

   Endowments, by contrast, tend to have a higher tolerance for risk. Their long-term time horizons and predictable cash flows, relative to their spending rate requirements, enable them to pursue more aggressive strategies than life companies can.
3. *Endowments are less able to assume risk than life insurance companies because of expectations that endowments should provide stable funding for charitable operations* is an inaccurate statement. Life insurance companies' ability to assume risk is circumscribed by their need to ensure the funding of liabilities to policyholders. The asset/liability management (ALM) focus of life insurance companies typically requires major holdings of bonds to offset the interest-sensitive nature of most life insurance liabilities. Regulations, including risk-based capital requirements, generally constrain the ability of life insurance companies to invest in higher risk assets.

   In contrast, the main risk facing an endowment is loss of purchasing power over time. Endowments have very long time horizons and are not focused on funding liabilities. Therefore, endowments should be able to accept higher volatility than life insurance companies in the short term to maximize long-term total returns.
4. *Endowments have lower liquidity requirements than life insurance companies because endowment spending needs are met through a combination of current income and capital appreciation* is an accurate statement. Life insurance companies face the need for liquidity as a key investment constraint, because life insurance products are promises to pay money depending on certain expected or unexpected events.

Endowments typically have low liquidity needs, except to fund periodic distributions and to cover emergency needs. Distributions are usually foreseeable and can usually be met from a combination of investment income and the sale of readily marketable securities.

5. *Both endowments and life insurance companies are subject to stringent legal and regulatory oversight* is an inaccurate statement. Life insurance companies are subject to relatively rigorous legal and/or regulatory oversight with respect to their portfolio composition and investment strategies.

   In contrast, endowments are relatively unburdened with legal and/or regulatory restraints, at least at the federal level in the United States, although some states do have specific rules and regulations regarding management of endowment assets.

8. Hannibal Insurance Company

   A. The investment strategy of Hannibal Insurance Company is inappropriate, because the company is ignoring interest rate risk and the strategy threatens both the surplus and policyholder reserves.

      Hannibal's investment strategy has three key negative consequences. First, the company faces major interest rate risk, as evidenced by the duration mismatch. Second, a focus on short-duration products will accelerate the mismatch. Finally, the company has not generated sufficient reserves and surplus relative to liabilities, given the risks it faces; thus it is increasing its risk of insolvency.

      Given the interest rate sensitivity of many life insurance products, controlling interest rate risk is one of the most challenging tasks facing portfolio managers in the insurance industry. Although tolerance for interest rate risk, or level of mismatch, varies from company to company, duration mismatch can become an acute problem in periods of rising interest rates. Meeting the return objective of earning a significant spread is important, but assets and liabilities must be managed in a way that offsets the effects of changes in interest rates.

      Confidence in an insurance company's ability to meet its obligations is so vital to the company's survival that special care must be taken to avoid any significant losses of principal. Hannibal has taken on a substantial amount of interest rate risk in recent years. Continuing a spread-maximization strategy in the face of rising interest rates threatens the firm's financial stability.

      The mismatch must be corrected. Continuing along the path outlined by the chief financial officer (CFO) will magnify the interest rate risk, which the CFO is ignoring because of the "increasing popularity" of a short-duration product. As the duration of the assets is held steady through the CFO's urging to invest in higher-yielding, longer-duration bonds, the duration of the liabilities will shrink. The CFO is focusing on a spread-maximization strategy and mistakenly relying on investment-grade securities to provide policyholder security. The real danger lies in another direction—namely, the potential forced sale of assets, with sizable losses resulting from interest rate increases, to pay off short-duration liabilities.

      The company has a relatively small surplus portfolio. Surplus is an indicator of an insurance company's financial health and is vital to expansion of the business. If interest rates continue to rise as expected, the market value of the portfolio assets will decline, which may wipe out the surplus and a portion of policyholder reserves. With the company unable to expand or meet its obligations, its viability becomes questionable.

   B. Two additional factors that affect liability duration for a life insurance company are (1) the duration of products sold and (2) policy surrenders and/or loans.

- The *duration of products sold* is a main driving force influencing the overall duration of liabilities. The extent to which a company directs marketing efforts toward short- or long-duration products will tilt overall duration. In this case, the company is placing a heavy emphasis on a two-year guaranteed investment contract product. The duration of this product will be much shorter than that of the overall portfolio. Management indicates that this product is popular, with sales increasing in recent years. This increase, all else being equal, will contribute to a decline in the duration of liabilities.
- Duration of liabilities is also driven by *policy surrender and/or loans*, either of which can be triggered by interest rate changes. Surrender rates triggered by interest rate changes are more difficult to predict than mortality rates and have become a critical variable for many life insurance companies. During periods of rising interest rates, policyholder redemptions accelerate as policyholders seek the most competitive rate. Such behavior would be typical in an environment in which "interest rates are rising and are expected to rise another 100 basis points." Accelerating surrenders could also influence an actuary to reduce the assumed duration of a company's liabilities.

C. Because of the varied features in life and annuity contracts, most life insurance companies segment their portfolios to group liabilities with similar interest-rate-sensitivity characteristics. Portfolios are then constructed by segment in such a way that the most appropriate securities fund each product segment. This practice also recognizes that particular product lines have unique time horizons and return objectives and should be managed accordingly.

Segmentation would be appropriate at Hannibal because of the problems arising from the popularity of a short-duration product. The portfolio manager could construct a portfolio targeted to the liabilities created by this product. Three arguments for the segmentation approach could be chosen from the following: Segmentation:

- Aids in managing liabilities of similar characteristics.
- Assists in the selection of the most appropriate assets to fund product segments (liabilities).
- Aids in the management and/or measurement of interest rate risk and duration mismatch by product line.
- Provides a framework for meeting return objectives by product line.
- Provides for accurate measurement of the profitability of product lines and/or manager performance.
- Provides for the allocation of investment income by line of business.
- Provides for the measurement of risk-adjusted returns.
- Facilitates accountability and allays regulatory concerns.

D. The focus of the return requirement for policyholder reserves is on earning a competitive return on the assets used to fund estimated liabilities. Life insurance companies are considered spread managers, in that they manage the difference between the return earned on investments and the return credited to policyholders. Spread management can take various forms, such as a yield approach versus a total-return approach, but the objective remains the same.

The focus of the return requirement for the surplus is on long-term growth. An expanding surplus is an important indicator of financial stability and the base for building the lines of business. When selecting investments for the surplus portfolio, managers typically seek assets with the potential for capital appreciation, such as common stocks, venture capital, and equity real estate.

9. A. Because the loan portfolio is now subject to greater interest rate risk although overall risk tolerance has not changed, the target maturity of the securities portfolio must be reduced to offset the loan portfolio's greater risk.
   B. Winthrop Bank should have more leeway to invest in below-investment-quality debt in its bond portfolio as a result.
   C. Winthrop's decision decreases the need for liquidity in its securities portfolio.
   D. The development suggests taking less risk in its securities portfolio.

CHAPTER 4

CAPITAL MARKET EXPECTATIONS

SOLUTIONS

1. The chief point is that extending the data series further back in time increases the risk of using data representing more than one regime. The analyst also needs to be aware of adjustments or revisions to the data, which can create inconsistencies in the data and make interpretation of those data difficult. The analyst must be sure that any adjustments to the data were made on a consistent and uniform basis. Furthermore, the analyst needs to be aware that variable definitions and calculation methods may have changed over the original and extended periods.
2. Drawing an inference that current sales expectations might be muted due to the weak sales numbers posted over the past several years is an example of the *status quo trap*. An objective assessment of early sales figures, surveys of shoppers, and collecting data about retail order patterns and shipments represent more unbiased bases for a year-end sales forecast.

   The *confirming evidence trap* was evident when Bildownes used the recent observation of the number of customers in a single department store as further support of his forecast for weak year-end retail sales. To help prevent this bias, an analyst could undertake more observations and then honestly and independently assess them with equal rigor before drawing a conclusion.

   Bildownes also seemed to be strongly influenced by his memory of previous weak year-end sales periods being associated with low pedestrian traffic during early December 1990. In assuming that a correlation witnessed in the past will repeat again without further analysis, Bildownes has fallen into the *recallability trap*. To counter this forecast-tainting bias, Bildownes should emphasize objective assessments of data, rather than personal memories, in forecasting.

   In drawing the conclusion that "there will be no overall year-over-year retail sales growth this holiday season," Bildownes has fallen into the *overconfidence trap*. This trap relates to the natural tendency for individuals to be overconfident about the accuracy of their forecasts. The easiest way to help prevent this trap from biasing a forecast is to admit the possibility that the forecast may be inaccurate and to increase the range of possible outcomes around the primary target outcome.

3. A.

	Real Risk-Free Rate	+	Expected Inflation	+	Spreads or Premiums	=	Expected Annual Fixed-Income Return
1-year U.S. T-note	1.2%	+	2.6%	+	0%	=	3.8%
10-year corp. bond	1.2%	+	2.6%	+	1.0% + 0.8% + 0.9%	=	6.5%
10-year MBS	1.2%	+	2.6%	+	0.95%	=	4.75%

Note: We assign the 10-year corporate a 1% maturity premium based on the 10-year over 1-year government spread.

Estimate of the expected return of an equal-weighted investment in the three securities: (3.8% + 6.5% + 4.75%)/3 = 5.02%.

B. The average spread at issue is [0 + (0.8% + 0.9%) + 0.95%]/3 = 0.88%. As 0.88 percent exceeds 0.5 percent, the investor will take an equally weighted position in the three securities. We exclude the 1 percent maturity premium for the 10-year corporate as the comparable is a 10-year T-bond also bearing the 1 percent maturity premium.

4. A. The historical equity risk premium is 0.7 percent, calculated as follows:

Historical Equity Returns	−	Historical 10-Year Government Bond Yield	=	Historical Equity Risk Premium
7.3%	−	6.6%	=	0.7%

B. The Grinold–Kroner model states that the expected return on equity is the sum of the expected income return (1.5%), the expected nominal earnings growth return (8.5% = 3.5% from inflation + 5.0% from real earnings growth), and the expected repricing return (−3.45%). The expected change in market valuation of −3.45% is calculated as the percentage change in the price-to-earnings ratio (P/E) level from the current 14.5x to the expected level of 14.0x: (14−14.5)/14.5 = −3.45%.

Thus, the expected return is 1.5% + 8.5% − 3.45% = 6.55%, or approximately 6.6%.

C. Using the results from Part B, the expected equity risk premium is 1.0 percent.

Expected Equity Return	−	Current 10-Year Government Bond Yield	=	Expected Equity Risk Premium
6.6%	−	5.6%	=	1.0%

5. A. Using the formula $RP_i = \sigma_i \rho_{iM} \left(\frac{RP_M}{\sigma_M}\right)$ we can solve for each expected industry risk premium. The term in brackets is the Sharpe ratio for the GIM, computed as 3.5/8.5 = 0.412.

i. $RP_{HealthCare} = (12)(0.7)(0.412) = 3.46\%$
ii. $RP_{Watch} = (6)(0.8)(0.412) = 1.98\%$
iii. $RP_{ConsumerProducts} = (7.5)(0.8)(0.412) = 2.47\%$

B. Based on the above analysis, the Swiss Health Care Industry would have the highest expected return. However, that return is expected compensation for systematic risk. We cannot conclude which industry is most attractive from a valuation standpoint.

6. A. The yield curve is inverting over the time period specified. This is an implicit forecast of an economic slowdown or a recession.

   B. Rolling over six-month Eurodollar securities would have provided superior results to rolling over one-month securities during the stated period. Extending the duration of the bond portfolio will be profitable when the yield curve subsequently flattens or inverts.

7. A. All of the measures in the table would lead an analyst to conclude that Brazil is currently experiencing an output gap. The economy, as measured by gross domestic product (GDP), has been contracting in each of the past two years. Thus, the economy has produced a higher level of output in the recent past. The unemployment rate has also been increasing steadily over the past two years and is quite high at over 10 percent. Thus, there is an ample supply of labor that could be put to work to increase economic output. Further, while the capacity utilization rate has been holding quite steady near 80 percent, it has declined from the reading posted two years ago. Thus, there is spare capacity that could be used to increase Brazil's economic output. Finally, the decline in inflation in the latest year confirms that there is an output gap. The decline in inflation is important because otherwise the economic slowdown could be from an extreme overheating position and might not have opened up an output gap as yet.

   B. Given the conclusion that Brazil is experiencing an output gap, an analyst would expect a further decline in the rate of inflation in the Brazilian economy in the next year.

8. The changes between Quarter 1 and Quarter 2 will be observed more clearly if we convert the economic measures from currency amounts into absolute percentage changes. The results are shown in the following table.

Economic Variable	Percentage Change: Qtr 1 to Qtr 2	
	Croatia	Czech Republic
Consumer spending	7.1%	10.3%
Business capital investment	8.3	22.0
Government investment/fiscal spending	10.0	27.3
Other miscellaneous GDP factors	100.0	91.4

Aggregate economic activity (including measures such as the components of GDP) is derived from many of the same factors from country to country. However, the proportion of economic activity derived from the multiple factors varies between economic regions and within a single region over time. Other issues that must be confronted when one analyzes across countries are the varying units of currency used and the differing levels of inflation between countries, which require an adjustment of some sort to be made before direct comparisons may be accomplished. Constant or inflation-adjusted measures may be used, and absolute currency measures may also be translated to a base currency to allow for direct comparisons. Alternatively, an analyst can examine the factors contributing to economic growth in proportion to an aggregate measure of activity such as GDP, as is shown in the following table.

Economic Variable	Absolute Currency Amounts Translated into Percentages of GDP			
	Croatia		Czech Republic	
	Qtr 1	Qtr 2	Qtr 1	Qtr 2
Consumer spending	57.1%	57.7%	57.7%	58.0%
Business capital investment	24.5	25.0	33.8	37.6
Government investment/fiscal spending	20.4	21.2	18.1	21.1
Other miscellaneous GDP factors	−2.0	−3.8	−9.6	−16.7

Finally, using the information in the two tables above allows one to analyze more clearly how meaningful the recent changes in economic output are to a specific economy. If we multiply the percentage change in GDP from Quarter 1 to Quarter 2 by the percentage of GDP that that factor represents in Quarter 2 to a particular economy, we can more clearly gauge the importance of the economic trends in the economic output data that we have collected.

Economic Variable	Percentage Change: Qtr 1 to Qtr 2 (weighted by each factor's GDP percentage)	
	Croatia	Czech Republic
Consumer spending	4.1%	6.0%
Business capital investment	2.1	8.3
Government investment/fiscal spending	2.1	5.8
Other miscellaneous GDP factors	−3.8	−15.3
Sum of weighted percentage change: Qtr 1 to Qtr 2	4.5	4.8

For example, the 7.1 percent increase in consumer spending in Croatia in Quarter 2 versus Quarter 1 is weighted quite heavily since the table above reflects that consumer spending represents about 57.7 percent of Croatia's total GDP as of the end of Quarter 2. Multiplying 7.1 percent by the 57.7 percent weighting that consumer spending represented to the Croatian economy produces a positive 4.1 percent weighted-average percentage change to the overall Croatian economy between Quarter 1 and Quarter 2. Here, we see the combined effect of underlying changes in each component of economic output and the relative importance of each component's change to overall economic output.

Analyzing the weighted percentage changes in the economic measures reflected in the table above shows that the Czech Republic would be expected to achieve a slightly higher economic growth rate relative to Croatia over the next year if current trends are sustained. However, the large and growing drag (negative absolute values) that other miscellaneous GDP factors are placing on the Czech economy should be explored further. This drag is probably due to factors such as a large amount of imports (relative to exports) of goods and supplies required to maintain the current robust pace of the economy.

9. A. The Taylor rule can be used to estimate the direction and magnitude of a short-term interest rate adjustment that could be made by central bank authorities. The calculation follows:

$$\begin{aligned} R_{optimal} &= R_{neutral} + [0.5 \times (GDPg_{forecast} - GDPg_{trend}) + 0.5 \times (I_{forecast} - I_{target})] \\ &= 4.0\% + [0.5 \times (2.6\% - 3.2\%) + 0.5 \times (4.0\% - 2.0\%)] \\ &= 4.70\% \end{aligned}$$

   B. The Taylor rule is a simple yet useful tool that an analyst can use to determine from macroeconomic factors when it might be appropriate for central bank authorities to push down short-term interest rates in order to monetarily stimulate an economy that is functioning below potential (i.e., has an output gap). Conversely, if an economy is operating above its long-term average rate (substantial growth) and there are signs of accelerating inflation or rising inflation expectations, the Taylor rule can signal the need for central bank authorities to raise the level of short-term interest rates so that economic activity and increasing inflation expectations may be mitigated.

   However, many other economic factors also affect aggregate output, inflation, and interest rates. Beyond economic factors, political and social factors come into the decision-making process when central bank authorities are setting interest rate targets. Central banks also typically take account of fiscal policies, wage behavior, asset prices, and developments in other economies. Periods of deflation would also call for more unorthodox central bank actions due to the fact that the central bank's ability to influence the economy is diminished once short-term interest rates approach zero during deflationary periods.

10. Comparing the broad economic output measures for Europe and the United States, the data show that both Europe and the United States have posted similar trends over the past few years and have had improving trends over the past year. The U.S. economy has posted higher absolute levels of GDP health care growth, which is expected to moderate over the next year. However, overall output and health care–related output are expected to continue to increase in Europe over the next year. Advantage: Europe.

    Recent consumer trends for Europe and the United States have also been quite correlated. However, the United States recently has registered higher absolute measures of overall consumer health care spending. Whereas this consumer impact is likely to be stable in the United States over the next year, Europe is expected to continue to show increased growth. Advantage: Europe.

    Regarding the economic impact of businesses, the United States posted better results than Europe over the past three years. However, over the past year, improving conditions have been seen for both regions. Currently, business profits have rebounded more in the United States. Thus, absolute economic measures look stronger in the United States than in Europe in the near term. However, over the next year, business-related economic impacts should be stronger in Europe. Advantage: Europe.

    Monetary authorities have been stimulative in both Europe and the United States over the past several years. However, the stimulation is expected to reverse in the United States over the next year, with short-term rates rising from 1 percent to 2.2 percent. Short-term rates are expected to rise only slightly over the next year in Europe. Thus, monetary policy will be a more neutral factor for both economies over the next year. The United States is expected to have lower overall interest rates and slightly lower inflation. Advantage: United States.

Fiscal policies for Europe and for the United States have been stimulative over the past few years but have been increasingly stimulative in the United States. Over the next year, the fiscal stimulation in the United States is expected to widen further in comparison to Europe. This trend is favorable to the United States as long as inflation is not an unexpected outcome of this fiscal stimulation and government borrowing caused by the fiscal stimulation does not crowd corporate borrowers out of the health care industry. Advantage: United States.

The higher average age of the aggregate general population in Europe relative to the United States is a positive factor for the health care industry from the perspective of Pharmavest. Advantage: Europe.

With more advantages pointing toward Europe's economies over the next year, Europe appears to be the economic region that should provide the stronger economic backdrop for the health care sector over the next year.

Matrix Summarization of Relative Advantages: Europe versus United States

	Recent Trends	Current Measures	1-Year Forecast
Broad economic measures	Similar (in Europe/U.S.)	Similar	Advantage: Europe
Impact of consumers	Similar	Similar	Advantage: Europe
Impact of businesses	Advantage: U.S.	Similar	Advantage: Europe
Impact of central bank	Similar	Similar	Advantage: U.S.
Impact of government	Similar	Advantage: Europe	Advantage: U.S.
Other/unique factors	Similar	Advantage: Europe	Advantage: Europe

11. To address the question, we first convert the data from the table into trend information (1-year, 3-year, and long-term 20-year trend information). The time periods are from the perspective of the end of 2004.

Trend Comparisons	1-Year Trend	3-Year Trend	20-Year Trend
GDP	2.5%	7.7% (2.5% compound average annual growth)	4.2%
Consumer spending	4.0	5.0 (1.6% compound average annual growth)	2.5
Business spending	2.7	11.8 (3.8% compound average annual growth)	2.6
Inflation	10.0	25.3 (7.8% compound average annual growth)	14.3
Govt spending (% of GDP)	−1.25	−2.5 (−0.8% compound average annual growth)	3.6

Based on the above comparisons, our conclusions about current trends witnessed over the past year for the Brazilian economy relative to longer-term 3-year and 20-year trends are reflected in the table below.

Trend Analysis	1-Year Trend	3-Year Trend	20-Year Trend
GDP	2.5%	1-year trend is the same as the average annual GDP growth 3-year trend of 2.5%.	1-year trend of GDP growth is weaker than the 20-year trends.
Consumer spending	4.0%	1-year trend is stronger than the average annual consumer spending growth 3-year trend of 1.6%.	1-year trend is stronger than the average annual consumer spending growth 20-year trend of 2.5%.
Business spending	2.7%	1-year trend is weaker than the average annual business spending growth 3-year trend of 3.9%.	1-year trend is stronger than the average annual business spending growth 20-year trend of 2.6%.
Inflation	10.0%	1-year trend is weaker (higher inflation) than the average annual inflation growth 3-year trend of 8.4%.	1-year trend is stronger (lower inflation) than the average annual inflation growth 20-year trend of 14.3%.
Govt spending (% of GDP)	−1.25%	1-year trend is weaker than the average annual govt spending growth 3-year trend of −0.8%.	1-year trend is weaker than the average annual govt spending growth 20-year trend of 3.6%.

12. A. Five elements of a pro-growth government structural policy are as follows:

- Fiscal policy is sound. Fiscal policy is sometimes used to control the business cycle.
- The public sector intrudes minimally on the private sector.
- Competition within the private sector is encouraged.
- Infrastructure and human capital development are supported.
- Tax policies are sound.

B. i. Declines in government tax receipts as a percent of GDP would be pro-growth because the equilibrium level of goods and services would increase. *Associated structural policy element: Tax policies are sound.*

ii. Declines in government tariff receipts would be pro-growth. Such declines would imply that government is fostering competition. By contrast, increases in tariff receipts would imply that government is protecting domestic businesses from international competition. *Associated structural policy element: Competition within the private sector is encouraged.*

iii. Increases in the number of publicly funded schools would be pro-growth because businesses stand to gain from a well-educated workforce. *Associated structural policy element: Infrastructure and human capital development are supported.*

iv. A negative net change in the number of state-owned businesses (that is, fewer such businesses) would be pro-growth. Such a change would increase the private sector's share of output, which would favor the efficient allocation of scarce resources. *Associated structural policy element: The public sector intrudes minimally on the private sector.*

v. A decrease in the long-term average budget deficit as a percent of GDP is pro-growth, because it would be a positive for controlling the current account deficit. *Associated structural policy element: Fiscal policy is sound.*

13. Four factors usually associated with emerging market economies are as follows:
    - Emerging market economies require high rates of investment, which is usually in short supply within the emerging economy itself. This situation creates a reliance on foreign capital. Areas of needed investment usually include both physical assets (capital equipment and infrastructure) and human capital (education and skills building).
    - Emerging economies typically have volatile political and social situations. Leaders usually acquire and maintain power using force and other less-than-democratic means. The social environment is usually strained by the fact that a large portion of the population possesses few assets, has little formal education, and is unable to generate income to feed/support family and neighbors.
    - To alleviate the first two factors above, organizations such as the IMF and World Bank provide conduits for external sources of investment and a means to push for structural reforms—political, social, educational, pro-growth, etc. The "conditions" usually prescribed by these institutions are often felt to be draconian.
    - Emerging countries typically have economies that are relatively small and undiversified. Those emerging economies that are dependent on oil imports are especially vulnerable in periods of rising energy prices and can become dependent on ongoing capital inflows.

14. The consumer-oriented aspect of the Australian economy (as measured by consumer orders) has been consistently strengthening over the past several months. The consumer measure had a negative reading in June, a slightly positive reading in July, and an even stronger August reading. From this information, we can state that the consumer-oriented aspect of the Australian economy appears to be improving.

    The business-oriented aspect of the Australian economy (as measured by business capital goods orders) has remained quite flat in the period reviewed. From this information, we can state that the business-oriented aspect of the Australian economy currently appears to be a positive contributor but is not necessarily showing signs of improvement or weakness. Thus, in recent months, the measure has been a stable but positive contributor.

    The central bank–oriented aspect of the Australian economy (as measured by central bank money supply) has also steadily improved over the period being analyzed.

    All of the leading indicator components have been positively contributing to the economy, and most have been contributing at an increasingly positive rate (all except business capital goods orders). These components are a sign of current economic activity and also typically create additional economic activity by their very nature. In addition, the total index of leading indicators, which includes all the components, has likewise moved upward steadily over the past few months. Thus, we can conclude from the measures in the table that the Australian economy should show continued growth over the next six to nine months.

15. Two factors that affect the yields available on inflation-indexed bonds (IIBs) are as follows:
    - Overall economic growth and its corresponding impact on real interest rates bear a direct impact on IIB yields. A growing economy places upward pressure on all bond yields. Though the impact may be muted due to the nature of the IIB structure, IIBs are not immune to interest rate risk.
    - Investor demand for bonds in general and for IIBs in particular has an inverse impact on IIB yields. As with non-IIBs, rising investor demand serves to drive interest rates lower and the lack of investor demand drives up the yields that issuers must pay in order to sell the bonds they need to issue.

16.

Index Data (South Korea)	Current Index Measure	Index 1-Year Forecast	South Korean Equity Market Impact	Corporate Fixed-Income Market Impact
GDP	159	173	Positive	Negative
Consumer spending	432	430	Negative	Positive
Business profits	115	100	Negative	Negative
Central bank money supply	396	455	Positive	Negative
Government spending relative to tax receipts	1,385	1,600	Positive	Negative

Justification:

GDP. A large 9 percent annual increase in GDP would give rise to strong corporate profits and would represent a favorable economic environment for equity investors (positive equity impact). However, such a strong economy would be a negative for corporate bond investors in that such economic growth and aggregate demand would place upward pressure on bond yields. In addition, in time, expectations of rising inflation could also hurt corporate bond investors (negative corporate bond impact).

Consumer spending. A slight decrease in consumer spending represents an economic drag on overall economic output. This drag serves to reduce real earnings growth (negative equity impact). A slight decrease in consumer spending will not place any upward pressure on corporate bond yields or inflation or generally impact a debt issuer's ability to pay back the bondholders (positive corporate bond impact).

Business profits. A 13 percent decline in business profits is a negative factor for both the equity market and the corporate bond market. Equity returns ultimately depend on businesses being able to earn a profit on the capital being employed. Thus, a steep decline in corporate profitability represents a negative equity impact. A severe decline in corporate profitability also increases the credit risk of corporate bondholders. Falling business profits can lead to corporate bond rating downgrades or insolvency (negative corporate bond impact).

Central bank money supply. A 15 percent increase in money supply represents central bank monetary stimulation. Such stimulation should foster stronger economic growth (positive equity impact). However, bond yields could be expected to increase because monetary stimulation may increase expectations for higher aggregate growth and because of the potential higher inflation that monetary stimulation can cause over time (negative corporate bond impact).

Government spending relative to tax receipts (government budget deficit spending): A large increase in government spending relative to tax receipts (fiscal budget deficit) also represents stimulation to the economy. This stimulation can create an attractive environment for increasing corporate profits (positive equity impact). However, bond yields could be expected to increase because fiscal stimulation may increase expectations for higher aggregate growth and because of the potential higher inflation that monetary stimulation can cause over time (negative corporate bond impact).

17. Four approaches to forecasting exchange rates are as follows:

    - PPP (or relative inflation rates), as exchange rate movements should offset inflation differentials.
    - Relative economic strength, because a strong pace of economic growth tends to attract investment.
    - Capital flows, as net inflows into a country, such as foreign direct investment, increase the demand for that country's currency.
    - Savings–investment imbalances, through their ultimate effect on the need for foreign savings.

18.

Observation	Canada	United Kingdom
Expected inflation over next year	2.0% ✓	3.0%
Real (inflation-adjusted) government 10-year bond rate	4.8%	5.1% ✓
Short-term (1-month) government rate	1.9%	5.0% ✓
Expected (forward-looking) GDP growth over next year	2.0%	3.3% ✓
New national laws have been passed that enable foreign direct investment in real estate/financial companies	Yes ✓	No
Government surplus (deficit)	3.0% ✓	−1.0%
Current account surplus (deficit)	8.0% ✓	−1.0%

A ✓ represents the comparatively stronger measure, where an analyst could expect to see a strengthening currency based on the factor being independently reviewed.

19. A. The Swiss price index has increased by $(150 - 100)/100 - 1.0 = 50\%$. The Fap price index has increased by $(140 - 100)/100 - 1.0 = 40\%$. The inflation differential is therefore 10 percent. According to PPP, to offset higher Swiss inflation, the fip should appreciate against the Swiss franc by approximately the same percentage to $0.90 \times$ (2.0 fips per 1 CHF) = 1.80 fips per 1 CHF.

    B. Contrasting the exchange rate of 1.8 fips per 1 CHF implied by PPP and the actual exchange rate of 2 fips per 1 CHF, we see that the fip is undervalued relative to its PPP value: At actual exchanges, more fips are required to purchase 1 CHF than PPP would predict.

CHAPTER 5

ASSET ALLOCATION

SOLUTIONS

1. A. The economic role of strategic asset allocation is to supply the investor's desired exposures to systematic risk. A single company's shares have substantial idiosyncratic or nonsystematic risk. By contrast, an indexed investment is a highly diversified portfolio with negligible nonsystematic risk. Representing an equity asset class with an indexed investment far better fulfills the purposes of strategic asset allocation.

   B. i. The more frequently RFM rebalances to its strategic asset allocation, the more important strategic asset allocation will appear in a time-series sense as in Brinson, Hood, and Beebower (1986).

   ii. If RFM chooses to index, the measured time-series importance of strategic asset allocation will increase, but it will decrease if RFM actively manages within asset classes, all else equal. This effect will occur because the percent of total variation explained by security selection will increase. Active management will also tend to decrease the measured cross-sectional importance of asset allocation.

   iii. By itself, choosing a policy portfolio that is distinct from peers' should not affect asset allocation's measured importance in a time-series sense. It will tend to differentiate RFM's returns from those of its peers, however, and tend to make asset allocation appear important in a cross-sectional sense.

   C. The institutional analyst is proposing a tactical asset allocation program because it involves making short-term adjustments to asset-class weights based on short-term expected relative performance differences between domestic and international equities. A problem with the TAA program is that the band of asset weights within which the proposed TAA would operate is too wide in relation to the permissible range for international equities determined by the Investment Policy Committee.

   D. A major concern of a DB pension plan is funding the pension liability. An ALM approach more directly and precisely addresses that concern than an asset-only approach to strategic asset allocation. A dynamic ALM approach considers the interperiod linkages of optimal investment decisions. By contrast, a static approach does not account for such linkages. A single-period mean–variance surplus optimization model is an example of a static ALM model. An advantage of a dynamic ALM approach is that it takes account of interperiod linkages; a disadvantage is that it is more costly and complex to implement than a static approach.

   E. Because the RFM pension liability can be modeled approximately as a short position in a long-term bond, the risk-minimizing strategic asset allocation is one 100 percent invested in long-term bonds.

2. Using Equation 5-1,

$$U_m = E(R_m) - 0.005R_A\sigma_m^2$$
$$= E(R_m) - 0.005(5)\sigma_m^2$$
$$= E(R_m) - 0.025\sigma_m^2$$

Therefore, for Allocation A, $U_A = E(R_A) - 0.025\sigma_A^2 = 11.5 - 0.025(18)^2 = 11.5 - 8.1 = 3.4$ percent; Allocation B, $U_B = E(R_B) - 0.025\sigma_B^2 = 8 - 0.025(14)^2 = 8 - 4.9 = 3.1$ percent; and for Allocation C, $U_C = E(R_C) - 0.025\sigma_C^2 = 6 - 0.025(10)^2 = 6 - 2.5 = 3.5$ percent.

Asset Allocation C appears best because it affords Lagland the highest risk-adjusted expected return.

3. We can use Roy's safety-first criterion with a return threshold (R_L) of 3.5 percent to decide which of the three allocations best meets the Garrett Foundation's objective. The asset allocation with the highest ratio $[E(R_P) - R_L]/\sigma_P$ is the one that minimizes the probability of not meeting the return threshold.

Allocation A: $0.444 = (11.5 - 3.5)/18$

Allocation B: $0.321 = (8 - 3.5)/14$

Allocation C: $0.250 = (6 - 3.5)/10$

Allocation A, with the largest ratio (0.444), is the foundation's best alternative according to Roy's safety-first criterion.

4. Because $(1.05)(1.024)(1.006) - 1 = 0.082$ or 8.2 percent, only Asset Allocation A with an expected return of 11.5 percent promises to satisfy Ernst's return requirement.
5. A. U.S. equities form a major part of world equities, so the specification does not meet the criterion that asset classes should be mutually exclusive. A possible additional criticism is that the asset classes may be nonhomogeneous. Narrower asset-class specifications may help control systematic risk.
   B. Alternative assets need to be subdivided further for asset allocation purposes because they are not homogeneous as a group. A further possible criticism is that the asset classes do not make up a preponderance of world wealth because Canadian markets are only a small fraction of world wealth (the text mentions that Canadian equity markets are one-tenth as large as U.S. equity markets).
   C. With the addition of U.S. fixed-income asset classes, this asset-class set should meet all the stated criteria. The specification between small- and large-cap stocks is frequently encountered because they are well differentiated; however, the argument could be made that mid-cap stocks should be added (or the limits of "small-cap" and "large-cap" defined to cover "mid-cap") to better cover investable wealth.
6. According to Equation 5-3, the new asset class's Sharpe ratio must exceed the quantity (Sharpe ratio of existing portfolio) × (Correlation of U.S real estate with the existing portfolio) $= 0.40(0.35) = 0.14$ for it to be optimal to add the new asset class. Thus, the foundation should add U.S. real estate if its predicted Sharpe ratio exceeds 0.14. Because the fund predicts a Sharpe ratio of 0.12 for U.S. real estate, the foundation should not add that asset class to the existing portfolio.
7. The relatively constant elements in the asset allocation process are the prediction procedure, the investor's risk tolerance function, and the optimizer. Most of the investor's expertise goes into formulating these stable elements. The prediction procedure represents

the investor's perception of best process for developing capital market expectations. The investor's risk tolerance function represents a quantification of his risk attitudes. The optimizer is the procedure for producing the best asset allocation. By contrast, the other elements of the process are inputs or outputs that are regularly revised.

8. The global minimum-variance portfolio has the smallest variance among all portfolios on the minimum-variance frontier. The concept is important in a mean–variance asset-only approach to asset allocation. By contrast, the minimum surplus variance portfolio concept is important in a mean–variance surplus optimization approach that focuses on surplus or net worth. The minimum surplus variance portfolio has minimum variance of surplus among all portfolios on the surplus efficient frontier.
9. A. Corner portfolios arise from a mean–variance optimization in which asset-class weights are constrained to be nonnegative. The global minimum variance portfolio is always included as a corner portfolio. Corner portfolios are minimum-variance portfolios in which an asset weight changes from zero to positive or from positive to zero along the minimum-variance frontier. The usefulness of corner portfolios comes from the fact that, although few in number, they can be used to find the composition of any minimum-variance portfolio.

   B. FRMC's return requirement is $(1.035)(1.0225)(1.00436) - 1.0 = 0.06290$ or 6.29 percent a year. This result contrasts to an additive return requirement of $3.5\% + 2.25\% + 0.436\% = 6.19\%$, which is lower.

   C. The highest Sharpe-ratio-efficient portfolio is close to Corner Portfolio 4. Corner Portfolio 4's expected return of 5.03 percent, however, does not satisfy FRMC's return objective of 6.29 percent. The efficient portfolio that just satisfies FRMC's return requirement must lie between Corner Portfolio 4 and Corner Portfolio 3, which has an expected return of 7.55 percent. The portfolio thus identified will have the highest Sharpe ratio among those efficient portfolios satisfying FRMC's return requirement.

   From the corner portfolio theorem, it follows that

$$6.29 = 7.55w + 5.03(1 - w)$$

   We find that the weight on Corner Portfolio 3 is $w = 0.500$ and the weight on Corner Portfolio 4 is $(1 - w) = 0.500$. Therefore,

   Weight of French equities $0.5(53.22\%) + 0.5(0.00\%) = 26.61\%$

   Weight of ex-France equities $0.5(37.23\%) + 0.5(24.70\%) = 30.97\%$

   Weight of French bonds $0.5(0\%) + 0.5(43.30\%) = 21.65\%$

   Weight of real estate $0.5(9.55\%) + 0.5(32.00\%) = 20.78\%$

   As an arithmetic check, $26.61\% + 30.97\% + 21.65\% + 20.78\% = 100\%$.

10. A. i. No. A conventional mean–variance efficient frontier is calculated using estimates of return distribution parameters. By assumption, the weights in Frontier B do not reflect estimation error, so the resulting efficient frontier must be superior to the conventional efficient frontier using estimates (in fact, it must be the best attainable). A frontier is superior to another frontier if it lies above it.

   ii. No. An efficient frontier reflecting the true return parameters must lie above the resampled efficient frontier. Resampled efficiency addresses estimation error by averaging portfolio weights across different simulations but cannot completely remove its impact.

B. The results of MVO, in particular the composition of efficient portfolios, are most sensitive to expected return inputs. As discussed in the text, estimation error in expected returns has been estimated to be roughly 10 times as important as estimation error in variances and 20 times as important as estimation in covariances.

11. A. The scatter of points in Exhibit 5–7 can be called a statistical equivalence region because these points represent possible efficient portfolios that could result from sampling based on the same underlying return parameters.

B. For each series of points, the numbering represents a rank order by mean return. The first point in the resampled efficient frontier is found by averaging the portfolio weights of assets in 1, 1′, and 1″; the second by averaging 2, 2′, and 2″; and so forth to the highest mean return resampled efficient portfolio (averaging the weights of 5, 5′, and 5″).

12. According to the Monte Carlo simulation the current asset allocation is not expected to satisfy Stevenson's requirement. The *y*-axis in Exhibit 5-8 is a logarithmic scale. Because $\log_{10}(630{,}000) = 5.8$ while $\log_{10}(100{,}000) = 5$ and $\log_{10}(1{,}000{,}000) = 6$, \$630,000 would be a point eight-tenths of the distance between the \$100,000 and \$1,000,000 hatch marks. Note that relevant line is the 10 percent one, because 90 percent of outcomes lie above it, and that in the year 2012 (10 years from 2002) the 10 percent line clearly is less than that "eight-tenths" point. Thus Stevenson cannot expect that portfolio value (in real dollars) to be at least \$630,000 with a probability of 90 percent at age 75.

13. A. We use Equation 5-4:

$$\begin{aligned} U_m^{\text{ALM}} &= E(SR_m) - 0.005R_A\sigma^2(SR_m) \\ &= E(SR_m) - 0.005(5)\sigma^2(SR_m) \\ &= E(SR_m) - 0.025\sigma^2(SR_m) \end{aligned}$$

For Allocation A,

$$U_A^{\text{ALM}} = E(SR_A) - 0.025\sigma^2(SR_A) = 6.5 - 0.025(14)^2 = 6.5 - 4.90 = 1.60$$

For Allocation B,

$$U_B^{\text{ALM}} = E(SR_B) - 0.025\sigma^2(SR_B) = 4.0 - 0.025(10)^2 = 4.0 - 2.50 = 1.50$$

For Allocation C,

$$U_C^{\text{ALM}} = E(SR_C) - 0.025\sigma^2(SR_C) = 0.0 - 0.025(2)^2 = 0.0 - 0.10 = -0.10$$

ILIC should prefer Asset Allocation A because it has the highest risk-adjusted expected return.

B. ILIC can use Monte Carlo simulation to obtain information concerning an asset allocation over time, as described in the text.

14. A. Long-term bond holdings are important for life insurers because of their asset/liability management (ALM) emphasis and the long-term nature of their liabilities. In contrast, individual investors do not have ALM concerns to the same degree, in general. As discussed in the text as well, because of the importance of human capital in relation to financial capital during youth, for many young investors equity investments will

be very large relative to fixed-income holdings. In conclusion, long-term bonds are generally more important in strategic asset allocation for life insurers than for young investors.

B. Banks are generally restricted by regulations in their holdings of common stock. Overall, common stock plays a minimal role in banks' securities portfolio. By contrast, because of human capital considerations mentioned in the solution to Part A, common stock investments tend to be very important for young investors (with the possible exception of those investors whose employment income is linked to equity market returns).

C. Because endowments are tax exempt, tax-exempt bonds play no role in their strategic asset allocation. In contrast, tax-exempt bonds sometimes play a substantive role for individual investors in high tax brackets, such as many midcareer professionals.

D. Private equity may play a role in the strategic asset allocation of substantial investors, both institutional and individual. A major foundation is much more likely to have the resources to research and invest in private companies than young investors and to play a role in strategic asset allocation.

15. A. At age 30, the closest Smith can get to his optimal 60/40 asset allocation is to invest 100 percent of his financial assets in stocks, a 100/0 stock/bond mix. Then his effective asset allocation for total wealth is $100,000/$2,200,000 = 4.55% stocks and 95.45% bonds.

B. At age 50, the closest Smith can get to his optimal 60/40 asset allocation is to invest 100 percent of his financial assets in stocks, 100/0 stock/bond mix. Then his effective asset allocation for total wealth is $900,000/$2,200,000 = 40.91% stocks and 59.09% bonds.

C. At age 65, Smith can attain his optimal 60/40 asset allocation by holding 0.60 × $2,200,000 = $1,320,000 in stocks for an asset allocation of $1,320,000/$2,000,000 = 66% stocks and 34% bonds, considering financial capital only.

D. At ages 30, 50, and 65, Smith's financial asset allocations were determined to be 100/0, 100/0, and 66/34, respectively. The results are consistent with the experience-based principle that for most individual investors, the allocation to stocks should be relatively large early in life and smaller later in life.

16. A. U.S. equities, and ex-U.S. equities represent respectively 30%/60% = 0.5 and 30%/60% = 0.5 of global equities. Therefore, for global equities,

$$A = (0.5 \times 8\%) + (0.5 \times 10\%) = 9\%$$

$$B = (0.5 \times 14\%) + (0.5 \times 10\%) = 12\%$$

Global equities' short-term expected return at 12 percent is above the long-term expectation of 9 percent because U.S. equities are expected in the short-term to outperform their long-term expected return.

U.S. bonds and ex-U.S. bonds represent respectively 30%/40% = 0.75 and 10%/40% = 0.25 of global fixed income. Therefore, for global fixed income,

$$C = (0.75 \times 6\%) + (0.25 \times 5\%) = 5.75\%$$

$$D = (0.75 \times 8\%) + (0.25 \times 4\%) = 7\%$$

Global fixed income's short-term expected return at 7 percent is above its long-term expectation of 5.75 percent. However within global fixed income U.S. bonds are expected short-term at 8 percent to outperform their long-term expected return while ex-U.S. bonds are expected short term at 4 percent to underperform their long-term expected return.

B. The results in Part A suggest three actions:

- In absolute terms, the global equities short-term expected return is 300 basis points above its expected long-term value of 9 percent; in relative terms, that is equivalent to a $12\%/9\% - 1.0 = 33\%$ higher expected return. For global fixed income, the absolute and relative expected return differences are 125 basis points and 22 percent, respectively. Because global equities appear more undervalued than global bonds, increase the weight on global equities from 60 percent and decrease the weight on global fixed income from 40 percent.
- Within global equities, overweight U.S. equities versus their target weight of 30 percent and decrease the weight on ex-U.S. equities from 30 percent. Although the short-term expected return on ex-U.S. equities is the same as the long-term expectation, U.S. equities are expected to outperform their long-term expected return by 600 basis points in the short term.
- Within the new global fixed-income allocation, overweight U.S. bonds and underweight ex-U.S. bonds, reflecting their short-term expected performance.

17. Portfolio C is the only appropriate choice. It is well diversified across all asset classes with minimal initial public offering (IPO)/technology exposure, and only 34 percent of the portfolio exposed to the riskier asset classes in total (IPO/tech, small-cap growth, and venture capital). IPO/Tech assets may be highly correlated with the plan sponsor's underlying business, thereby exposing both the company and the plan beneficiaries to excessive risk in the event of a sharp downturn in the company's business. Portfolio C has a Sharpe ratio higher than that of the current portfolio; Portfolio C's Sharpe ratio is lower than, but in line with, those of Portfolios A and B. Portfolio C is better diversified across asset classes and substantially less volatile. Finally, Portfolio C has minimal reserves, which is appropriate given the plan's long time horizon and minimal liquidity needs.
18. To avoid a repetition of last year's shrinkage in the plan's surplus, BI's board must consider both surplus management and the level of total return produced. As such, Donovan should recommend that the board consider Portfolio E. Portfolio E minimizes surplus volatility while meeting the board's expected return objective of 9 percent. Its absolute volatility is only slightly more than that of the current portfolio (which offers a lower rate of return) and equals that of Portfolio B (which offers a slightly higher expected return but also higher surplus volatility). Adopting Portfolio E would minimize surplus volatility without significantly increasing absolute risk or sacrificing expected return.
19. The real return from the recommended allocation should meet the minimum required return identified in the IPS. The allocation philosophy will reflect the Foundation's return objective, above-average risk tolerance, low liquidity requirements, and tax-exempt status. In general the portfolio allocation should include the following:

    - An allocation to fixed-income instruments of less than 50 percent, because real returns of bonds are forecasted to be lower than those of stocks. Bonds will be included primarily for diversification and risk reduction. The ongoing cash flow from the bond portfolio should easily provide for all normal working capital needs.
    - An allocation to equities greater than 50 percent. A number of factors support a high allocation to equities: historical and expected real returns are high, the horizon is long, risk tolerance is above average, and taxes are not a consideration.

- Within the equity universe, large-cap, small-cap, international stocks and venture capital should be considered. Diversifying within the equity universe will contribute to risk reduction, and total return could be enhanced.
- Real estate should be included in the portfolio as an alternative to stocks and bonds. It will provide diversification as well as inflation protection in the long term.

An example of an appropriate modestly aggressive allocation is shown below:

Asset Class	7-Year Forecast of Real Returns	Recommended Allocation	Real Return Contribution
Cash (U.S.):			
T-bills	0.7%	0%	–
Bonds			
Intermediate	2.3	5	0.115%
Long Treasury	4.2	10	0.420
Corporate	5.2	10	0.520
International	4.9	10	0.490
Stocks			
Large cap	5.5	30	1.650
Small cap	8.5	10	0.850
International	6.6	10	0.660
Venture capital	12.0	5	0.600
Real estate	5.0	10	0.500
Total expected real return		100%	5.805%

CHAPTER 6

FIXED-INCOME PORTFOLIO MANAGEMENT

SOLUTIONS

1. The tracking risk is the standard deviation of the active returns. For the data shown in the problem, the tracking risk is 19.728 bps, as shown below:

Period	Portfolio Return	Benchmark Return	Active Return	(AR – Avg. AR)^2
1	14.10%	13.70%	0.400%	0.00090%
2	8.20	8.00	0.200	0.00010
3	7.80	8.00	−0.200	0.00090
4	3.20	3.50	−0.300	0.00160
5	2.60	2.40	0.200	0.00010
6	3.30	3.00	0.300	0.00040
Average active return per period =				0.100%
Sum of the squared deviations =				0.00400%
Tracking risk (std. dev.) =				0.28284%

2. A. Equity = E = 40 percent of €5 million = €2 million

$$\text{Borrowed funds} = B = 60 \text{ percent of €5 million} = \text{€3 million}$$

$$k = \text{Cost of borrowed funds} = 4.6 \text{ percent per year}$$

$$= 4.6/12 \text{ or } 0.3833 \text{ percent per 30 days}$$

$$r_F = \text{Return on funds invested} = 0.5 \text{ percent}$$

Therefore,

$$R_E = \text{Return on equity} = r_F = 0.5 \text{ percent}$$

$$R_B = \text{Return on borrowed funds} = r_F - k = 0.5 - 0.3833 = 0.1167 \text{ percent}$$

B. R_P = Portfolio rate of return = (Profit on borrowed funds + Profit on equity)/ Amount of equity = $[B \times (r_F - k) + E \times r_F]/E$ = [€3 million × (0.5 − 0.3833) + €2 million × 0.5]/€2 million = 0.6750 percent

C. R_P = Portfolio rate of return = (Profit on borrowed funds + Profit on equity)/Amount of equity = $[B \times (r_F - k) + E \times r_F]/E$ = [€3 million × (0.3 − 0.3833) + €2 million × 0.3]/€2 million = 0.1751 percent

D. If the return on funds invested exceeds the cost of borrowing, then leverage magnifies the portfolio rate of return. This condition holds for the case in Part B, where the return on funds of 0.5 percent exceeds the cost of borrowing of 0.3833 percent, and therefore, the portfolio return (0.6750 percent) is greater than the return on funds.

If the return on funds invested is less than the cost of borrowing, then leverage is a drag on the portfolio rate of return. This condition holds for the case in Part C, where the return on funds of 0.3 percent is less than the cost of borrowing of 0.3833 percent, and therefore, the portfolio return (0.1751 percent) is less than the return on funds.

E. The bond dealer faces a credit risk even if he holds the collateral. The reason is that the value of the collateral may decline to such an extent that its market value falls below the amount lent. In such a situation, if the borrower defaults, the market value of the collateral will be insufficient to cover the amount lent.

3. The portfolio is more sensitive to changes in the spread because its spread duration is 3.151 compared with the benchmark's 2.834. The portfolio's higher spread duration is primarily a result of the portfolio's greater weight on agency securities. The spread duration for each can be calculated by taking a weighted average of the individual sectors' durations. Because there is a difference between the portfolio's and the benchmark's spread duration, the tracking risk will be higher than if the two were more closely matched.

	Portfolio			Benchmark		
Sector	% of Portfolio	Spread Duration	Contribution to Spread Duration	% of Portfolio	Spread Duration	Contribution to Spread Duration
Treasury	22.70	0.00	0.000	23.10	0.00	0
Agencies	12.20	4.56	0.556	6.54	4.41	0.288
Financial institutions	6.23	3.23	0.201	5.89	3.35	0.197
Industrials	14.12	11.04	1.559	14.33	10.63	1.523
Utilities	6.49	2.10	0.136	6.28	2.58	0.162
Non-U.S. credit	6.56	2.05	0.134	6.80	1.98	0.135
Mortgage	31.70	1.78	0.564	33.20	1.11	0.369
Asset backed	—	2.40	0.000	1.57	3.34	0.052
CMBS	—	5.60	0.000	2.29	4.67	0.107
Total	100.00		3.151	100.00		2.834

4. Dollar duration is a measure of the change in portfolio value for a 100 bps change in market yields. It is defined as

$$\text{Dollar duration} = \text{Duration} \times \text{Dollar value} \times 0.01$$

A. A portfolio's dollar duration is a weighted average of the dollar durations of the component securities. The dollar duration of this portfolio at the beginning of the period is $54,212, which is calculated as

$$\text{Portfolio Dollar Duration} = \frac{0.01}{3}[(1{,}060{,}531)(5.909) + (981{,}686)(3.691) + (1{,}090{,}797)(5.843)] = \$54{,}212.$$

or

Initial Values

Security	Price	Market Value	Duration	Dollar Duration
Bond 1	$106.110	$1,060,531	5.909	$62,667
Bond 2	98.200	981,686	3.691	36,234
Bond 3	109.140	1,090,797	5.843	63,735
		Portfolio Dollar Duration =		$54,212

At the end of one year, the portfolio's dollar duration has changed to $45,439, as shown below.

After 1 Year

Security	Price	Market Value	Duration	Dollar Duration
Bond 1	$104.240	$1,042,043	5.177	$53,947
Bond 2	98.084	980,461	2.817	27,620
Bond 3	106.931	1,068,319	5.125	54,751
		Portfolio Dollar Duration =		$45,439

B. The rebalancing ratio is a ratio of the original dollar duration to the new dollar duration:

$$\text{Rebalancing ratio} = \$54{,}212/\$45{,}439 = 1.193$$

C. The portfolio requires each position to be increased by 19.3 percent. The cash required for this rebalancing is calculated as:

$$\text{Cash required} = 0.193 \times (\$1{,}042{,}043 + 980{,}461 + 1{,}068{,}319) = \$596{,}529$$

5. A. Because you are considering bonds with embedded options, the returns of portfolios are unlikely to be normally distributed. Because shortfall risk is not based on normality assumption, however, it may be used as a risk measure. Furthermore, because the client has specified a minimum target return (£25,000/£2,000,000 or 1.25 percent over the next six months), shortfall risk could be a useful measure to look at.
   B. One of the shortcomings of shortfall risk is that it is not as commonly used as standard deviation, and there is relatively less familiarity with shortfall risk. Also, its statistical properties are not well known. Unlike VAR, it does not take the form of a dollar amount. Finally, the shortfall risk gives the probability of the returns from the

portfolio falling below the specified minimum target return, but it does not provide any information about the extent to which the return may be below the specified minimum target.

6. A. Because the fund desires to increase the duration, it would need to buy futures contracts.

   B. D_T = target duration for the portfolio = 10

   D_I = initial duration for the portfolio = 8.17

   P_I = initial market value of the portfolio = €75 million

   D_{CTD} = the duration of the cheapest-to-deliver bond = 9.35

   P_{CTD} = the price of the cheapest-to-deliver bond = €130,000

   Conversion factor for the cheapest-to-deliver bond = 1.06

   Approximate number of contracts

$$= \frac{(D_T - D_I)P_I}{D_{CTD}P_{CTD}} \times \text{Conversion factor for the CTD bond}$$

$$= \frac{(10.0 - 8.17) \times 75{,}000{,}000}{9.35 \times 130{,}000} \times 1.06 = 119.69.$$

   Thus, the pension fund would need to buy 119 futures contracts to achieve the desired increase in duration.

7. Covered call writing is a good strategy if the rates are not going to change much from their present level. The sale of the calls brings in premium income that provides partial protection in case rates increase. The additional income from writing calls can be used to offset declining prices. If rates fall, portfolio appreciation is limited because the short call position is a liability for the seller, and this liability increases as rates go down. Consequently, there is limited upside potential for the covered call writer. Overall, this drawback does not have negative consequences if rates do not change because the added income from the sale of calls would be obtained without sacrificing any gains. Thus, Consultant A, who suggested selling covered calls, probably believes that the interest rates would not change much in either direction.

   Doing nothing would be a good strategy for a bondholder if he believes that rates are going down. The bondholder could simply gain from the increasing bond prices. Thus, Consultant B, who suggested doing nothing, likely believes that the interest rates would go down.

   If one has no clear opinion about the interest rate outlook but would like to avoid risk, selling interest rate futures would be a good strategy. If interest rates were to decline, the loss in value of bonds would be offset by the gains from futures. Thus, Consultant C, who suggested selling interest rate futures, is likely the one who has no opinion.

   Paying the premium for buying the puts would not be a bad idea if a bondholder believes that interest rates are going to increase. Thus, Consultant D is likely the one who believes that the interest rates are headed upward.

8. The payoff to More Money Funds would be:

$$\text{Payoff} = (0.030 - \text{Credit spread at maturity}) \times \$10{,}000{,}000 \times 5$$

   A. Payoff = (0.030 − 0.025) × $10,000,000 × 5 = $ 250,000.
   B. Payoff = (0.030 − 0.035) × $10,000,000 × 5 = −$250,000, or a loss of $250,000.

C. The maximum gain would be in the unlikely event of credit spread at the forward contract maturity being zero. So, the best possible payoff is $(0.030 - 0.000) \times \$10{,}000{,}000 \times 5 = \$1{,}500{,}000$.

9. First, let us compute the amount in each of the three tranches in the CDO. The senior tranche is 70 percent of \$250 million = \$175 million. The junior tranche is 20 percent of \$250 million = \$50 million. The rest is the equity tranche = \$250 million − \$175 million − \$50 million = \$25 million.

   Now let us compute the amount that would be received by the equity tranche. Annual interest generated by the collateral would be $6 + 5 = 11$ percent of \$250 million = \$27.5 million. Annual interest received by the senior tranche would be $7.5 + 0.5 = 8$ percent of \$175 million = \$14 million. Annual interest received by the junior tranche would be $6 + 3 = 9$ percent of \$50 million = \$4.5 million. So, the amount to be received by the equity tranche is $27.5 - 14 - 4.5 = \$9$ million. This amount represents a return of $9/25 = 0.36$ or 36 percent.
10. The mispricing occurs because the forward rate doesn't conform to the covered interest rate parity theorem.

   A. The current discount rate is −2.48 percent [i.e., (\$1.18 − \$1.21)/\$1.21]
   B. The covered interest rate parity theorem states that the forward foreign exchange rate for a fixed period must be equal to the interest rate differentials between the two countries.

   $$\text{Forward rate} = \text{spot rate} \times (1 + \text{domestic interest rate})/(1 + \text{foreign interest rate})$$

   Substituting into the formula:

   $$\text{Forward rate} = \$1.21(1 + 0.02)/(1 + 0.03)$$

   $$\text{Forward rate} = \$1.198$$

11. The investor can evaluate the change in value of the Canadian bond if U.S. rates change by 80 bps as follows:

   $$\Delta \text{ in value of Canadian bond} = \text{Canadian bond's duration} \times \text{Canada country beta} \times \Delta \text{ in U.S. rates}$$

   $$\Delta \text{ in value of Canadian bond} = 8.40 \times 0.63 \times 0.80 \text{ percent}$$

   $$\Delta \text{ in value of Canadian bond} = 4.23 \text{ percent}$$

12. Let W denote the spread widening.

   $$\text{Change in price} = \text{Duration} \times \text{Change in yield}$$

   $$\text{Change in price} = 8.3 \times W$$

   Assuming, the increase in price caused by the spread widening will be 0.75 percent.

   $$0.75\% = 8.3 \times W$$

Solving for the spread widening, W,

$$W = 0.0904\% = 9.04 \text{ bps}$$

Thus, a spread widening of 9.04 bps would wipe out the additional yield gained from investing in the U.S. bond. The 0.0904 percent change in rates would wipe out the quarterly yield advantage of 75 bps.

13. The forward premium on the Japanese yen is $2.7 - 1.6 = 1.1\%$. So, the portfolio manager should hedge using a forward contract if the anticipated return on yen is less than 1.1 percent.

    A. Because the anticipated return on yen of 1.5 percent is greater than 1.1 percent, the portfolio manager should not hedge.
    B. Because the anticipated return on yen of 0.5 percent is less than 1.1 percent, the portfolio manager should hedge.

14. The interest rate differential between the U.K. pound and the U.S. dollar is $4.7 - 4.0 = 0.7\%$. Because this differential is greater than the 0.4 percent return on the U.S. dollar expected by the fund manager, the forward hedged position has a higher expected return than the unhedged position.

CHAPTER 7

EQUITY PORTFOLIO MANAGEMENT

SOLUTIONS

1. A. The three main large-cap styles are value, growth, and market oriented.
   B. Value managers seek to buy stocks below their intrinsic value. That said, the stocks may be cheap for good reason. Also, it may take a long time for stocks to reach their intrinsic value. Growth managers buy stocks of companies with either steadily growing earnings or companies whose earnings they expect to sharply appreciate. However, they may overpay for these earnings or the expected earnings may not materialize. Managers following the third style, market oriented, may forecast stock returns using a combination of growth or value considerations but endeavor to build portfolios that more closely resemble the market than either value or growth managers. If their fees are relatively high for achieving market-like returns, indexing or enhanced indexing may be a more cost-effective alternative.
2. The portfolio managed by Galicia is experiencing style drift. The threefold increase in the weighting of growth stocks suggests that Galicia has decided to shift to more of a market orientation, although some or all of the drift may have occurred because the stocks in the portfolio have become less value-like during the two-year period. The relatively low percentages given to "Other" suggest that Galicia's style exposures explain the overwhelming majority of the portfolio's performance.
3. The fund has a modest value orientation. Dividend yield, price-to-earnings ratio (P/E), price-to-book ratio (P/B), and earnings per share (EPS) growth are all slightly lower than the market benchmark. The sector weights are a bit more mixed. Some sectors that typically contain stocks with value characteristics (consumer discretionary and utilities) are overweight, while others (finance and energy) are underweight or equal weight to the benchmark. Also, traditionally growth-oriented sectors like health care and information technology are modestly overweight—unlikely in a deep value portfolio.
4. A better approach would be full replication. The main justification for using full replication is that all the components of the FTSE 100 are very liquid, so full replication can be accomplished readily and inexpensively. Because full replication minimizes tracking risk, it is the preferred method when the index consists of liquid securities. Another point is that full replication allows for the creation of a self-rebalancing portfolio in the case of a value-weighted (or float-weighted index): Trading is required only to reinvest dividends and to reflect changes in index composition. A self-rebalancing portfolio is one in which the portfolio moves in line with the index without any need for trading activity. An

optimized portfolio may indeed hold fewer than 100 stocks. Because it does not contain every stock in the index in the proper capitalization weight, however, periodic trading will be required (even in the absence of index changes and dividend flows) simply to realign the portfolio's characteristics with those of the index. Over time, the trading-related costs will drag down performance. In general, optimization should be used only in situations in which full replication would result in substantial transaction costs.

5. A. The principal benefit of all stocks being categorized as either growth or value (Morgan Stanley Capital International [MSCI] approach) is that it is collectively exhaustive. That said, many stocks are "border" stocks (i.e., have characteristics that place them near the value/growth border) that don't really exhibit significant value or growth characteristics but are categorized in one of these styles anyway. The Dow Jones method's neutral/core category eliminates this problem, but the value and growth indices by definition do not contain all of the stocks in the broad index.

   B. Either set of indices can be used for returns-based style analysis. That said, Miller is likely to obtain a higher R^2 in a regression of the portfolio returns on the style index returns if he uses the more "granular" set of style indices—those by Dow Jones. For example, if the portfolio is a deep value portfolio or a strong growth portfolio, the Dow Jones indices are more likely to better explain the portfolio's style than a set of style indices in which every stock is forced into either value or growth. Specifically, the deep value portfolio will be better represented by the Dow Jones Value Index because that index focuses more on deep value stocks. That same portfolio's returns regressed versus the MSCI Value Index is likely to show a lower R^2.

6. The principal benefit of a market-neutral long–short portfolio is absence of a long-only constraint. A long-only constraint penalizes portfolios in two ways. First, it prevents the portfolio manager from fully exploiting a negative forecast on a given stock. Secondly, in a long-only portfolio, being unable to fully exploit a negative forecast also limits the ability of the portfolio manager to maximize positive forecasts. The main risk with long–short portfolios is the unlimited liability on the short trades. If a stock in which an investor has a long position loses all of its value, the most that could happen is that the investor loses his entire investment. With a short position, however, the investor's upside is limited (stock goes to zero) but the liability is unlimited (theoretically, a stock can appreciate infinitely).

7. Hayes can produce such a portfolio through the use of a portable alpha. He submits a proposal to manage a market-neutral long–short portfolio of U.K. stocks. This strategy generates alpha (α). To produce beta (β), the Japanese equity exposure, Hayes takes a long position in a notional value of futures equal to the size of the portfolio.

8. Suzuki tells her client that although she can certainly double the portfolio's tracking risk to 4 percent, the portfolio's alpha will increase but not double. The problem is that as an investor increases a portfolio's tracking risk, the long-only constraint increasingly limits the portfolio manager from taking full advantage of her investment insights. Remember, $IR \approx IC\sqrt{Breadth}$. If the breadth is constant but the information coefficient (IC) falls because a smaller portion of the manager's insight is translated into the portfolio, then the information ratio (IR) must also fall.

9. The short-side alpha is likely the larger of the two. Many investors look for cheap stocks in which to take long positions, but comparatively few look for expensive stocks to short. Shorting is operationally more cumbersome than taking a long position, which contributes to the limited use of shorting by most investors. Also, sell recommendations from the analyst community are relatively uncommon. Analysts are more likely to simply not cover a stock on which they have an unfavorable opinion. Also, analysts working

for investment banking firms have a strong incentive not to issue negative reports on companies with which the bank may wish to do business.

10. A. The change is in fact positive (assuming that Johnson is willing to accept a slightly higher level of tracking risk) because the information ratio improves. Her current portfolio has an information ratio of 0.87 (2.4%/2.75%). The portfolio with the enhanced indexer has an information ratio of 0.97 (2.8%/2.9%).

    B. Stock-based enhanced indexing begins with an index portfolio and then over- or underweights individual stocks based on the portfolio manager's return expectations for those stocks. The portfolio is built to look like its target benchmark but to add some level of outperformance on a fairly consistent basis. The advantage of this approach is greater breadth than the synthetic approach. That said, as with all active strategies, obtaining a satisfactory IC or level of investment insight is the challenge. Synthetic enhanced index strategies involve gaining exposure to the benchmark with futures (or a swap) while generating an alpha, typically using fixed income. This strategy has the advantage of being straightforward. It generally has narrower breadth (usually a duration or credit bet) and so requires a high IC to produce the same level of IR as the stock-based approach.

11. A. The total active risk is greater than 6 percent because in the calculation, the long–short manager would be benchmarked to the Russell 1000 rather than the manager's normal benchmark, which most closely captures the manager's orientation. We can see this by noting the positive level of misfit risk. The misfit risk is calculated with the equation $\sqrt{6.0\%^2 + (\text{Misfit risk})^2} = 6.1\%^2$, which equals 1.1%.

    B. The total active risk is $\sqrt{5\%^2 + 7.13\%^2} = 8.71\%$.

    C. The expected active return is $(0.3 \times 0\%) + (0.7 \times 1\%) = 0.7\%$.

    The expected total active risk for the portfolio is
    $\sqrt{(0.3^2 \times 0\%^2) + (0.7^2 \times 1.5\%^2)} = 1.05\%$.

    The expected IR is $0.7\%/1.05\% = 0.67$.

    D. The efficient combination of managers leads to a portfolio with an IR of $1.59\%/1.10\% = 1.45$. Hence, despite the slightly greater active risk exposure, the overall portfolio IR increases by a factor of 2.17 versus the current mix.

    E. In general, the exposures to non-U.S. equities in the long–short portfolio should not concern Whitmore as long as she believes that the manager has skill in managing non-U.S. equities. As shown in Part A of this problem, the misfit risk for the strategy is relatively small because the manager overlays the long–short portfolio with Russell 1000 futures and thus has a high correlation with the Russell 3000 benchmark. The large majority of the strategy's total active risk is driven by the manager's active return volatility.

CHAPTER 8

ALTERNATIVE INVESTMENTS PORTFOLIO MANAGEMENT

SOLUTIONS

1. Direct (physical) investments in real estate tend to be much less liquid than investments in real estate investment trusts (REITs), which are indirect investments. Reasons for the illiquidity of direct investments include the following:

   - The large transaction sizes when buying/selling commercial/industrial buildings and land or residential apartment buildings is in contrast to the flexibility of trading small amounts in REITs on public exchanges.
   - The lack of availability and timeliness of information with respect to direct real estate investment results in extensive valuation and due diligence issues, whereas REITs are exchange traded in real time on a daily basis, and information about them is readily available and accessible.
   - The high transaction costs of direct investments in terms of broker commissions and the financing costs of buying physical assets require long-term investment horizons. Exchange-traded REITs have low transaction costs, and reallocation of funds is easy.

2. A. Direct investment in real estate includes individual residences, agricultural land, and commercial real estate. The category of commercial real estate can be subdivided into industrial, office, retail, and apartment complexes. Indirect investment is achieved via REITs, which can be subdivided into equity, mortgage, and hybrid (a combination of first two) investment trusts.

   Using the unsmoothed National Council of Real Estate Investment Fiduciaries (NCREIF) Index as a benchmark for direct investment in commercial real estate indicates that the long-term (1990–2004) correlation of direct real estate investment with the S&P 500 is slightly negative; the correlation of direct real estate investment with bonds (the Lehman Aggregate Bond Index) is significantly negative, indicating that adding physical real estate to a 50 percent stock/50 percent bond portfolio would have provided very substantial diversification benefits.

   The correlations of the National Association of Real Estate Investment Trusts (NAREIT) Index with both the S&P 500 and bonds were both moderately positive for the period examined. This fact indicates that indirect investment in real estate had diversification benefits relative to a 50/50 stock bond portfolio, but that the diversification benefits were not as large as those resulting from direct real estate investment.

3. A. Semyonova's recommendation can be critiqued along the following dimensions:

    - *Return.* The long-term returns for bonds and direct investment in real estate (unsmoothed NCREIF) are similar (7.70 percent and 7.27 percent); therefore, reallocating 10 percent of bond investments to direct real estate investment would not sacrifice much return.
    - *Risk.* (a) The standard deviation for the unsmoothed NCREIF Index is more than twice that for the Lehman Aggregate; therefore, this reallocation does not reduce risk as measured by standard deviation. (b) Downside volatility, as represented in this table by the minimum quarterly return, is much greater for real estate than for bonds. (c) The NCREIF Index is a compilation of many types of real estate, whereas the trustees would have to choose a specific asset, possibly incurring higher risk than indicated by the NCREIF data.
    - *Diversification.* The correlation between the Lehman Aggregate and the unsmoothed NCREIF Index is significantly negative, which would indicate good potential for diversification.
    - *Liquidity.* Investment in physical real estate is the least liquid of the asset classes shown in the table. A transaction could probably not be reversed quickly or easily.

   B. Pearson's recommendations can be criticized along the following dimensions:

    - *Return.* The unhedged return of REITs is almost 2 percentage points greater than the return of the S&P 500, whereas the hedged return is about 2 percentage points less than the S&P. Therefore, taking into account the equity return component of the NAREIT Index, this reallocation could represent a slight sacrifice in return.
    - *Risk.* The standard deviation of the NAREIT Index and the hedged NAREIT Index was approximately 2 and 3 percentage points below that of the S&P 500, respectively. Thus, no matter which index we use to represent indirect real estate investment, the reallocation would satisfy the objective of risk reduction, based on historical experience. Additionally, downside risk (as measured by the minimum quarterly return) was much less for REITs than for the S&P 500, so the reallocation could reduce downside risk as well.
    - *Diversification.* The correlation between the S&P 500 and the hedged NAREIT Index is zero, indicating that REITs have sources of return that are different from those for large-cap equities, which would enhance diversification.
    - *Liquidity.* REITs and S&P 500 equities are exchange traded and, therefore, are both liquid.

   C. The second scenario—that is, reallocation of 10 percent of large-cap equities to REITs—is the best choice to fulfill the trustees' stated goals for the following reasons:

    - *Return.* Using the long-term data provided in the table, the first scenario (based on unsmoothed NCREIF data) would have a mean return of $10.94\% \times 0.5 + 7.70\% \times 0.4 + 7.27\% \times 0.1 = 9.28\%$, whereas the second scenario (using hedged NAREIT) would yield 9.12 percent. If the unhedged NAREIT returns are used in the calculation, the expected return rises to 9.5 percent. Therefore, a 10 percent investment in REITs (even those least correlated with equities—e.g., mortgage REITs) and corresponding 10 percent reduction in S&P 500 stocks would represent a return similar to that of the first scenario.

- *Risk.* The second scenario is superior in terms of risk reduction because it maintains a higher allocation to bonds, which show a much lower correlation with unhedged REITs than does the S&P 500. Additionally, the minimum quarterly return is worst (most negative) for the unsmoothed NCREIF Index and the S&P 500. Therefore, the second scenario would reduce allocation to an asset class with high downside risk and reallocate money to REITs, which have a lower downside risk. Finally, REITs are highly liquid and can be easily divested, whereas physical real estate necessitates a long-term commitment and entails high transaction costs.

Note: Although bonds have a negative correlation with the NCREIF Index (the first scenario), which suggests a superior reduction in risk through diversification, the three points provided here indicate that the reallocation from equities to REITS more closely fulfills the stated objectives of the trustees.

- *Index construction.* The choice of real estate index is pertinent to the assumptions used in calculating expected results for asset allocation decisions. The use of the unsmoothed NCREIF Index can be substantiated because more frequent, market-based (transaction) data are more timely and accurate than the smoothed, annually calculated, appraisal-based data. This method suggests higher expected returns—and significantly greater risk.

The use of the hedged NAREIT Index could be justified by the concept of eliminating double counting (the equity return component in equity REITs). Additionally, the use of mortgage and hybrid REITs would reduce the redundancy of the more highly correlated equity REITs. Nevertheless, equity REITs compose about 95 percent of the NAREIT Index, so the unhedged data show a significant increase in return with less risk, as demonstrated by the high Sharpe ratio of the NAREIT Index relative to most other asset classes.

4. A. The roll yield for Year 1 is 29.1% − 9.6% − 6.1% = 13.4%.
   B. The collateral yield for Year 2 is −30.5% − (−14.2%) − (−24.3%) = 8.0%.
   C. Collateral yield is earned because of the assumption that when investing in a commodity futures index, the full value of the underlying futures contract is invested at a risk-free rate as the investor posts 100 percent margin with T-bills. Therefore, the position is fully collateralized, and for every dollar invested in the commodity futures index, the investor receives a dollar of commodity exposure plus interest on a dollar invested in T-bills. This is the *implied yield* or *collateral return.*
   D. Changes in commodity futures prices are highly correlated with changes in spot prices. In periods of financial, economic, or political distress, and sometimes after natural disasters, short-term commodity prices tend to rise because most such events create shocks with respect to physical commodities that reduce current supply and cause prices to rise. This is called *positive event risk.*
5. A. Two points can be made that relate to the value of the Goldman Sachs Commodity Index (GSCI) as a risk diversifier and the interpretation of the Sharpe ratio. First, the negative correlation of the GSCI with the S&P 500 and the low positive correlation of the GSCI with the Lehman Government/Corporate Bond Index suggest good risk reduction benefits when the GSCI is added to a portfolio of U.S. stocks and bonds. Second, in interpreting the low Sharpe ratio for the GSCI, account must be taken of the appropriateness of the Sharpe ratio for measuring commodity returns. The validity of standard deviation as a measure of risk in the denominator of the Sharpe ratio is compromised when returns are skewed and/or have high kurtosis. Because commodity

returns exhibit skewness, the Sharpe ratio is not necessarily the best representation of the risk–return trade-off with respect to this asset class.

B. McCoy is evaluating a short time series. Because investment performance depends on the time period studied, the high returns generated by commodities in 2000–2004 may not be representative of long-term performance. In fact, we know this is the case when the data are compared with data for the longer period documented in Problem 4. This does not necessarily suggest that investment in commodities is not appropriate. However, it raises a caveat about comparing expectations of future returns for a period when the economic environment may be different from that of the short-term period that generated the results in the table given. This information also suggests that commodities may provide benefits as a tactical asset class.

The same concerns with respect to the short time frame covered by the table can be expressed for the correlation data. However, the values are virtually the same for the longer-term data, which suggests that commodity returns are not correlated with the other asset classes; as a result, inclusion of commodities in the portfolio could provide both long- and short-term diversification benefits.

6. A. Survivorship bias occurs when returns of managers who have failed or exited the market are not included in the data analyzed over a specific time frame. This results in overestimation of historical returns in the range of 1.5 to 3.0 percent per year. The timing of survivorship bias may be concentrated during certain economic periods, further complicating analysis of persistence of returns over short timeframes. Additionally, age (vintage) effects make it difficult to compare performance of hedge funds that have track records of different lengths. This is especially important when researching hedge funds, which have average track records of two to five years.

B. Indices that are value weighted as opposed to equally weighted may take on the return characteristics of the best-performing hedge fund in them over a given period. These indices thus reflect the weights of popular bets by hedge fund managers, because the asset values of the various funds change as a result of asset purchases as well as price appreciation.

C. Lack of security trading leads to stale price bias and can cause measured standard deviation to be over- or understated, depending on the time period being studied. This could result in measured correlations being lower than expected. This issue is not a significant concern in the creation of hedge fund indices because monthly data are used. Furthermore, the underlying holdings in many hedge fund strategies are relatively liquid; therefore, positions reflect market prices.

7. A. Equity market-neutral strategies identify over- and undervalued stocks while neutralizing the fund's exposure to market risk by combining long and short positions with similar exposure to related market or sector factors. Therefore, as their name suggests, they have little or no market risk. They also have low credit risk because their long–short positions result in net low leverage. As expected, there is virtually no correlation between funds using this strategy and the S&P 500.

Convertible arbitrage strategies exploit anomalies in the prices of corporate convertible bonds, warrants, and preferred stock. The convertible arbitrage funds buy or sell these securities and then hedge the risk of changes in price and volatility of the underlying securities, changes in interest rates, and changes in the issuers' credit ratings. The many small, individual positions taken, and hedging of these risks, result in low market exposure. However, this strategy also increases credit risk considerably because hedging via derivative instruments creates high leverage exposure. Convertible arbitrage strategies have a relatively low correlation with the S&P 500 or the Lehman Government/Corporate Bond Index because hedging the risks mitigates underlying market exposure.

Global macro strategies trade on systematic moves in major financial and nonfinancial markets by using futures and options contracts. They may also take positions in traditional equity and fixed-income markets. Because they tend to make large bets on the direction of currencies, commodities, or stock and bond markets globally, they have high market exposure. Given their extensive use of leverage via futures and options, they are also exposed to significant credit (leverage) risk. Because of their large positions with regard to anticipated changes in market levels, the correlation of global macro with the S&P 500 and Lehman Government/Corporate Bond Index tends to be greater than those of the first two strategies discussed here.

B. The usefulness of historical hedge fund data continues to be controversial. Research has shown that the volatility of returns is more persistent through time than the level of returns. Issues such as survivorship and backfill bias have a significant impact on historical tests of performance persistence. Additionally, lock-up periods, restrictions on redemptions/withdrawals, and the relatively short track record of many hedge funds complicate the extrapolation of past performance to expected (future) performance of hedge funds.

8. The fee structures charged by hedge fund managers often have two components: management fees and incentive fees. The "1 and 20" refers to a 1 percent per year management fee based on net asset value plus a 20 percent incentive, or profit-sharing, fee that is earned only if assets exceed a specified value. This value may be the high-water mark of the fund—that is, the highest previous NAV. Typically, drawdowns (declines/losses in net asset value) must be recouped before any incentive fees are charged.

9. Farkas's statement is not valid if the hedge fund has a lock-up period. During this time, the investor cannot redeem any part of the investment. Additionally, once the lock-up period has expired, redemption rights may be limited to a quarterly or semiannual schedule and the investor generally must give advance notice, ranging from 30 to 90 days, of an intention to redeem.

10. A. Any of the following reasons could cause an upward bias in the Sharpe ratio:

- Lengthening the measurement interval: This will result in a lower estimate of volatility. For example, the annualized standard deviation of daily returns is generally higher than of weekly returns, which is, in turn, higher than of monthly returns.
- Compounding the monthly returns but calculating the standard deviation from the (not compounded) monthly returns.
- Writing out-of-the-money puts and calls on a portfolio: This strategy can potentially increase the return by collecting the option premium without paying off for several years. Strategies that involve taking on default risk, liquidity risk, or other forms of catastrophe risk have the same ability to report an upwardly biased Sharpe ratio. (An example is the Sharpe ratios of market-neutral hedge funds before and after the 1998 liquidity crisis.) This is akin to trading negative skewness for a greater Sharpe ratio by improving the mean or standard deviation of the investment.
- Smoothing of returns: Using certain derivative structures, infrequent marking to market of illiquid assets, or using pricing models that understate monthly gains or losses can reduce reported volatility.

- Eliminating extreme returns: Because such returns increase the reported standard deviation of a hedge fund, a manager may choose to attempt to eliminate the best and the worst monthly returns each year to reduce the standard deviation. Operationally, this entails a total-return swap, in which one pays the best and worst returns for one's benchmark index each year and the counterparty pays a fixed cash flow and hedges the risk in the open market. If swaps are not available, one can do it directly with options.

B. Because of the option-like payoff characteristics of many hedge fund strategies, their returns are not normally distributed, but normality is an assumption inherent in the computation of standard deviation in the denominator of the Sharpe ratio. Hedge fund returns, on average, display some skewness (asymmetry of the return distribution), as well as high kurtosis (relatively frequent extreme returns). These effects are not captured by standard deviation, the risk measure used in the Sharpe ratio. Also, Sharpe ratios are overestimated when investment returns are serially correlated (i.e., returns trend), which causes a lower estimate of the standard deviation. This occurs with certain momentum (trend-following) hedge fund strategies and those that may have a problem with stale pricing or illiquidity (e.g., distressed securities).

11. A. The hedge fund's average nine-month rolling return:

$$RR_{9,1} = (2.7 + 1.7 - 1 + 0.9 - 1 - 2 - 2 + 4 + 3.5)/9 = 0.7556\%$$
$$RR_{9,2} = 0.7778\%$$
$$RR_{9,3} = 0.3778\%$$
$$RR_{9,4} = 0.2444\%$$
$$\text{Average} = (0.7556 + 0.7778 + 0.3778 + 0.2444)/4 = 0.54\%$$

B. Rolling returns can show how consistent the returns are over the investment period and whether there is any cyclicality in the returns.

12. A. A hurdle rate of 5% per year equates to a monthly hurdle rate of $5\%/12 = 0.4167\%$. The downside deviation for the hedge fund $= \sqrt{28.78/(12-1)} \times \sqrt{12} = 5.60\%$.

The downside deviation for the index $= \sqrt{65.04/(12-1)} \times \sqrt{12} = 8.42\%$.

The downside deviation is lower than the standard deviation because downside deviation takes into account only the deviations on the downside. The downside deviation of the hedge fund is lower than that of the index in this case.

B. Annualized return for the hedge fund $= 0.6613\% \times 12 = 7.9356\%$.

Annualized return for the index $= 0.449\% \times 12 = 5.388\%$.

The Sortino ratio for the hedge fund $= (7.94 - 5)/5.6 = 0.53$.

The Sortino ratio for the index $= (5.39 - 5)/8.42 = 0.05$.

The Sortino ratio of the hedge fund is much higher than that of the index, indicating that it provides greater return per unit of downside risk.

13. A. Managed futures are often considered a subgroup of global macro hedge funds because both strategies attempt to take advantage of systematic moves in major financial and nonfinancial markets.

B. The primary similarity between managed futures and absolute-return hedge fund strategies is that they seek positive returns regardless of market direction. Managed futures strategies invest exclusively in the forward and derivatives markets on a leveraged basis by trading futures and options contracts in the financial, commodity, and currency markets. In contrast, other hedge fund strategies invest in underlying markets; some, depending on their strategies, also use derivatives.

14. The theory of market efficiency suggests that news is simultaneously available to all market participants and is quickly incorporated into market prices. However, research in behavioral finance indicates that investors may systematically underreact to information; consequently, security prices may trend, particularly in traditional investment vehicles (stocks and bonds). Actively managed derivative strategies that follow momentum, or trend-based, models have been shown to be profitable by capturing these trends.
15. Similarly to market-neutral funds, managed futures programs can replicate many strategies available to cash market investors at lower transaction costs and can also trade on strategies by using derivatives that are unavailable to cash market investors. Research has shown that when returns are segmented according to whether the stock/bond markets rose or fell, managed futures have negative correlation cash market portfolios when cash market portfolios post significant negative returns and are positively correlated when cash portfolios reported significant positive returns. Therefore, managed futures may offer unique asset allocation characteristics in different market environments.

    Also, hedging demands of cash market participants may create investment situations where hedgers are required to offer derivative investors a risk premium, or positive return, for holding open long or short offsetting positions. Option traders may be able to create positions that offer this "risk premium" for holding various option contracts when cash market participants increase purchases of options to protect themselves in markets with trending prices or volatility. This return (i.e., the convenience yield) can be earned simply by buying and holding a derivatives portfolio.
16. The term *fallen angels* refers to debt securities that were originally deemed investment grade when issued by financially healthy companies but have subsequently been downgraded to below investment grade. In contrast, companies with high-risk profiles and existing senior debt issues can seek additional (subordinated) financing via originally issued high-yield securities.
17. The private equity approach of investing is considered an active approach. New investors in the debt and/or equity of a troubled company (distressed securities) participate on creditor committees and assist in the recovery or reorganization process to maximize their return on investment. Under the relative-value approach, passive investors buy the distressed securities and either hold them until they appreciate to the desired level or trade them within a relatively short period of time.
18. The results of a prepackaged bankruptcy have different effects on the various parties involved:

    (a) In a prepackaged bankruptcy, the prebankruptcy creditors of the company have already agreed in advance with the debtor company on a plan or reorganization before the debtor company actually files for bankruptcy. This may involve the creditors making concessions in return for equity of the reorganized company.

    (b) Prebankruptcy shareholders do not have nearly as much leverage as the creditors. The prebankruptcy shareholders typically lose their entire stake in the company because in a prepackaged bankruptcy, a private equity firm (the vulture investor) seeks to become a majority owner of a new private company.

(c) The vulture investor is bearing a lot of risk in a transaction like this but may come out with a substantial profit if things work out well. The vulture investor hopes to end up with a healthy company that can be sold to private or public investors.

19. The statement is correct. When the economy is in a downturn, there are more bankruptcies, thereby increasing the supply of distressed securities at relatively low (or falling) prices.

CHAPTER 9

RISK MANAGEMENT

SOLUTIONS

1. Centralized risk control systems bring all risk management activities under the responsibility of a single risk control unit. Under decentralized systems, each business unit is responsible for its own risk control. The advantages of a centralized system are that it brings risk control closer to the key decision makers in the organization and enables the organization to better manage its risk budget by recognizing the diversification embedded across business units. The decentralized approach has the advantage of placing risk control in nearer proximity to the source of risk taking. However, it has the disadvantage of not accounting for portfolio effects across units.
2. The following risk exposures should be reported as part of an Enterprise Risk Management System for Ford Motor Company:

    - *Market risks:*

        - Currency risk, because expenditures and receipts denominated in nondomestic currencies create exposure to changes in exchange rates.
        - Interest rate risk, because the values of securities that Ford has invested in are subject to changes in interest rates. Also, Ford has borrowings and loans, which could be affected by interest rate changes.
        - Commodity risk, because Ford has exposure in various commodities and finished products.

    - *Credit risk,* because of financing provided to customers who have purchased Ford's vehicles on credit.
    - *Liquidity risk,* because of the possibility that Ford's funding sources may be reduced or become unavailable and Ford may then have to sell its securities at a short notice with a significant concession in price.
    - *Settlement risk,* because of Ford's investments in fixed-income instruments and derivative contracts, some of which effect settlement through the execution of bilateral agreements and involve the possibility of default by the counterparty.
    - *Political risk,* because Ford has operations in several countries. This exposes it to political risk. For example, the adoption of a restrictive policy by a non-U.S. government regarding payment of dividends by a subsidiary in that country to the parent company could adversely affect Ford.

3. Two types of risk that were inadequately managed were model risk and operational risk. Systematic errors in a major input of the options pricing model, implied volatility, resulted

in mispricing options and trading losses. Thus model risk was inadequately managed. Furthermore, the systems and procedures at NatWest failed to prevent or detect and bring to the attention of senior management the trading losses. Thus, operational risk also was not well managed.

4. Trader 1's statement is incorrect. Buyers are concerned about the transaction costs of trades as much as sellers, so a security's liquidity is highly relevant to buyers. In certain cases, such as a short position in a stock with limited float, the liquidity risk for the purchase side of a trade can be considerable.

   Trader 2's statement is incorrect. Derivatives usually do not help in managing liquidity risk because the lack of liquidity in the spot market typically passes right through to the derivatives market.

   Trader 3's statement is correct. Businesses need to take risks in areas in which they have expertise and possibly a comparative advantage in order to earn profits. Risk management can entail taking risk as well as reducing risk.

5. A. Assuming that the desk pays its traders a percentage of the profits on their own trading books, the −€20 million loss generated by an individual trader implies that the rest of the desk made €30 million and that the bank will have to pay the other traders an incentive fee on this larger amount, even though it generated only €10 million in net revenues. By contrast, if every trader had made money and the revenues to the desk were €10 million, the incentive payouts to traders would have been much lower and the net profits to the bank much higher.

   B. In the scenario described above, the trader in question appears to have increased his risk exposure at year-end. The asymmetric nature of the incentive fee arrangement may induce risk taking because it is a call option on a percentage of profits and the value of a call option increases in the volatility of the underlying. In this sense, the interests of the bank and the trader diverged to the detriment of the bank.

   C. First and foremost, it is clear that senior management was out of touch with the risk dynamics of the desk because it should have known that the trader in question was over his limits at some points much earlier in the scenario. The fact that management discovered this violation only after the loss occurred reflects poor risk governance.

6. *Strengths*. The sensitivity analysis reported by Ford is useful in highlighting the possible adverse effect of a 1 percent decline in interest rates on Ford Credit's net income. It also is based on an objective measure of interest rate risk, duration.

   Weaknesses. The sensitivity analysis reported in the table assumes that interest rate changes are instantaneous, small, parallel shifts in the yield curve. From a risk management perspective, one would have a special interest in the effects of larger interest rate changes, including major discontinuities in interest rates. The inclusion of value at risk would help fill this gap in the analysis. Furthermore, changes in the yield curve other than parallel shifts should be examined, such as nonparallel shifts (twists) in the yield curve. The text mentions the recommendation of the Derivatives Policy Group to examine both parallel shifts and twists of the yield curve.

7. A. There is a 1 percent chance that the portfolio will lose at least £4.25 million in any given week.

   B. There is a 99 percent chance that the portfolio will lose no more than £4.25 million in one week.

8. Statement A, which is the definition of value at risk (VaR), is clearly correct. Statement B is also correct, because it lists the important decisions involved in measuring VaR. Statement D is correct: The longer the time period, the larger the possible losses. Statement

C, however, is incorrect. The VaR number would be larger for a 1 percent probability than for a 5 percent probability. Accordingly, the correct answer is C.

9. A. The probability is 0.005 that the portfolio will lose at least 50 percent in a year. The probability is 0.005 that the portfolio will lose between 40 percent and 50 percent in a year. Cumulating these two probabilities implies that the probability is 0.01 that the portfolio will lose at least 40 percent in a year. So, the 1 percent yearly VaR is 40 percent of the market value of $10 million, which is $4 million.
   B. The probability is 0.005 that the portfolio will lose at least 50 percent in a year, 0.005 that it will lose between 40 and 50 percent, 0.010 that it will lose between 30 and 40 percent, 0.015 that it will lose between 20 and 30 percent, and 0.015 that it will lose between 10 and 20 percent. Cumulating these probabilities indicates that the probability is 0.05 that the portfolio will lose at least 10 percent in a year. So, the 5 percent yearly VaR is 10 percent of the market value of $10 million, which is $1 million.

10. First, we must calculate the monthly portfolio expected return and standard deviation. Using "1" to indicate the U.S. government bonds and "2" to indicate the U.K. government bonds, we have

$$\mu_P = w_1\mu_1 + w_2\mu_2 = 0.50(0.0085) + 0.50(0.0095) = 0.0090$$

$$\sigma_P^2 = w_1^2\sigma_1^2 + w_2^2\sigma_2^2 + 2\,w_1\,w_2\sigma_1\sigma_2\rho$$

$$= (0.50)^2(0.0320)^2 + (0.50)^2(0.0526)^2 + 2(0.50)(0.50)(0.0320)(0.0526)(0.35)$$

$$= 0.001242$$

$$\sigma_P = \sqrt{0.001242} = 0.0352$$

   A. For a 5 percent monthly VaR, we have $\mu_P - 1.65\sigma_P = 0.0090 - 1.65(0.0352) = -0.0491$. Then the VaR would be $100 million(0.0491) = $4.91 million.
   B. For a 1 percent monthly VaR, we have $\mu_P - 2.33\sigma_P = 0.0090 - 2.33(0.0352) = -0.0730$. Then the VaR would be $100 million(0.0730) = $7.30 million.
   C. There are 12 months or 52 weeks in a year. So, to convert the monthly return of 0.0090 to weekly return, we first multiply the monthly return by 12 to convert it to an annual return, and then we divide the annual return by 52 to convert it to a weekly return. So, the expected weekly return is 0.0090(12/52) = 0.0021. Similarly, we adjust the standard deviation to $0.0352(\sqrt{12}/\sqrt{52}) = 0.01691$. The 5 percent weekly VaR would then be $\mu_P - 1.65\sigma_P = 0.0021 - 1.65(0.01691) = -0.0258$. Then the VaR in dollars would be $100 million(0.0258) = $2.58 million.
   D. The 1 percent weekly VaR would be $\mu_P - 2.33\sigma_P = 0.0021 - 2.33(0.01691) = -0.0373$. Then the VaR would be $100 million(0.0373) = $3.73 million.

11. A. For the five-year period, there are 60 monthly returns. Of the 60 returns, the 5 percent worst are the 3 worst returns. Therefore, based on the historical method, the 5 percent VaR would be the third worst return. From the returns given, the third worst return is −0.2463. So, the VaR in dollars is 0.2463($25,000) = $6,157.50.
   B. Of the 60 returns, the 1 percent worst are the 0.6 worst returns. Therefore, we would use the single worst return. From the returns given, the worst return is −0.3475. So, the VaR in dollars is 0.3475($25,000) = $8,687.50.

12. A. Of the 700 outcomes, the worst 5 percent are the 35 worst returns. Therefore, the 5 percent VaR would be the 35th worst return. From the data given, the 35th worst return is −0.223. So, the 5 percent annual VaR in dollars is 0.223($10 million) = $2,230,000.
    B. Of the 700 outcomes, the worst 1 percent are the 7 worst returns. Therefore, the 1 percent VaR would be the seventh worst return. From the data given, the seventh worst return is −0.347. So, the 1 percent annual VaR in dollars is 0.347($10 million) = $3,470,000.
13. A. The analytical or variance–covariance method begins with the assumption that portfolio returns are normally distributed. A normal distribution has an unlimited upside and an unlimited downside. The assumption of a normal distribution is inappropriate when the portfolio contains options because the return distributions of options are far from normal. Call options have unlimited upside potential, as in a normal distribution, but the downside return is truncated at a loss of 100 percent. Similarly, put options have a limited upside and a large but limited downside. Likewise, covered calls and protective puts have limits in one direction or the other. Therefore, for the portfolio that has options, the assumption of a normal distribution to estimate VaR has a number of problems. In addition, it is very difficult to calculate a covariance between either two options or an option and a security with more linear characteristics—among other reasons because options have different dynamics at different points in their life cycle.
    B. Portfolios with simple, linear characteristics, particularly those with a limited budget for computing resources and analytical personnel, might select the variance/covariance method. For more complex portfolios containing options and time-sensitive bonds, the historical method might be more appropriate. The Monte Carlo simulation method typically would not be a wise choice unless it were managed by an organization with a portfolio of complex derivatives that is willing to make and sustain a considerable investment in technology and human capital.
14. A. The observed outcomes are consistent with the VaR calculation's prediction on the frequency of losses exceeding the VaR. Therefore, the VaR calculation is accurate.
    B. The VaR results indicate that under "normal" market conditions that would characterize 19 out of 20 days, the portfolio ought to lose less than €3 million. It provides no other information beyond this.
    C. The portfolio certainly lends itself to scenario analysis. In this particular case, given the substantial short options position, it might be instructive to create a customized scenario under which the portfolio was analyzed in the wake of a large increase in option-implied volatility.
15. The fact that credit losses occur infrequently makes Statement A incorrect. Unlike a European-style option, which cannot be exercised prior to expiration and thus has no current credit risk, an American-style option does have the potential for current credit risk. Therefore, Statement C is incorrect. Statement B, however, is correct.
16. A. The decision not to hedge this risk was correct. Suppose the company had hedged this risk. If the price of oil were to increase, the favorable effect of the increase on income would be offset by the loss on the oil futures, but the home currency should appreciate against the U.S. dollar, leaving the company worse off. If the price of oil were to decrease, the unfavorable effect on income would be offset by the futures position and the home currency should depreciate, leaving the company better off. In

short, the company would remain exposed to exchange rate risk associated with oil price movements.

B. The decision not to hedge this risk was correct. The company should remain exposed to market risk associated with exchange rate movements (i.e., currency risk). Hedging would remove currency risk but leave the company with market risk associated with oil price movements. If the home currency declined, the price of oil would likely decline because it is positively correlated with the U.S. dollar value of the home currency. That would be a negative for income. On the other hand, appreciation of the home currency is likely to be accompanied by an oil price increase, which would be positive for income.

C. The risk management strategy adopted is logical because it exploits a natural hedge. A decline in the price of oil (a negative) is likely to be accompanied by a depreciation of the home currency relative to the U.S. dollar (a positive), and an increase in the price of oil (a positive) is likely to be accompanied by appreciation of the home currency (a negative). Hedging both currency and market risk would be an alternative risk management strategy to consider, but in comparison to the strategy adopted, it would incur transaction costs.

17. A. Because the option is a European-style option, it cannot be exercised prior to expiration. Therefore, there is no current credit risk.

B. The current value of the potential credit risk is the current market value of the option, which is $6. Of course, at expiration, the option is likely to be worth a different amount and could even expire out of the money.

C. Options have unilateral credit risk. The risk is borne by the buyer of the option, Tony Smith, because he will look to the seller for the payoff at expiration if the option expires in the money.

18. The Sharpe ratio uses standard deviation of portfolio return as the measure of risk. Standard deviation is a measure of total risk. The Sortino ratio measures risk using downside deviation, which computes volatility using only rate of return data points below a minimum acceptable return. In contrast to the Sharpe ratio, its focus is on downside risk. Return over maximum drawdown (RoMAD) uses maximum drawdown as a risk measure. Maximum drawdown is the difference between a portfolio's maximum point of return and the lowest point of return over a given time interval.

CHAPTER 10

EXECUTION OF PORTFOLIO DECISIONS

SOLUTIONS

1. A. Quoted spread is the difference between the ask and bid prices in the quote prevailing at the time of the trade is entered. The prevailing quote is the one at 10:50:06, with a bid of $4.69 and an ask of $4.75. So, Quoted spread = Ask − Bid = $4.75 − $4.69 = $0.06.

   B. The time-of-trade quotation midpoint = ($4.69 + $4.75)/2 = $4.72.
   Effective spread = 2 × (Trade price − Time-of-trade quotation midpoint) = 2 × ($4.74 − $4.72) = 2 × $0.02 = $0.04.

   C. The effective and quoted spreads would be equal if a purchase took place at the ask price and a sale took place at the bid price.

2. A. The difference between quoted spreads and effective spreads reflects the price improvement provided by dealers. If the effective spreads are lower than the quoted spreads, dealers are providing price improvements. Since the effective spreads are lower than the quoted spreads on both the New York Stock Exchange (NYSE) and National Association of Securities Dealers Automated Quoting system (NASDAQ), dealers in both markets provided price improvements in the period being examined.

   B. The difference between the quoted and effective spreads is much greater on the NYSE (0.301 cents) than on NASDAQ (0.087 cents). Therefore, the dealers on the NYSE provided greater price improvement than those on NASDAQ.

3. E-Crossnet should not disclose unmatched quantities. Crossing networks maintain complete confidentiality not only in regard to the size of the orders and the names of the investors placing the orders, but also in regard to the unmatched quantities. If E-Crossnet were to disclose the unmatched quantities, it would provide useful information to other parties that would affect the supply and demand of these stocks in which clients want to transact. As a result of the information leakage, transaction costs for its clients would likely rise.

4. A. The second order will have a greater market impact because it is bigger in size.

   B. The second order will have a greater market impact because the trader placing it has a reputation of representing informed investors in the stock. Thus, other traders may believe that the stock's intrinsic value differs from the current market price and adjust their quotations accordingly. In contrast to most other situations in which a reputation of being smart is beneficial, in stock trading, it is not to one's advantage.

C. By definition, orders executed on crossing networks, such as POSIT, avoid market impact costs because the orders are crossed at the existing market price determined elsewhere, regardless of size. Therefore, the first order will have greater market impact. Note, however, that a part of a large order may go unfilled on the crossing network.

5. A. Missed trade opportunity cost is the unfilled size times the difference between the subsequent price and the benchmark price for buys (or times the difference between the benchmark price and the subsequent price for sells). So, using the closing price on February 8 as the subsequent price, the estimated missed trade opportunity cost is 460,000 × ($23.60 – $21.35) = $1,035,000.

   B. Using the closing price on February 14 as the subsequent price, the estimated missed trade opportunity cost is 460,000 × ($21.74 – $21.35) = $179,400.

   C. One of the problems in estimating missed trade opportunity cost is that the estimate depends upon when the cost is measured. As the solutions to Parts A and B of this problem indicate, the estimate could vary substantially when a different interval is used to measure the missed trade opportunity cost. Another problem in estimating the missed trade opportunity cost is that it does not consider the impact of order size on prices. For example, the estimates above assume that if the investment manager had bought the 500,000 shares on February 8, he would have been able to sell these 500,000 shares at $23.60 each on February 8 (or at $21.74 each on February 14). However, an order to sell 500,000 shares on February 8 (or on February 14) would have likely led to a decline in price, and the entire order of 500,000 shares would not have been sold at $23.60 (or at $21.74). Thus, the missed trade opportunity costs above are likely to be overestimates.

6. Since the portfolio manager does not want to pay more than £45 per share, he should place a limit order to buy 5,000 shares at no more than £45 per share. An advantage of placing the limit order is that he avoids the risk of paying too high a price and then suffering substantial losses if the stock price subsequently declines. However, a disadvantage is that his order may not be filled because the market price may never touch his limit order price of £45, incurring a missed trade opportunity cost. For example, consider a situation in which the stock's ask price is £47 when the order to buy at £45 limit is placed and the stock trades up to £80. If the portfolio manager had placed a market order, he would have been able to purchase the stock at £47 and make a profit by selling the stock at the current price of £80. An advantage of a market order is certainty of execution. The disadvantage of a market order is uncertainty concerning the price at which the order will be executed. Because the portfolio manager's chief focus is on execution price, the limit order would be preferred.

7. One negative of shopping the order is that it could delay the execution of the order, and the stock price could increase in the meantime. Another important negative of shopping the order is that it leaks information to others about the buying intention of the asset management firm. This information leakage could result in an adverse price movement in the shares that the asset management firm wants to buy because the broker/dealers could revise their quotes or trade based on the information gained.

8. A. Estimated implicit costs = Trade size × (Trade price – Benchmark price) for a buy, or Trade size × (Benchmark price – Trade price) for a sale. In this problem, Trade size = 100 and Trade price = $2.66.

   i. Opening price = $2.71

   Estimated implicit costs = 100 × ($2.71 – $2.66) = $5

ii. Closing price = $2.65

$$\text{Estimated implicit costs} = 100 \times (\$2.65 - \$2.66) = -\$1$$

iii. We need to first calculate the volume-weighted average price (VWAP).

$$\text{VWAP} = \text{Dollar volume/Trade volume}$$

$$\text{Dollar volume} = (200 \times \$2.71) + (200 \times \$2.72) + (100 \times \$2.76) + (100 \times \$2.77) + (1100 \times \$2.70) + (100 \times \$2.66) + (100 \times \$2.65) = \$5,140$$

$$\text{Trade volume} = 200 + 200 + 100 + 100 + 1100 + 100 + 100 = 1,900 \text{ shares}$$

So, VWAP = $5,140/1,900 = $2.7053 per share.

$$\text{Estimated implicit costs} = 100 \times (\$2.7053 - \$2.66) = \$4.53$$

B. Using VWAP as a benchmark, implicit costs are $4.53, whereas implicit costs are −$1 if the closing price is used as a benchmark. Estimated implicit costs may be quite sensitive to the choice of benchmark.

9. A. If the order is received late in the day, the broker would act based on how the prices have changed during the day. If the order is a sell order and prices have increased since the opening, the broker would immediately fill the order so that the sale price is greater than the benchmark price. If prices have fallen during the day, the broker would wait until the next day to avoid recording a low-priced sale on a day when the market opened higher. The broker would do the opposite if the order is a buy order. If prices have increased since the opening, the broker would wait until the next day to avoid recording a high-priced buy on a day when the market opened lower. If the prices have fallen during the day, the broker would immediately fill the order so that the purchase price is lower than the benchmark price.

B. The broker would execute the order just before closing so that the transaction price is the same as the closing price.

C. The broker would split the order and spread its execution throughout the day so that the transaction price is close to the market VWAP.

10. A. For a sale,

$$\text{Estimated cost} = \text{Trade size} \times (\text{Benchmark price} - \text{Trade price}).$$

Using €52.87 as the benchmark price, the transaction cost estimate of the first trade is 10,000 × (€52.87 − €53.22) = −€3,500. The transaction cost estimate of the second trade is 10,000 × (€52.87 − €53.06) = −€1,900. The transaction cost estimate of the third trade is 10,000 × (€52.87 − €52.87) = €0. The total transaction cost estimate =

$$-€3,500 + (-€1,900) + €0 = -€5,400$$

B. The quotation midpoint that prevailed at the time of the decision to trade was €53.25. This is the benchmark price, and the implementation shortfall estimate of the cost of executing the first order is 10,000 × (€53.25 − €53.22) = €300. The implementation shortfall estimate of the cost of executing the second order is 10,000 × (€53.25 − €53.06) = €1,900. The implementation shortfall estimate of the cost of executing the third order is 10,000 × (€53.25 − €52.87) = €3,800. So, the implementation shortfall estimate of the total cost of executing the three orders is €300 + €1,900 + €3,800 = €6,000.

C. The estimated transaction cost using the closing price as the benchmark is negative. This result makes it seem as if the trader had a trading profit. This conclusion is not reasonable because the trader did pay the bid–ask spread and her trades had a market impact, making prices less favorable in her subsequent trades. For example, in the first trade, the trader sold the shares close to the bid price and the trade resulted in a decline in prices. Overall, the use of closing price as the benchmark is not appropriate in this problem because the benchmark itself is significantly affected by the large size of the order.

In contrast, the implementation shortfall estimate uses a benchmark which is determined before the order has an impact on prices. The implementation shortfall approach, which results in a reasonable estimate of €6,000 as the total cost of executing the sale, is the appropriate approach in this problem.

11. A. The paper portfolio traded 1,000 shares on Monday for \$10.00 per share. The value of the portfolio at the close on Wednesday is \$10,050. The net value is \$50.

The real portfolio contains only 700 shares and was traded over the course of two days. On Wednesday's close, it is worth 700 × \$10.05 = \$7,035.

The cost of the portfolio is \$7,052:

$$\text{Monday}: 600 \times \$10.02 = \$6{,}012 + \$20 \text{ commissions} = \$6{,}032$$

$$\text{Tuesday}: 100 \times \$10.08 = \$1{,}008 + \$12 \text{ commissions} = \$1{,}020$$

The net value of the real portfolio is \$7,035 − 7,052 = −\$17.

Thus, the implementation shortfall is \$50 − (−\$17) = \$67, or 67 bps.

B. Implementation shortfall broken into components is as follows:

- Delay

$$\text{Monday}: 600/1{,}000 \times [(\$10.00 - \$10.00)/\$10.00] = 0.00\%$$

$$\text{Tuesday}: 100/1{,}000 \times [(\$9.99 - \$10.00)/\$10.00] = -0.01\%$$

- Realized profit and loss

$$\text{Monday}: 600/1{,}000 \times [(\$10.02 - \$10.00)/\$10.00] = 0.12\%$$

$$\text{Tuesday}: 100/1{,}000 \times [(\$10.08 - \$9.99)/\$9.99] = 0.09\%$$

- Missed trade opportunity cost

$$300/1{,}000 \times [(\$10.05 - \$10.00)/\$10.00] = 0.15\%$$

Commissions are 0.20% + 0.12% = 0.32%.

Total implementation shortfall is 0.67 percent, or 67 bps.

12. Portfolio trades involve the purchase or sale of a basket of stocks, with the buy or sell orders placed as a coordinated transaction. Jane Smith could ask a broker for a quote for the entire basket of telecommunications stocks that she wants to purchase. Because there are multiple stocks in the basket being purchased, it is clear to the counterparty that the purchase is not motivated by information about a particular stock and the market impact of the trade is likely to be less. As a consequence, the cost of trading the basket of stocks is expected to be lower than the total trading cost of buying each stock individually.
13. The average execution cost for a purchase of securities is 75 basis points, or 0.75 percent, and the average execution cost for a sale of securities is also 0.75 percent. So, the average execution for a round-trip trade is $2 \times 0.75\%$, or 1.5%. Since the portfolio is expected to be turned over twice, expected execution costs are $1.5\% \times 2 = 3\%$. Therefore, the expected return net of execution costs is $8\% - 3\% = 5\%$.
14. Just as some traders in London possess information about stocks that traders in New York may not, some New York-based traders possess information that London-based traders may not. When New York-based traders begin to trade with the opening of U.S. markets, their trades reveal new information. The new information is incorporated into prices not only in New York but also in London during the hours of overlap between the markets. This incorporation of additional information from New York in London results in higher volatility of prices in London after the opening of the U.S. markets.
15. One reason the manager may have chosen not to trade more aggressively is that he does not think there are other informed traders who have the same information he has about the company's stock. That is, he does not expect other traders to trade in the stock based on information, thus quickly eliminating his informational advantage. By trading in smaller sizes over a period of time, the manager attempts to reduce the chance that other traders will infer that the fund manager is trading based on special information. By spreading his trades over time, the manager is trying to reduce the price impact of trading by not revealing his full trading intentions.
16. Liquidity-motivated traders transact only to meet liquidity needs and desire low transaction costs. So, they would prefer the market with the lower bid–ask spreads. The information-motivated traders trade strategically to maximize the profits from their information. Some of their profits are made in trades in which liquidity-motivated traders are the counterparty. Since the liquidity-motivated traders trade in the market with the lower spreads, information-motivated traders will trade with them in that market. Also, information-motivated traders prefer to place larger orders to profit from any superior information they have. Such traders with large orders are particularly concerned about the market impact cost in the form of a price change for large trades. Since the quoted prices are firm for only a fixed depth, larger orders may move the bid (ask) price downward (upward). In a market with greater depth, the market impact cost is less. Thus, the market with greater depths would be preferred by information-motivated traders. Overall, between the two alternate trading venues, the one with lower spreads and greater depths would be preferred by both types of traders.
17. *Trade A.* In spite of the high urgency level, this trade represents 3 percent ADV. This trade is suitable for an implementation shortfall algorithm.
    Trade B. This trade represents 75 percent ADV and has high spreads. It is not suitable for an algorithmic trade and should be traded using a broker.
18. Although the goal is to minimize explicit transaction costs, the trader needs also to consider the opportunity cost of not being invested in the S&P 500 portfolio. The trader

should use an implementation shortfall strategy to control the risk of this rebalance. In short, he should minimize explicit costs by waiting for trades to cross in an electronic crossing network, such as the POSIT trading system, but he should also submit names not likely to cross to a broker in order to minimize opportunity costs. Such a strategy would balance the costs of a delay in implementing a strategic asset allocation against the concern to minimize explicit transaction costs.

CHAPTER 11

MONITORING AND REBALANCING

SOLUTIONS

1. A. Accumulating funds for the child's education is a new investment goal. Prior to the adoption, the couple's time horizon was two-stage (preretirement and postretirement). In their late 40s, they will have a period in which they need to pay for the cost of the child's education; this will involve substantial costs for which they must plan. The couple's multistage time horizon now includes the period up to the child's entering college, the child's college years, the remaining period to retirement, and retirement.

   B. Given the investor's circumstances, the decision to buy a house in one year's time makes the addition of a shortfall risk objective appropriate. He needs to earn at least 2 percent if he is to have sufficient funds to buy the house. An appropriate shortfall risk objective is to minimize the probability that the return on the portfolio falls below 2 percent over a one-year horizon. The decision also creates a liquidity requirement. The need for $102,000 in cash at the end of the investment period means that the investor cannot tie up his money in a way such that he does not have ready access to it in a year's time.

   C. The approval of the grant has created a liquidity requirement of €15 million − €1 million = €14 million.

2. The first action ("Revise the investment policy statement of the pension scheme to take into account a change in the forecast for inflation in the United Kingdom") is incorrect. The investment policy statement (IPS) depends on the client's particular circumstances, including risk tolerance, time horizon, liquidity and legal constraints, and unique needs. Therefore, a change in economic forecast would not affect the IPS. The IPS also considers a client's return requirement. This return requirement may change over the long term if the inflation outlook has changed over the long term. A change in the inflation outlook over a short period, such as in this question, would not necessitate a change in the return portion or any other aspect of the IPS.

   The second action ("Reallocate pension assets from domestic (U.K.) to international equities because he also expects inflation in the United Kingdom to be higher than in other countries") is correct. A change in economic forecast might necessitate a change in asset allocation and investment strategy. An expectation of increased inflation in the United Kingdom might lead to expectations that U.K. equity performance will slow and would likely result in both weaker U.K. equity returns and stronger returns from overseas markets. This would justify an increased allocation to international equities.

The third action ("Initiate a program to protect the financial strength of the pension scheme from the effects of U.K. inflation by indexing benefits paid by the scheme") is incorrect. The implementation of an inflation index adjustment program would protect the plan participants, not the plan itself, from the effects of higher U.K. inflation. With an inflation index adjustment program, Summit's costs of funding the defined benefit scheme would actually increase (thereby weakening the plan's financial position) as U.K. inflation increases.

3. A. The return requirement should be higher to:

- Fund her additional living expenses.
- Meet her new retirement goals.

The following calculations are not required but provide basis for the statement that the return must be higher than the previous 7 percent to generate a retirement portfolio that will support the desired retirement spending level (at a reasonable retirement spending rate). The portfolio must now produce a return of approximately 9 percent, depending on the retirement spending rate assumption made.

Current portfolio (gross)	\$3,700,000
Less surgery	214,000
Less house down payment	430,000
Less living expenses	1,713,000
Current portfolio (net)	1,343,000
After-tax return = Before-tax return(1 − T) = 9.0% (0.7) = 6.3%	
Years = 25	
Retirement portfolio	$\$6{,}185{,}967 = \$1,343,000(1.063)^{25}$
Retirement spending (after tax)	280,000
Retirement spending (before tax)	400,000
Spending rate (before tax)	$6.47\% = \$400,000/\$6,185,967$

Risk tolerance should be higher. Wisman's risk tolerance should be higher because:

- Her husband's intention to work for another 25 years gives her the ability to assume more risk.
- The increase in assets affords her the ability to assume more risk.

Her time horizon is still multistage, but the stages have changed. In the first stage, expected to last 25 years, her husband will be working. The second stage is retirement.

The liquidity requirement should be higher. Wisman has a higher liquidity requirement because of the cost of the surgery for her son and the down payment for the house.

B. The allocation to Spencer Design Stock (currently 39.1 percent) should be decreased. Having a large percentage of her portfolio in one risky and potentially illiquid equity security exposes the portfolio to unnecessary and significant security-specific risk.

The allocation to cash (currently 2.4 percent) should be increased. Wisman needs \$430,000 for a house down payment, \$214,000 for her son's surgery, and the current year's portion of the \$1,713,000 present value of ongoing living expenses.

The allocation to the diversified bond fund (currently 30.5 percent) should be increased. The couple's portfolio must support the \$1,713,000 present value of ongoing living expenses and can sustain only moderate portfolio volatility. The regular income stream and diversification benefits offered by bonds are consistent with those needs.

The allocation to large-capitalization equities (currently 10.4 percent) should be increased. Wisman requires growth and inflation protection to meet her current and future spending needs. A diversified equity portfolio is likely to meet these requirements over time without imparting unacceptable volatility to principal values.

The allocation to emerging market equities (currently 11 percent) should be decreased. Wisman requires high returns but cannot afford to sustain large losses. Having a large percentage of total assets in volatile emerging markets securities is too risky for Wisman.

The allocation to undeveloped commercial land (currently 6.6 percent) should be decreased. Wisman needs income and liquidity to meet ongoing portfolio disbursement requirements. Undeveloped land requires cash payments (taxes, etc.) and is often illiquid.

4. The Javier–Campbell Trust's willingness to take risk is now below average because of its need to have a high probability of covering Javier's living expenses during the remainder of her lifetime, which encompasses a short time horizon. Javier's below-average willingness to take risk (coupled with her short time horizon) dominates Campbell's above-average willingness (coupled with his long time horizon). Of course, once Javier is no longer living, the Trust can reflect Campbell's higher willingness to take risk.
5. A. The suggested approach has several disadvantages:
   - A fixed ±5 percent corridor takes no account of differences in transaction costs among the asset classes. For example, private equity has much higher transaction costs than inflation-protected bonds and should have a wider corridor, all else equal.
   - The corridors do not take account of differences in volatility. Rebalancing is most likely to be triggered by the highest volatility asset class.
   - The corridors do not take account of asset class correlations.

   B. i. The corridor for international equities should be narrower than it was previously.
   ii. The corridor for inflation-protected bonds should be unaffected. The transaction costs should have an effect on the relative widths of the corridors for private equity and international equities.
   iii. The corridor for private equity should be narrower than that for domestic equities.
   iv. The corridor for domestic equities should be narrower than that for inflation-protected bonds.
6. A. Calendar rebalancing at a relatively high frequency such as weekly or monthly would be appropriate. In contrast to percentage-of-portfolio rebalancing, calendar rebalancing does not require continuous monitoring of portfolio values. The riskiness of the portfolio suggests frequent rebalancing to control drift.

   B. Such markets tend to be characterized by reversal and enhance the investment results from rebalancing to the strategic asset allocation, according to Perold–Sharpe analysis.
7. A. i. *Buy and hold.* The buy-and-hold strategy maintains an exposure to equities that is linearly related to the value of equities in general. The strategy involves buying, then holding, an initial mix (equities/bills). No matter what happens to relative values, no rebalancing is required; hence, this is sometimes termed the *do nothing* strategy. The investor sets a floor below which he or she does not wish the portfolio's value to fall. An amount equal to the value of that floor is invested in some nonfluctuating asset (e.g., Treasury bills or money market funds). The payoff diagram for a

buy-and-hold strategy is a straight line, so the portfolio's value rises (falls) as equity values rise (fall), with a slope equal to the equity proportion in the initial mix. The value of the portfolio will never fall below the specified floor, and the portfolio has unlimited upside potential. Increasing equity prices favor a buy-and-hold strategy; the greater the equity proportion in the initial mix, the better (worse) the strategy will perform when equities outperform (underperform) bills.

The strategy is particularly appropriate for an investor whose risk tolerance above the specified floor varies with wealth but drops to zero at or below that floor. After the initial portfolio transaction, transaction costs are not an issue. The strategy is tax efficient for taxable investors.

ii. *Constant mix.* The constant-mix strategy maintains an exposure to equities that is a constant percentage of total wealth. Periodic rebalancing to return to the desired mix requires the purchase (sale) of equities as they decline (rise) in value. This strategy, which generates a concave payoff diagram, offers relatively little downside protection and performs relatively poorly in up markets. The strategy performs best in relatively flat (but oscillating or volatile) markets and capitalizes on market reversals. The constant-mix strategy performs particularly well in a time period when equity values oscillate greatly but end close to their beginning levels; greater volatility around the beginning values accentuates the positive performance.

The constant-mix strategy is particularly appropriate for an investor whose risk tolerance varies proportionately with wealth; such an investor will hold equities at all levels of wealth. This strategy requires some rule to determine when rebalancing should take place; typical approaches avoid transaction costs until asset-class weights have changed by a given percentage. At this point, transaction costs are incurred to rebalance. Taxes can be material for taxable investors.

iii. *Constant-proportion portfolio insurance.* The constant-proportion portfolio insurance (CPPI) strategy maintains an exposure to equities that is a constant multiple greater than 1 of a "cushion" specified by the investor. The investor sets a floor below which he does not wish assets to fall, and the value of that floor is invested in some nonfluctuating asset (e.g., Treasury bills or money market funds). Under normal market conditions the value of the portfolio will not fall below this specified floor. As equity values rise (fall), the CPPI strategy requires the investor to purchase (sell) additional equities. Thus following this strategy keeps equities at a constant multiple of the cushion (assets–floor) and generates a convex payoff diagram. The CPPI strategy tends to give good downside protection and performs best in directional, especially up, markets; the strategy does poorly in flat but oscillating markets and is especially hurt by sharp market reversals.

The strategy is particularly appropriate for an investor who has zero tolerance for risk below the stated floor but whose risk tolerance increases quickly as equity values move above the stated floor. To control transaction costs, this strategy requires some rule to determine when rebalancing takes place. One approach avoids transaction costs until the value of the portfolio has changed by a given percentage. At this point, transaction costs are incurred to rebalance. Taxes can be a material consideration for taxable investors.

B. The CPPI strategy is the most appropriate rebalancing strategy for the MU endowment fund, taking into account the major circumstances described: the endowment's increased risk tolerance, the outlook for a bull market in growth assets over the next five years, the expectation of lower than normal volatility, and the endowment's desire to limit downside risk.

The CPPI strategy is consistent with higher risk tolerance, because the strategy calls for purchasing more equities as equities increase in value; higher risk tolerance is reflected in the resulting increased allocation to equities over time.

- The CPPI strategy will do well in an advancing equities market; because equities are purchased as their values rise, each marginal purchase has a high payoff.
- The CPPI strategy would do poorly in a higher-volatility environment for equities, because the strategy would sell on weakness but buy on strength, only to experience reversals; conversely, the strategy does much better in the face of lower volatility.
- The CPPI strategy provides good downside protection, because the strategy sells on weakness and reduces exposure to equities as a given floor is approached.

In summary, given that MU receives little other funding, the endowment fund must produce the maximum return for a specified level of risk. Given that the level of acceptable risk is generally higher, although with a very specific downside floor, the market outlook suggests that the constant-proportion strategy is the endowment fund's best rebalancing strategy.

CHAPTER 12

EVALUATING PORTFOLIO PERFORMANCE

SOLUTIONS

1. In this simplest rate-of-return calculation, the portfolio experiences no external cash flows. In this situation, the account's rate of return during evaluation period t equals the market value (MV_1) at the end of the period less the market value at the beginning of the period (MV_0), divided by the beginning market value:

$$r_t = \frac{MV_1 - MV_0}{MV_0} \text{ or } (€523{,}500 - €453{,}000)/€453{,}000$$
$$= 0.1556 = 15.56\%$$

Joubert earned a 15.56 percent rate of return on his portfolio during the year 2002.

2. A. The contribution was received at the end of the evaluation period, and it should be subtracted from the account's ending value. The external cash flow had no opportunity to affect the investment-related value of the account, and hence, it should be ignored.

$$r_t = \frac{(MV_1 - CF) - MV_0}{MV_0} \text{ or}$$
$$r_t = \frac{(42{,}300 - 500) - 42{,}000}{42{,}000}$$
$$= -0.48\%$$

Even though Smith actually ended up with a larger amount in his account at the end of the period as compared to the beginning of the period (£42,300 versus £42,000), he actually lost money on his investments. His rate of return was −0.48 percent. The slight increase in his account balance was due to the contribution at the end of the month rather than to a positive return.

B. In this case, the contribution was received at the beginning of the evaluation period, and it should be added to the account's beginning value. This sum is then subtracted from the ending value of the account, and the result is divided by the same sum (see formula below). In this case, the external cash flow did have an opportunity to affect the investment-related value of the account and it should be included in the calculation.

$$r_t = \frac{MV_1 - (MV_0 + CF)}{MV_0 + CF}$$

$$r_t = \frac{42{,}300 - (42{,}000 + 500)}{(42{,}000 + 500)} = -0.47\%$$

This rate of return is slightly higher (a smaller negative number) than the −0.48 percent return calculated in Part A. The slight increase in investment performance was due to the contribution made at the beginning of the month. In this case, the numerator of the formula yields an identical answer to that of Part A (−£200). But the denominator is larger (£42,500 vs. £42,000), giving a slightly higher return than in Part A.

3. A. Yes, an accurate rate of return can be calculated. The appropriate calculation is the time-weighted rate of return. The time-weighted rate of return (TWR) reflects the investment growth in the account as if the account began with one dollar. Its calculation requires that the account be valued every time an external cash flow occurs. If no cash flows take place, then the calculation of the TWR is simple; the change in the account's value is expressed relative to its beginning value. If external cash flows do occur, then the TWR requires computing a set of subperiod returns. These subperiod returns must then be linked together to compute the TWR for the entire evaluation period.

First, we determine the appropriate subperiods by reviewing the dates of the contributions to the account. Contributions were made on September 14th and 21st. The appropriate subperiods are as shown:

Subperiod 1 = Days 1 through 14

Subperiod 2 = Days 15 through 21

Subperiod 3 = Days 22 through 30

Next, we calculate the rate of return for each subperiod:

For subperiod 1:

$$r_{t,1} = [(\$105{,}000 - \$3{,}000) - \$100{,}000]/\$100{,}000$$
$$= 0.02 \text{ or } 2.00\%$$

For subperiod 2:

$$r_{t,2} = [(\$108{,}000 - \$2{,}500) - \$105{,}000]/\$105{,}000$$
$$= 0.0048 \text{ or } 0.48\%$$

For subperiod 3:

$$r_{t,3} = (\$110{,}000 - \$108{,}000)/\$108{,}000$$
$$= 0.0185 \text{ or } 1.85\%$$

Converting the subperiod returns into decimal form, we use the following expression to compute the time-weighted rate of return:

$$r_{twr} = (1 + r_{t,1}) \times (1 + r_{t,2}) \times \ldots \times (1 + r_{t,n}) - 1$$

In the case of Mary's portfolio:

$$r_{twr} = (1 + 0.02) \times (1 + 0.0048) \times (1 + 0.0185) - 1$$
$$= 0.0439 \text{ or } 4.39\%$$

4. A. The time-weighted rate of return for the investment manager is:

$$r_{twr} = (1 + 0.0125)(1 + 0.0347)(1 + [-0.0236])(1 + 0.0189)$$
$$(1 + [-0.0267])(1 + 0.0257) - 1$$
$$= 0.0405 \text{ or } 4.05\%$$

B. Adding the subperiod rates of return gives $0.0125 + 0.0347 + (-0.0236) + 0.0189 + (-0.0267) + 0.0257 = 0.0415$ or 4.15 percent.

Characteristically, the additive calculation gives a higher return number (4.15 percent) than the time-weighted calculation (4.05 percent). In general, the time-weighted rate of return is a better indicator of long-term performance because it takes account of the effects of compounding.

5. The TWR reflects the investment growth of one unit of money initially invested in the account. If external cash flows occur, then the account must be valued as of the date of each of these cash flows; the calculation of the TWR then requires computing a series of subperiod returns for the subperiods defined by the external cash flows. The subperiod returns are then combined by chain-linking, and 1 is subtracted from the result to arrive at the TWR.

The money-weighted rate of return (MWR) measures the compound growth rate in the value of all funds invested in the account over the evaluation period. The MWR is also called internal rate of return (IRR). The MWR is the growth rate that will link the ending value of the account to its beginning value plus all external cash flows. The MWR is computed using an iterative procedure.

The MWR represents the average growth rate of all dollars invested in an account, while the TWR represents the growth of a single unit of money invested in the account. Consequently, the MWR is sensitive to the size and timing of external cash flows contributed to and withdrawn from the account, while the TWR is not affected by the cash flows. Under "normal" conditions, these two return measures will produce similar results. However, when external cash flows occur that are large relative to the account's value (rule of thumb: greater than 10 percent) and the account's performance fluctuates significantly, then the MWR and the TWR can differ substantially.

6. A. The correct methodology for approximating a time-weighted rate of return for the entire year of 2003 is to use a linked internal rate of return (LIRR) approach. This approach takes the money-weighted rate-of-return values and then chain-links the returns over the entire evaluation period.

B. The calculation is:

$$r_{\text{LIRR}} = (1 + 0.0535) \times (1 + [-0.0234]) \times (1 + 0.0462) \times (1 + 0.0125) - 1$$
$$= 0.0898 \text{ or } 8.98\%$$

7. A. For Swennson, the annualized rate of return is:

$$r_a = [(1 + 0.275)(1 - 0.189)(1 + 0.146)(1 - 0.324)(1 + 0.123)]^{1/5} - 1$$
$$= -0.0209 = -2.09\%$$

For Mattsson, the annualized rate of return is:

$$r_a = [(1 + 0.057)(1 + 0.049)(1 + 0.078)(1 - 0.067)(1 + 0.053)]^{1/5} - 1$$
$$= 0.0327 \text{ or } 3.27\%$$

B. Mattsson's annualized rate of return of 3.27 percent was higher than Swennson's at −2.09 percent.

8. In this problem, the Wilshire 5000 represents the market index for U.S. equities, the Russell 1000 Value Index represents the portfolio benchmark, and Anderson's account is the portfolio.

A. The return due to style is the difference between the benchmark and the market index, or S = (B − M) = (21.7 percent − 25.2 percent) = −3.5 percent.

B. The return due to active management is the difference between the portfolio and the benchmark, or $A = (P - B) = (18.9\% - 21.7\%) = -2.8\%$.

C. The implication of the style calculation is that large-cap value is out of favor: i.e., the Russell 1000 Value Index underperformed the Wilshire 5000 by 3.5 percent. In and of itself, this should not be a large concern for an investor with a properly diversified portfolio. Certain styles will periodically outperform and underperform the market index.

The implication of the active management calculation is that Anderson is not adding value as compared to the benchmark, since its portfolio underperformed the portfolio benchmark. If Anderson is indeed a large-cap value manager and the Russell 1000 Value Index is an appropriate benchmark, then the client may be better off investing in the passive alternative. Of course, one period is not enough to make a judgment such as this. However, sustained underperformance of an active manager as compared to an appropriate benchmark should be cause for concern.

9. To verify the choice of the benchmark, a potential client could compare the market capitalization (median, average, weighted average) of the subject portfolio with the respective benchmark index. This can help identify a good match (or mismatch) based on the size (market capitalization) of the stocks in the portfolio versus the index. In addition, the historical beta of the portfolio can be calculated relative to the potential benchmark. On average, it should be close to 1.0. If the beta is significantly larger (smaller) than the benchmark, it would indicate that the portfolio is substantially riskier (less risky) than the benchmark.

10. A. Overall, the domestic equities asset class has performed well relative to the benchmark (4.54 percent vs. 4.04 percent). However, only one of the two domestic equities managers has outperformed his respective benchmark. Equity manager A has outperformed by 15 basis points, while equity manager B has underperformed by 18 basis points.

    The international equity asset class as a whole has outperformed its benchmark. In addition, both international equity managers have also outperformed their respective benchmarks.

    The fixed-income asset class underperformed its benchmark. Both fixed-income managers have underperformed their respective benchmarks as well.

    B. Overall, the total fund has outperformed its benchmark by 11 basis points. Nevertheless, the fund may be able to improve its relative performance by considering some changes to the manager lineup.

    C. For each manager that underperformed his or her assigned benchmark (equity manager B and both fixed-income managers), the plan sponsor should first verify that the benchmarks in place are appropriate for the particular managers' investment styles. If the benchmarks are appropriate, and if performance is not expected to improve (based on many factors, including quality of people, organizational issues, etc.), then the plan sponsor may consider replacing these managers with other active managers following similar investment disciplines, or perhaps replacing them with passive investment alternatives corresponding to the benchmarks those managers are being measured against.

11. In practice, an acceptable benchmark is one that both the investment manager and the plan sponsor agree represents the manager's investment process. However, in order to function effectively in performance evaluation, a benchmark should possess certain basic properties. It should be:

    - *Unambiguous.* The names of securities and their corresponding weights in the benchmark should be clearly noted.
    - *Investable.* The benchmark should be available as a passive option.
    - *Measurable.* It should be possible to calculate the benchmark's return on a timely basis, for various time periods (e.g., monthly, quarterly, annually).
    - *Appropriate.* The benchmark should be consistent with the manager's investment style or area of expertise.
    - *Reflective of current investment opinions.* The manager should have opinions and investment knowledge of the individual securities within the benchmark.
    - *Specified in advance.* The benchmark should be specified prior to the beginning of an evaluation period and known to both the investment manager and the fund sponsor.
    - *Owned.* The investment manager should be aware of and accept accountability for the constituents and performance of the benchmark.

12. Kim Lee Ltd.'s benchmark is not valid. The chief criticism of this type of benchmark is that it is not, and cannot be, specified in advance. Furthermore, since no one knows who the top-quartile managers will be at the beginning of an evaluation period, the benchmark is not investable; that is, there is no passive option for investment. Kim Lee Ltd. can inform existing and prospective clients where the firm's past performance has ranked in its peer group, but the universe should not be used *ex ante* as a performance benchmark.

Furthermore, the firm should disclose sufficient information about the composition of the peer group for recipients to evaluate the meaningfulness of the firm's *ex post* ranking.

13. A one-factor model can be used to predict the return on Jones' portfolio and the benchmark. In this case, the returns can be expressed as a linear function of the return on the entire U.S. equity market (as represented in the problem statement by the Wilshire 5000), as shown below:

$$R_p = a_p + \beta_p R_I + \varepsilon_p$$

where R_p is the return on the portfolio and R_I is the return on U.S. equities. The term ε_p is the residual, or nonsystematic, element of the relationship. Finally, the term β_p measures the sensitivity of the portfolio to the return on the U.S. equities market.

Calculating the expected return on Jones's portfolio gives:

$$R_{\text{Jones}} = 0.5 + 1.15(5.9) = 7.29\%$$

Calculating the expected return on the custom benchmark gives:

$$R_{\text{Benchmark}} = 1.5 + 0.95(5.9) = 7.11\%$$

The incremental expected return of the portfolio versus the benchmark is 0.18 percent. This can be calculated by computing the difference between the two expected returns. It can also be calculated by combining the two formulas as shown below:

$$R_{\text{Difference}} = (0.5 - 1.5) + (1.15 - 0.95)(5.9) = 0.18\%$$

Since the portfolio actually returned 8.13 percent during the period, the total differential return is 1.02 percent (the difference between the actual return of 8.13 percent and the expected benchmark return of 7.11 percent). However, based on the one-factor model, an outperformance of 0.18 percent was expected. The difference between the 1.02 percent and the 0.18 percent (or 0.84 percent) can be attributed to the value-added investment skill of Susan Jones.

14. We begin by calculating the information ratio for each of the two managers. The formula for the information ratio is:

$$\text{IR}_A = \frac{\overline{R}_A - \overline{R}_B}{\hat{\sigma}_{A-B}}$$

In our problem statement, the value-added for Manchester (1.5 percent) is the numerator in this formula, and the variability of excess returns (2.24 percent) is the denominator. Thus, for Manchester we can calculate an information ratio of 0.67.

Similarly, for Oakleaf we can calculate an information ratio of 0.4 (4 percent excess returns divided by 10 percent variability).

When we review our table, it gives the probability of outperformance. Since the question refers to underperformance, we must subtract the values in the table from 1 to determine the probability of underperformance.

Year	Manchester Outperformance	Manchester Underperformance	Oakleaf Outperformance	Oakleaf Underperformance
1	74.75%	25.25%	65.54%	34.46%
5	93.20	6.80	81.45	18.55
10	98.25	1.75	89.70	10.30

In this case, Oakleaf has a larger chance of underperforming the benchmark at all three time periods: 1, 5, and 10 years. This is interesting, since Oakleaf has a much larger expected value-added return (4 percent annually versus 1.5 percent for Manchester). However, the much larger variability of excess returns (10 percent for Oakleaf versus 2.24 percent for Manchester) clearly is an important factor in this situation.

15. In general terms, equity will earn higher returns than cash on average over the long term. However, there are periods of declining equity performance when cash may outperform equities.

    In the case of Acorn and Zebra, Acorn would be preferable over Zebra, all else but the cash levels being equal. During most time periods when equities are outperforming cash, it would be better to have less cash and more equities in the portfolio. But during the time periods when equities are declining, it may be preferable to have more cash. Unfortunately, it is extremely difficult to forecast ahead of time when these time periods of declining equity performance will occur.

16. There are performance measurement issues that are created when there are short positions in a portfolio. The basic equation for the return on an account is:

$$r_t = \frac{MV_1 - MV_0}{MV_0}$$

In theory, the net assets of a long–short portfolio could be zero. If the value of the portfolio's long positions is equal to the value of the portfolio's short positions, then the beginning market value, MV_0, would be zero and the account's rate of return would be either positive infinity or negative infinity.

To address this problem, we need to revise our performance measurement methodology. One approach would be to determine returns by summing the performance impacts of the individual security positions (both long and short). A return could be calculated for the period that the individual security positions were maintained. Once an individual security position changed, the return period would end and a new return period would start.

Regarding performance evaluation, if we have information regarding the historical returns and holdings of a long–short equity manager's long and short portfolios, we could use either returns-based or security-based benchmark building approaches to construct separate long and short benchmarks for the manager. These benchmarks could then be combined in appropriate proportions to create an appropriate benchmark for the manager.

Another possible option for performance evaluation is the use of the Sharpe ratio to evaluate hedge fund manager performance. It can be calculated without reference to the manager's underlying investment universe. Typically, a hedge fund manager's Sharpe ratio is compared to that of a universe of other hedge fund managers whose investment mandates are similar to those of the manager under evaluation.

17. Both macro attribution and micro attribution are different facets of performance attribution. The basic tenet behind performance attribution is that an account's performance is compared to a designated benchmark, then the sources of differential returns are identified and quantified. The main difference between macro and micro attribution is the definition of which "account's" performance we are analyzing. Macro attribution is done at the fund sponsor level; that is, analysis is typically done for a grouping of investment managers or investment accounts. Micro attribution is carried out at the level of the individual investment manager.

    There are three main inputs to the macro attribution approach:

    1. Policy allocations.
    2. Benchmark portfolio returns.
    3. Fund returns, valuations, and external cash flows.

    Fund sponsors determine policy allocations, or "normal" weightings, for each asset class and individual manager. These are typically determined after some sort of asset liability analysis and/or determination of the risk tolerance of the governing body of the fund.

    Benchmark portfolio returns are an important factor in determining the value added by the fund. If the benchmarks do not adequately match the managers' investment styles, the performance attribution will have little value. Fund sponsors may use broad market indexes as the benchmarks for asset categories (the Wilshire 5000 as the benchmark for overall U.S. domestic equities, for example) and may use more focused indexes to represent managers' investment styles (such as the Russell 2000 Value Index for a small-cap value manager).

    Fund returns, valuations, and external cash flows are all critical elements for determining the relevant performance for the portfolio as a whole and for each individual investment manager's account.

    A return metric implies that fund returns are used at the level of the individual management account to allow an analysis of the fund sponsor's decisions regarding manager selection. A dollar-metric approach uses account valuation and external cash flow data to calculate rates of return and also to compute the dollar impacts of the fund sponsor's investment policy decision making.

CHAPTER 13

GLOBAL INVESTMENT PERFORMANCE STANDARDS

SOLUTIONS

1. The Global Investment Performance Standards (GIPS standards) must be applied on a firmwide basis, and the firm must be defined as an investment firm, subsidiary, or division held out to clients or potential clients as a distinct business entity (Provisions II.0.A.1–2). A *distinct business entity* is a unit, department, or office that is organizationally and functionally segregated from other units, divisions, departments, or offices and that retains discretion over the assets it manages and autonomy over the investment decision-making process (GIPS glossary). If Walker, Pierce & Company of Frankfurt satisfies these criteria, it may define itself as a firm and undertake meeting all the requirements of the GIPS standards in order to claim compliance. The fact that Walker, Pierce & Company of Frankfurt has its own head of marketing suggests that it does hold itself out as a distinct business entity, and the fact that it is geographically separated from its parent company headquarters suggests that it may be organizationally and functionally segregated, but we lack sufficient information to determine if it retains discretion over the assets it manages and autonomy over the investment decision-making process. If Walker, Pierce & Company of Frankfurt does in fact qualify as a firm and achieve compliance, it must disclose the definition of the firm used to determine total firm assets and firmwide compliance (Provision II.4.A.1).
2. The standard compliance statement must accompany performance presentations prepared by firms claiming GIPS compliance. The statement cannot claim compliance with the GIPS standards "except for" anything (Provision II.0.A.8). In spite of the prior years' compliance with the then-prevailing Standards, Larson Dynamic Management may no longer claim compliance if it has failed to meet the January 1, 2005 deadline for trade-date accounting. The only acceptable compliance statement is: "[Name of firm] has prepared and presented this report in compliance with the Global Investment Performance Standards (GIPS®)." The compliance statement may be used only if the firm complied with all requirements of the GIPS standards (Provision II.0.A.7).
3. A and B. To calculate annual performance for Year 1 and Year 2, convert the quarterly returns to relative form $(1 + r)$, link them multiplicatively, and subtract 1.

For Year 1:

$$1Q\text{ Year 1: } 1 + 4.76\% = 1.0476$$

$$2Q\text{ Year 1: } 1 + 12.08\% = 1.1208$$

$$3Q\text{ Year 1: } 1 + (-4.88\%) = 0.9512$$

$$4Q\text{ Year 1: } 1 + 7.14\% = 1.0714$$

$$r_{\text{Year1}} = (1.0476 \times 1.1208 \times 0.9512 \times 1.0714) - 1 = 0.1966 = 19.66\%$$

For Year 2:

$$1Q\text{ Year 2: } 1 + (-13.57\%) = 0.8643$$

$$2Q\text{ Year 2: } 1 + 17.65\% = 1.1765$$

$$3Q\text{ Year 2: } 1 + 1.08\% = 1.0108$$

$$4Q\text{ Year 2: } 1 + 0.97\% = 1.0097$$

$$r_{\text{Year2}} = (0.8643 \times 1.1765 \times 1.0108 \times 1.0097) - 1 = 0.0378 = 3.78\%$$

C. To calculate cumulative performance, convert the quarterly returns for the entire two-year period to relative form $(1 + r)$, link them multiplicatively, and subtract 1:

$$\begin{aligned} r_{Cum} &= (1.0476 \times 1.1208 \times 0.9512 \times 1.0714 \times 0.8643 \times 1.1765 \\ &\quad \times 1.0108 \times 1.0097) - 1 \\ &= 0.2418 = 24.18\% \end{aligned}$$

Alternately, express the annual returns for Year 1 and Year 2 in relative form, multiply them together, and subtract 1:

$$\begin{aligned} r_{Cum} &= (1.1966 \times 1.0378) - 1 \\ &= 0.2418 = 24.18\% \end{aligned}$$

D. To calculate annualized compound performance, convert the cumulative rate of return to relative form $(1 + r_{Cum})$ and raise it to the reciprocal of the number of years in the period $(1/n)$, and subtract 1. In this problem, there are two years in the period, so the compound annual rate of return is:

$$\begin{aligned} 1.2418^{(1/2)} - 1 &= \sqrt{1.2418} - 1 \\ &= 0.1144 = 11.44\% \end{aligned}$$

4. The GIPS standards allow the linking of noncompliant performance, provided that no noncompliant performance is shown after January 1, 2000 (Provision II.5.A.2). Firms must disclose which periods are not in compliance and the reasons for noncompliance during any time period for which the composite is not in compliance (Provision II.4.A.10). In the example given, Smith & Jones may link noncompliant performance prior to January 1, 2000 but must disclose that the market value of fixed-income securities did not include

accrued income for periods prior to 1999. If the use of derivatives in some accounts was material, the nature and extent of such use must be disclosed (Provision II.4.A.5). It might be appropriate to place portfolios that use leverage or derivatives into different composites from those that do not.

5. Smith & Jones may not claim to be GIPS-compliant if model performance is linked to actual performance. The GIPS standards state that composites must include only actual assets under management within the defined firm, and they expressly prohibit linking simulated or model portfolios with actual performance (Provision II.3.A.8). This requirement does not restrict investment managers from showing model results as supplemental information, but linking model returns to actual returns and showing the combined history as a continuous record would be misleading and thus is not permitted. If a firm presents model results as supplemental information, it must clearly label them.
6. Barry, Smith must have a documented, composite-specific policy for the treatment of external cash flows and must compute time-weighted total returns that adjust for external cash flows. For periods beginning January 1, 2005, rate-of-return approximation methods must adjust for cash flows on a day-weighted basis (Provision II.2.A.2). Accordingly, Barry, Smith must use a return-calculation methodology that adjusts for daily-weighted external cash flows, such as the Modified Dietz method. However, the March 12, 2006, contribution to the Dennett portfolio represents 13.67 percent of the portfolio's value, and it may be classified as a large external cash flow. Barry, Smith must establish in advance a policy for determining what is considered a "large" external cash flow for the Balanced Tax-Exempt composite. Large external cash flows may distort approximated returns. The GIPS standards recommend that portfolios be valued as of the date of all large external cash flows (Provision II.2.B.3), and this treatment will be mandatory for periods beginning January 1, 2010 (Provision II.2.A.2). If the portfolio is valued as of the end of the day on March 12, then Barry, Smith can compute subperiod returns and link them to calculate a true time-weighted rate of return for the month of March. The firm could also treat the cash flow as a temporary new account. Alternately, if Barry, Smith has adopted a Significant Cash Flow policy for this composite, the firm could determine that this account should be excluded from the composite for the month.
7. A. Approximate return for March using the Modified Dietz formula:

$$r_{ModDietz} = \frac{\text{MV}_1 - \text{MV}_0 - \text{CF}}{\text{MV}_0 + \sum(\text{CF}_i \times w_i)}$$

$$w_i = \frac{31 - 12}{31} = 0.6129$$

$$r_{ModDietz} = \frac{19{,}250{,}000 - 16{,}575{,}000 - 2{,}265{,}000}{16{,}575{,}000 + (2{,}265{,}000 \times 0.6129)} = 0.0228 = 2.28\%$$

B. True time-weighted return for March:

$$r_t = \frac{\text{MV}_1 - \text{MV}_0}{\text{MV}_0}$$

$$r_{t,1} = \frac{(19{,}550{,}000 - 2{,}265{,}000) - 16{,}575{,}000}{16{,}575{,}000} = 0.0428 = 4.28\%$$

$$r_{t,2} = \frac{19{,}250{,}000 - 19{,}550{,}000}{19{,}550{,}000} = -0.0153 = -1.53\%$$

$$r_{\text{twr}} = (1 + r_{t,1}) \times (1 + r_{t,2}) \times \ldots \times (1 + r_{t,n}) - 1$$

$$r_{\text{twr}} = (1 + 0.0428) \times (1 + (-0.0153)) - 1 = 0.0268 = 2.68\%$$

C. The capital markets in which the Dennett portfolio was invested were volatile during the month of March. The portfolio had a 4.28 percent return in the first 12 days of the month but a -1.53 percent return for the rest of the month. The portfolio had a large external cash inflow during March. In these circumstances, the approximate return may be distorted. The approximate return calculated using the Modified Dietz method differs by 40 basis points (0.40 percent) from the true time-weighted return calculated by geometrically linking subperiod returns.

8. Performance must be calculated after actual trading expenses are deducted (Provision II.2.A.5). Trading expenses are the costs of buying or selling a security, and they typically take the form of brokerage commissions or spreads. Only actual trading expenses are used; estimates are not permitted. The reason for this requirement is that trading expenses must be incurred in order to implement the investment strategy, and performance should reflect those expenses.
9. A. Portfolio returns:

$$r_A = \frac{85.3 - 74.9 - 7.5}{74.9 + (7.5 \times 0.613)}$$

$$= \frac{2.9}{79.5} = 0.0365 = 3.65\%$$

$$r_B = \frac{109.8 - 127.6 - (-15) - (-5)}{127.6 + (-15 \times 0.742) + (-5 \times 0.387)}$$

$$= \frac{2.2}{114.535} = 0.0192 = 1.92\%$$

$$r_C = \frac{128.4 - 110.4 - 15}{110.4 + (15 \times 0.387)}$$

$$= \frac{3}{116.205} = 0.0258 = 2.58\%$$

B. To calculate the composite return based on beginning assets, first determine the percent of beginning composite assets represented by each portfolio; then determine the weighted-average return for the month.

$$\text{Beginning composite assets} = 74.9 + 127.6 + 110.4 = 312.9$$

$$\text{Portfolio A} = \frac{74.9}{312.9} = 0.239 = 23.9\%$$

$$\text{Portfolio B} = \frac{127.6}{312.9} = 0.408 = 40.8\%$$

$$\text{Portfolio C} = \frac{110.4}{312.9} = 0.353 = 35.3\%$$

$$r_{Comp} = (0.0365 \times 0.239) + (0.0192 \times 0.408) + (0.0258 \times 0.353) = 0.0257$$

$$= 2.57\%$$

C. To calculate the composite return based on beginning assets plus cash flows, first use the denominator of the Modified Dietz formula to determine the percentage of total beginning assets plus weighted cash flows represented by each portfolio, and then calculate the weighted-average return.

Beginning composite assets + Weighted cash flows = $[74.9 + (7.5 \times 0.613)] + [127.6 + (-15 \times 0.742) + (-5 \times 0.387)] + [110.4 + (15 \times 0.387)] = 79.5 + 114.535 + 116.205 = 310.24$

$$\text{Portfolio A} = \frac{79.5}{310.24} = 0.256 = 25.6\%$$

$$\text{Portfolio B} = \frac{114.535}{310.24} = 0.369 = 36.9\%$$

$$\text{Portfolio C} = \frac{116.205}{310.24} = 0.375 = 37.5\%$$

$$r_{Comp} = (0.0365 \times 0.256) + (0.0192 \times 0.369) + (0.0258 \times 0.375) = 0.0261 = 2.61\%$$

10. The GIPS standards require that all of the compliant firm's actual, fee-paying, discretionary portfolios must be included in at least one composite. This requirement prevents firms from presenting only the best-performing portfolios to prospective clients. A key term in the Standards is "discretionary." As defined in the Guidance Statement on Composite Definition, "Discretion is the ability of the firm to implement its intended strategy." Restrictions placed on the manager that impede the investment process to such an extent that the strategy cannot be implemented may render the portfolio nondiscretionary. A firm's composites cannot include nondiscretionary portfolios (Provision II.3.A.1). The firm's documented policies should include a definition of discretion, and the firm should review the client's investment guidelines periodically to confirm whether a portfolio is discretionary.
11. The GIPS standards prohibit including nondiscretionary portfolios in composites. IPS restrictions do not necessarily render a portfolio nondiscretionary. It is up to the investment management firm to define discretion and to determine whether it has the discretion to implement the investment strategy, given the restrictions of the IPS. In this case, however, it appears likely that SMERF's policy requiring transactions to be approved in advance by the Investment Committee and the pension plan's liquidity needs prevent Midwest National Bank from fully implementing the investment objective of achieving long-term capital appreciation through active management. If so, Midwest National Bank should classify the SMERF portfolio as nondiscretionary and exclude it from all composites.
12. The guiding principles for firms to consider when defining composites include the following:

- Composites must be defined according to objective or strategy.
- Composite definitions should be stated clearly.
- Because the GIPS standards promote comparability among firms, composite definitions ought to take into account how other firms define similar products.

- Firms must consistently apply the criteria so that the composite includes all actual, fee-paying, discretionary portfolios that meet the composite definition.
- Firms cannot include portfolios with different investment strategies or objectives in the same composite. Firms may need to create multiple composites to ensure that this circumstance does not occur.

The following hierarchy is useful for defining composites that represent the firm's investment strategies:

Investment mandate. Portfolios with a similar strategy or product description; for example, "Small-Cap Domestic Equity."

Asset classes. Composites based on broad asset classes; for example, equity, fixed-income, balanced, and the like.

Style or strategy. Composites defined by the style employed by the manager; for example, value, growth, passive or sector.

Benchmarks. Composites based on a specific index or custom benchmark against which the portfolio is managed.

Risk/return characteristics. Portfolios grouped together based on shared, distinctive risk/return characteristics.

Other criteria should also be considered, including the extent and use of derivatives, hedging and/or leverage, tax status, type of client, instruments used, client characteristics, and portfolio types.

13. Balanced or multiasset composites may come in a wide range of equity and fixed-income exposure levels. The GIPS standards do not specify how many or what composites a firm should create. Firms themselves must direct the creation of composites, including how many to define and what portfolios they contain. Smith & Jones must determine how many different balanced composites are needed to provide an adequate representation of the firm's distinct investment strategies. The key to defining multiasset composites is determining the base or strategic asset mix and the tactical asset ranges for each composite. For example, if Smith & Jones manages four base strategies with 20 percent, 40 percent, 60 percent, and 80 percent equity exposure and manages them within a tightly constrained allowable range of 2 percent to 3 percent before rebalancing (that is, without tactical asset management), it could create four balanced composites that reflect those base mixes. If Smith & Jones *also* manages four base strategies with 20 percent, 40 percent, 60 percent, and 80 percent equity exposure *with* allowances for tactical asset allocation, eight composites could be created—one for each of the four base exposure levels without tactical management and one for each of the four base exposures with tactical management.
14. Composites must include new portfolios on a consistent and timely basis after the portfolio comes under management, unless specifically mandated by the client (Provision II.3.A.3). It is up to the firm to establish and document a policy that includes new portfolios in composites as soon as possible. The firm may define composite-specific policies on the timing of the inclusion of new portfolios, taking into account the time required to implement the investment strategy represented by each composite. Once the policy has been defined, it must be applied consistently.
15. As a general rule, a firm should not switch portfolios from one composite to another. Unless documented changes are made to a client's objectives or investment guidelines, or the composite is redefined, portfolios should remain in the appropriate composite

throughout their lives (Provision II.3.A.5). In cases of documented changes in the client's objectives or guidelines, a portfolio may be moved to a new composite but the historical record must stay with the old composite. This standard is designed to prevent the movement of outperforming portfolios into and underperforming portfolios out of a composite, thereby improving the composite's reported performance.

Take, for example, a case in which a middle-aged client's portfolio was included in an investment management firm's balanced growth composite and all of the component portfolios in the balanced growth composite (including the client's) were invested in a 60 percent large-cap value equity/40 percent intermediate-term municipal bond mix for the 1996–2003 period. If the client retired in 2004 and instructed the manager to reduce equity exposure and emphasize tax-exempt income, the portfolio could at that point be moved to another composite reflecting the new objective. The portfolio's performance from 1996 through 2003 must remain in the balanced growth composite, and future performance would be included in an appropriate income-oriented composite. Anytime a portfolio is moved from one composite to another, the move must be based on a change in client objectives, a change in directive from the client, or a redefinition of the composite, and the change and move must be clearly documented.

16. Under the Standards, there is no minimum or maximum number of portfolios that a composite may include. The Standards require that firms disclose the number of portfolios in each composite as of the end of each period presented, unless there are five or fewer portfolios.
17. The head of performance measurement is correct in stating that the GIPS standards require the presenting firm to disclose significant events that may assist a prospective client in interpreting the performance record (Provision II.4.A.19). Such events include, but are not limited to, the loss of key personnel such as portfolio managers. In this case, the small firm lost not one but seven investment decision-makers. Shelbourne Capital Company must include a disclosure that equity investment professionals left the firm, and it must indicate when they left.
18. A. Under the beginning-of-period allocation method, cash is allocated to the equity segment in proportion to stocks as a percentage of invested assets excluding cash.

$$\text{Allocated Cash}_{\text{Beginning}} = 8{,}514{,}010 \times \frac{96{,}425{,}706}{96{,}425{,}706 + 20{,}777{,}934}$$
$$= 7{,}004{,}641$$

The equity segment return is the weighted-average return of the stock and cash components.

$$r_B = \left(0.0079 \times \frac{96{,}425{,}706}{96{,}425{,}706 + 7{,}004{,}641}\right) + \left(0.0021 \times \frac{7{,}004{,}641}{96{,}425{,}706 + 7{,}004{,}641}\right) = 0.0075 = 0.75\%$$

B. Under the strategic asset allocation method, the cash position associated with the equity segment is assumed to be total assets multiplied by the percentage difference between the strategic and the actual allocation to stocks. The strategic allocation to stocks is 80 percent, and the actual allocation to stocks is 76.7 percent.

$$\text{Allocated Cash}_{\text{Strategic}} = 125{,}717{,}650 \times (0.800 - 0.767) = 4{,}148{,}682$$

$$r_S = \left(0.0079 \times \frac{96{,}425{,}706}{96{,}425{,}706 + 4{,}148{,}682}\right) + \left(0.0021 \times \frac{4{,}148{,}682}{96{,}425{,}706 + 4{,}148{,}682}\right) = 0.0077 = 0.77\%$$

19. A long-standing principle in performance record reporting is that performance belongs to the firm, not to the individual or individuals managing accounts for the firm. The GIPS standards stipulate that performance track records of a past firm or affiliation must be linked to or used to represent the historical record of a new firm or new affiliation if (1) substantially all the investment decision-makers are employed by the new firm (i.e., research department, portfolio managers, and other relevant staff); (2) the staff and decision-making process remain intact and independent within the new firm; and (3) the new firm has records that document and support the reported performance (Provision II.5.A.4.a). Although a new team of equity managers joined Claiborne and Jackson, there is no evidence that the entire decision-making team, including analysts and traders, also joined Claiborne and Jackson. Indeed, three members of the old firm's investment strategy committee did not join the new firm. It also appears that Claiborne and Jackson may lack data documenting and supporting the reported performance. Consequently, Claiborne and Jackson may not use the historical performance record that the new equity portfolio managers claim to have achieved while they were employed at Shelbourne Capital Company.
20. The GIPS standards recommend presenting performance gross of investment management and administrative fees and before taxes, except nonreclaimable withholding taxes (Provision II.5.B.1.a). Returns must be clearly labeled as gross of fees or net of fees (Provision II.4.A.6). In addition, the firm's fee schedule must be presented (Provision II.4.A.12). When net-of-fees returns are presented, the firm must disclose if any other fees are deducted in addition to direct trading expenses and investment management fees (Provision II.4.A.16). Philosophically, gross-of-fees returns are more directly comparable to benchmark returns and the returns earned by other firms, compared with net-of-fees returns, which reflect the actual benefit the client has received from the firm's management of portfolio assets. There is no reason for Smith & Jones not to present properly calculated and labeled net-of-fees returns, but management should additionally consider presenting gross-of-fees returns as recommended by the GIPS standards.
21. The GIPS standards require that at least five years of GIPS-compliant performance be reported (or a record for the period since firm inception if inception is less than five years ago). After presenting five years of performance, the firm must present additional annual performance up to 10 years (Provisions I.E.12.a–b and II.5.A.1.a). Bentwood Institutional Asset Management could not drop the years prior to 2001 at the time Cooper suggests it do so. In addition to violating a specific requirement, Cooper's suggestion was not in the spirit of fair representation and full disclosure of performance. Technically, the firm will be able drop the early years of its composite presentation once it has established a 10-year GIPS-compliant record, as long as it continues to show at least the most recent 10 years. For instance, it will be able to show just the 10 calendar years 2001–2010 after the composite returns for 2010 become available. The GIPS standards are ethical standards, however, and it would be most appropriate for Bentwood to show its entire GIPS-compliant performance record.
22. The GIPS standards are ethical standards for fair representation and full disclosure of investment performance. A primary purpose of a benchmark is to allow clients and

prospective clients to conduct meaningful analysis of a portfolio's performance over time. The GIPS standards define *benchmark* as "an independent rate of return (or hurdle rate) forming an objective test of the effective implementation of an investment strategy" (GIPS Glossary). The firm should accordingly select or construct a benchmark appropriate for the investment objectives, strategy, or style represented by the composite. The GIPS standards recognize that benchmarks evolve and that a new benchmark that better represents the intended investment strategy may become available. Changing benchmarks solely or primarily to improve the firm's relative performance, however, is not in keeping with the spirit of the GIPS standards. If a firm decides to change a composite benchmark, it must disclose when and why it made the change (Provision II.5.A.6). The GIPS standards do not prohibit a firm from making the change of benchmark retroactive, but normally it is most fitting for the change to become effective prospectively. Firms are encouraged to continue to present the old benchmark for prior periods. (GIPS Interpretations, question and answer dated September 19, 2001.)

23. The GIPS standards require that the total return of a benchmark (or benchmarks) that reflects the investment strategy or mandate represented by the composite must be presented for each annual period. If no benchmark is presented, the presentation must explain why not (Provision II.5.A.6). Benchmarks provide an objective test of a firm's implementation of an investment strategy in the spirit of fair representation and full disclosure of investment results. Stating that most of the firm's clients are uninterested in performance relative to a benchmark does not give a compelling reason for failing to provide the independent returns of an appropriate benchmark. Renner, Williams & Woods should attempt to identify a benchmark that reflects the income-oriented strategy of the fixed-income composite.
24. *High/low* presents the highest and lowest portfolio returns in the composite, and the high/low range is the arithmetic difference between the return earned by those best-performing and the worst-performing portfolios in the composite. These values are easy to understand, but the presence of outliers may result in high/low measures that do not represent the normal dispersion of portfolio returns within the composite.

    The *interquartile range* is the spread between the return of the portfolio at the 25th percentile and the return of the portfolio at the 75th percentile of an ordered distribution of returns. It has the advantage of eliminating the impact of outliers, but prospective clients may be unfamiliar with this measure.

    If returns are normally distributed, approximately two-thirds of the returns will fall within one *standard deviation* of the mean return. In this case, if the returns of the individual portfolios are normally distributed, approximately two-thirds of the portfolio returns will lie between 2.02 percent and 3.12 percent. This calculation is somewhat difficult by hand, especially for a large number of portfolios, but spreadsheet software typically includes a standard deviation routine. Standard deviation is a well-known and generally valid measure of dispersion.
25. A. The first step in calculating the capital return is to determine the capital employed.

$$C_E = C_0 + \sum(\mathrm{CF}_i \times w_i)$$

$$C_E = 8{,}000{,}000 + (1{,}000{,}000 \times 0.51) = 8{,}510{,}000$$

The formula for capital return for a single period (in this case, the second quarter) reduces the change in market value by capital expenditures during the period (E_C)

and increases it by the proceeds of property sales (S).

$$r_C = \frac{(\text{MV}_1 - \text{MV}_0) - E_C + S}{C_E}$$

$$r_C = \frac{8{,}375{,}000 - 7{,}450{,}000 - 1{,}750{,}000 + 2{,}250{,}000}{8{,}510{,}000} = 0.1675 = 16.75\%$$

B. The income return calculation requires reducing accrued investment income by nonrecoverable expenditures (E_{NR}), interest on debt (INT_D), and property taxes (T_P).

$$r_I = \frac{\text{INC}_A - E_{NR} - \text{INT}_D - T_P}{C_E}$$

$$r_I = \frac{75{,}000 - 200{,}000 - 137{,}500 - 20{,}000}{8{,}510{,}000} = -0.0332 = -3.32\%$$

C. The total return for the quarter is the sum of the capital return and the income return.

$$r_T = r_C + r_I$$

$$r_T = 0.1675 + (-0.0332) = 0.1343 = 13.43\%$$

26. Under the GIPS standards, a single verification report is issued with respect to the whole firm. Verification cannot be carried out for a single composite, and the term "verification" may never be applied to an individual composite (see Provisions III.A.1 and III.C). A qualified, reputable verification firm will not accept an assignment from Renner, Williams & Woods to conduct verification only with regard to the firm's equity and balanced account composites while excluding the fixed-income composites from the scope of the verification.

27. A. Anticipated income tax rate:

Federal income tax rate + [State income tax rate × (1 − Federal income tax rate)]

+ [City income tax rate × (1 − Federal income tax rate)]

$= 0.172 + [0.043 \times (1 - 0.172)] + [0.021 \times (1 - 0.172)] = 0.225 = 22.5\%$

B. Pretax return:

$$r_{ModDietz} = \frac{123{,}159{,}825 - 127{,}945{,}000 - (-8{,}950{,}000)}{127{,}945{,}000 + \left(-8{,}950{,}000 \times \frac{30-17}{30}\right)}$$

$$= \frac{4{,}164{,}825}{124{,}066{,}667} = 0.0336 = 3.36\%$$

C. Preliquidation after-tax return:

$$\text{T}_{\text{real}} = (12{,}545{,}000 \times 0.15) + (975{,}000 \times 0.225) + (533{,}105 \times 0.225)$$

$$= 2{,}221{,}074$$

$$r_{PLATModDietz} = r_{ModDietz} - \frac{T_{real}}{\text{MV}_0 - \sum(\text{CF}_i \times w_i)}$$

$$r_{PLATModDietz} = 0.0336 - \frac{2{,}221{,}074}{124{,}066{,}667}$$

$$= 0.0336 - 0.0179 = 0.0157 = 1.57\%$$

D. To add back the hypothetical return effect of nondiscretionary asset sales, one must first calculate the gain ratio (GR), the weighted-average capital gains tax rate, and the adjustment factor (F).

$$GR = \frac{G_{real} + G_{unreal}}{MV_1 + CF_{NetOut}}$$

$$G_{real} = 975{,}000 + 12{,}545{,}000 = 13{,}520{,}000$$

$$G_{unreal} = 123{,}159{,}825 - 85{,}676{,}400 = 37{,}483{,}425$$

$$CF_{NetOut} = 8{,}950{,}000 - 533{,}105 = 8{,}416{,}895$$

$$GR = \frac{13{,}520{,}000 + 37{,}483{,}425}{123{,}159{,}825 + 8{,}416{,}895} = 0.3876$$

The weighted-average capital gains tax rate is calculated by weighting the short-term capital gains tax rate in proportion to realized short-term capital gains as a percentage of total realized capital gains, and the long-term capital gains tax rate in proportion to realized long-term capital gains, as a percentage of total realized capital gains:

$$T_{cgr} = \left(0.225 \times \frac{975{,}000}{975{,}000 + 12{,}545{,}000}\right) + \left(0.15 \times \frac{12{,}545{,}000}{975{,}000 + 12{,}545{,}000}\right)$$

$$= 0.1554 = 15.54\%$$

$$F = CF_{NetOut} \times T_{cgr} \times GR$$

$$F = 8{,}416{,}895 \times 0.1554 \times 0.3876 = 506{,}975$$

Then the after-tax return adjusted for the impact of nondiscretionary capital gains is

$$r_{AdjPLATModDietz} = r_{PLATModDietz} + \frac{F}{MV_0 + \sum(CF_i \times w_i)}$$

$$= 0.0157 + \frac{506{,}975}{124{,}066{,}667}$$

$$= 0.0157 + 0.0041 = 0.0198 = 1.98\%$$

28. The report has a significant number of omissions and errors.

Omissions that prevent the Bristol Capital Management performance report from being GIPS compliant are as follows:

- The availability of a complete list and description of all of Bristol's composites is not disclosed as is required (Provision II.4.A.2).

- The availability of additional information regarding policies for calculating and reporting returns in compliance with the GIPS standards is not disclosed (Provision II.4.A.17).
- Although Bristol does disclose the use of derivatives, the firm has omitted the required description of the extent of use, frequency, and characteristics of the instruments that must also be disclosed in sufficient detail to identify the risks (Provision II.4.A.5).
- If the firm has included non-fee-paying accounts in its composite, the percentage of the composite represented by these accounts must be disclosed as of the end of each annual period (Provision II.5.A.7).
- The composite creation date must be disclosed (Provision II.4.A.24).
- Because the composite represents a global investment strategy, the presentation must include information about the treatment of withholding tax on dividends, interest income, and capital gains (Provision II.4.A.7).
- A description of the composite's strategy must be disclosed (Provision II.4.A.20).

Items included in the Bristol Capital Management performance report that are *not compliant* with GIPS Standards are as follows:

- The GIPS standards state that performance periods of less than one year must not be annualized, as Bristol does for the first quarter of 2007 (Provision II.5.A.3).
- GIPS verification cannot be performed for a single composite as is stated in the notes to the Bristol report. Third-party verification is performed with respect to the entire firm (Provisions III.A.1 and III.C).
- For periods beginning January 1, 2001, portfolios must be valued at least monthly. Bristol is valuing portfolios quarterly (Provision II.1.A.3).
- A firm must use the compliance statement as specified in the GIPS. There are no provisions for partial compliance. If a firm does not meet all the GIPS requirements, then it is not in compliance with the GIPS standards. Bristol's use of the "except for" compliance statement violates the Standards (Provisions II.0.A.7–8).
- The firm must disclose which measure of composite dispersion is presented (Provision II.4.A.26).
- The GIPS standards state that accrual accounting must be used for fixed-income securities and all other assets that accrue interest income (Provision II.1.A.6). Bristol states that it uses cash-basis accounting for the recognition of interest income.

ABOUT THE CFA PROGRAM

The Chartered Financial Analyst® designation (CFA®) is a globally recognized standard of excellence for measuring the competence and integrity of investment professionals. To earn the CFA charter, candidates must successfully pass through the CFA Program, a global graduate-level self-study program that combines a broad curriculum with professional conduct requirements as preparation for a wide range of investment specialties.

Anchored by a practice-based curriculum, the CFA Program is focused on the knowledge identified by professionals as essential to the investment decision-making process. This body of knowledge maintains current relevance through a regular, extensive survey of practicing CFA charterholders across the globe. The curriculum covers 10 general topic areas ranging from equity and fixed-income analysis to portfolio management to corporate finance, all with a heavy emphasis on the application of ethics in professional practice. Known for its rigor and breadth, the CFA Program curriculum highlights principles common to every market so that professionals who earn the CFA designation have a thoroughly global investment perspective and a profound understanding of the global marketplace.

www.cfainstitute.org

QUANTITATIVE
INVESTMENT
ANALYSIS

QUANTITATIVE
INVESTMENT
ANALYSIS
WORKBOOK

FIXED
INCOME
ANALYSIS

FIXED
INCOME
ANALYSIS
WORKBOOK

EQUITY
ASSET
VALUATION